DATE DUE

13773   77-14460

280
Bac   Backman, Milton V
            Christian churches of America; origins
         and beliefs.   Brigham Young Univ. Pr. 1976
            230p illus

            1 Sects   2 U.S.-Religion   3 Religions
         I Title

Christian Churches of America

Origins and Beliefs

Christian
Churches of America

Origins and Beliefs

13773

Milton V. Backman, Jr.
Brigham Young University Press

77–14460

Library of Congress Cataloging in Publication Data

Backman, Milton V., Jr.
    Christian Churches of America

    Includes bibliography
        1. Sects—Religion.   2. United States—
Religion.   I. Title.
BR516.5.B33   280'.0973   75-30772
ISBN 0-8425-0028-6
ISBN 0-8425-0029-4 (pbk.)

Library of Congress Catalog Card Number: 75-30772
International Standard Book Number: 0-8425-0028-6 (hardback)
                                       0-8425-0029-4 (paperback)
Brigham Young University Press, Provo, Utah 84602
© 1976 by Brigham Young University Press. All rights reserved
Second printing 1976
Printed in the United States of America
76 3Mc 19955

Table of Contents

To my family:
My wife, Kathleen, and Kristine, Karl, and Karen

Preface and Acknowledgments

Throughout the history of mankind, individuals have engaged in a fervent quest for religious truth. This seeking and inquiring has precipitated the rise of countless churches and many of these institutions have had a profound impact on the thinking and actions of their adherents. For some, religion is one of the most powerful motivating forces in their lives and pervades many aspects of their active existence.

In light of man's abiding interest in spiritual themes, I launched a study of America's Christian faiths, asking the questions, "What were the circumstances leading to the rise of the major Christian denominations in contemporary America? What were some of the most important historical developments of these religions in the United States? And what are the most distinguishing beliefs of the various religious communities in this land?"

The pursuit of these themes led to many interesting avenues of historical exploration, a myriad of ideas, and countless contacts with sincere Christians who willingly revealed their innermost spiritual convictions. This search also increased my impression that many people are misunderstood, that their basic theological concepts are sometimes misrepresented, and that ecclesiastical histories do not always unfold events as they are seen by members of the various religious communions in America.

One objective of this study is to relate the history and beliefs of the major denominations in America that have a Christian historic heritage as they might be described by members of the respective denominations. To achieve this goal, I frequently turned to the writings of those who initiated powerful religious movements and sought to recapture the flavor of their testimonies. I also attempted to employ the terminology which various Christians use to express their innermost religious convictions.

The work begins with a brief introduction of religion in America followed by a sketch of the history and beliefs of Roman Catholics and Eastern Christians. Catholicism is then contrasted with Protestantism, including both classical and modern reorientations of Protestant thinking. The last two sections of this work describe the transplanted and native American non-Catholic faiths. Since there are many similarities in the pattern of belief of many of these religious communities, I have included at the end of most of these chapters a list of distinguishing beliefs, concepts which most members of the respective churches endorse that are different from tenets generally held by Protestants.

Many members of different denominations have read portions of the manuscript at various stages of its development and to them I am greatly indebted for their discerning suggestions and timely advice. Included among those whose penetrating criticisms helped improve the accuracy of this work are John Stephen Staley, Ph.D. (for his suggestions on Roman Catholicism); Rev. Fr. Elias K. Stephanopoulos (Greek Orthodox); Clayton W. Hammell, pastor (Lutheran); Father Walter Ellingson (Episcopalian); Rebecca Robinson, Ralph Rudd, and William Lake (Cleveland Meeting, Religious Society of Friends); Rev. David A. Mote (United Church of Christ); Ellis M. Keck, pastor (Baptist); Don Plott, pastor (Baptist); Rev. Charles Graham and Curtis Ledbetter (Methodism); Rev. William Spangler (Christian Church); Roy Doxey (Latter-day Saint); Gary John Jewkes (Christian Science Committee on Publication); Robert Curtis (Watch Tower Bible and Tract Society); R. E. Ansel, pastor (Assembly of God); officers of the Seventh-day Adventist, General Conference, and Milton V. Backman, Sr.

Introduction: Religious Trends in Modern America

America is frequently referred to as a cosmopolitan nation whose inhabitants represent various cultures, races, and religions. In this land of liberty and opportunity, many people of different religious persuasions are worshipping God in harmony with traditional Christian practices. All of the major and many of the minor faiths of Europe have been transplanted to the New World and a myriad of theological concepts and practices have become an accepted characteristic of the American religious life. Since the early nineteenth century, the American environment has also been a productive spring issuing a continual flow of new religious communities. While Americans have listened attentively to old and new theological voices of Europe and have constantly absorbed European patterns of thought, they have also responded to the challenges of the modern world by constantly producing their versions of a new theology. The result of this transplanting, blending, and innovating has been an astounding increase in religious pluralism. Nowhere else in the world can one find such a variety of Christian churches.

America's religious mosaic is so complex that no one has succeeded in enumerating all of the faiths worshipping in this land. Many groups that gather in homes, halls, schools, and auditoriums are not included in any interdenominational reports. Probably hundreds of such religious groups are not classified by ordinary statistical processes. One of the most comprehensive lists of American denominations appears in the annual *Yearbook* published by the National Council of Churches. In 1972 this body provided statistical information on 236 American religious societies.

Another characteristic of religion in modern America is that a wide latitude of belief exists within many congregations. The theological pluralism within many bodies is almost as significant as the diversity which divides many churches. The views, for example, of what might be referred to as a liberal Methodist might harmonize to a greater degree with the beliefs held by a liberal Baptist or a liberal Presbyterian than with the tenets held by an orthodox Methodist. Since a variety of theological ideas is so evident in many bodies of Christians, Catholic and Protestant, a person who launches a quest to better understand the beliefs of Americans might easily become confused in a maze of conflicting thoughts.

In an attempt to distinguish the more popular patterns of religious beliefs, authors, teachers, and preachers have adopted a variety of labels. Some Protestants are classified as fundamentalists. Others are referred to as orthodox or conservative Protestants. Another group is sometimes called the neoorthodox, while other Christians are called liberals. Precise definitions of what is meant by these classifications are difficult to make and have never been universally adopted. Sometimes fundamentalists are grouped with the orthodox; sometimes the neoorthodox and humanists are classified with the liberals. Liberal Protestantism is further identified occasionally with popular patterns of thought such as existentialism; and some individuals divide the liberals into categories identified by the names of celebrated theologians, such as Karl Barth, Reinhold Niebuhr, Paul Tillich, Rudolf Bultmann, Dietrich Bonhoeffer, and Teilhard de Chardin.

The problem of classifying Protestants by employing contemporary terms is aggravated because many Christians do not appreciate being referred to by any of the commonly used labels. A Lutheran minister might refer to one of his friends as a liberal, but deny that he is himself a fundamentalist or a conservative. His friend, on the other hand, might refer to the minister as a fundamentalist, denying that he is himself a liberal. Both men might insist that they be referred to as a Lutheran, might reject the modern terms applied to them by others, and yet might employ many of these classifications to describe the beliefs of others.

A few doctrines have also been identified with wings of Protestant thought. The belief, for example, in the verbal inerrancy of the Bible is referred to as a fundamentalist tenet. A Lutheran, however, who endorses this doctrine might deny that it is a fundamentalist belief, insisting that it is a Lutheran belief. Another Lutheran who rejects the concept will contend that the tenet is not Lutheran but a fundamentalist notion, possibly mentioning that the concept was not taught by Martin Luther.

Although many have become disenchanted with the use of labels, and problems are created by employing names to distinguish patterns of thought, the classification of beliefs provides a convenient mechanism for summarizing contemporary Protestant thought. Two major classifications are therefore employed in this work. Individuals who are striving to preserve the historic Protestant theology are classified as orthodox or conservative Protestants.

Traditional Protestant beliefs, popular beliefs held by a high percentage of the Protestants prior to the late nineteenth century, are also referred to as the classical Protestant theology. Modern restatements, beliefs representing the views of contemporary theologians who have and are reinterpreting traditional Protestant concepts, are referred to as liberal views or the new or contemporary theology.

The religious pluralism in America is not only evident in the multiple Protestant faiths that have either been transplanted to America or have originated in this land, but also in the fact that America has become a three-religion culture. During the nineteenth and early twentieth centuries large numbers of Catholic and Jewish immigrants established their homes in the United States. Of the 131 million church members enumerated by the National Council of Churches in 1971, 55 percent were classified as Protestant, 40 percent as Catholic (37 percent being Roman Catholic), and approximately 5 percent as Jewish.[1] When Americans were asked in a Gallup Poll conducted in the preceding year to state their religious preference, 65 percent of the population indicated a Protestant preference; 26 percent Roman Catholic; 3 percent Jewish; 2 percent membership in smaller American faiths, such as Eastern Orthodoxy; and 4 percent indicated that they had "no formal" religion.[2]

A deep interest in humanitarian programs is another characteristic of religion in twentieth century America. As a result of the post-Civil War industrial revolution, the new immigration, the rise of cities, and the disappearance of the frontier, many new problems emerged in this nation. Inequalities of wealth, unemployment, labor unrest, and poverty in urban America led some reformers to inaugurate a variety of programs designed to alleviate the economic and social ills of society. As the nineteenth century drew to a close, many ministers (inspired by the humanitarian impulses of that age and cognizant of new challenges) renewed their interest in the social significance of Christianity. Reshaping of goals was followed by action, resulting in the rise of the social gospel. Various programs launched in the late nineteenth century have been retained and expanded, and new agencies designed to help people have been added, so that religious communities are currently supporting innumerable social service programs, including hospitals, clinics, dispensaries, loan and employment agencies, counseling services, condominiums for the elderly, orphanages, boys' camps, and work projects for the unemployed. Church groups are also striving to help people help themselves through educational opportunities. Many faiths are supporting schools, from nurseries and elementary schools to colleges and universities. Christians are also serving others by visiting the sick, counseling prisoners, assisting drug addicts, and preparing Thanksgiving and Christmas baskets for various groups in society.

One of the active supporters of the social gospel movement is the Salvation Army. This nonsectarian organization, founded by William Booth in London in 1865, was transplanted to America in 1880. Evangelists of this religious philanthropic society are well known for the assistance they render alcoholics, drug addicts, and poverty stricken individuals. In addition to this service, the Salvation Army provides shelter, rehabilitation centers, clinics, children's homes, employment bureaus, summer camps, and social and religious instruction to Americans of various creeds, races, and nationalities.

Social Christianity has expanded from the United States to many other lands. In addition to offering people in other lands spiritual and moral instruction, American Protestants and Catholics have provided educational programs, economic assistance, and medical aid to people throughout the world. By 1960 citizens of this nation were providing at least one-half of all Protestant and one-ninth of all Roman Catholic personnel serving in mission fields and were contributing 80 percent of all Protestant and one-half of all Roman Catholic financial support for foreign missionary work. Currently Latin American and African nations are among the major recipients of these missionary endeavors.[3]

Not all American missionary programs have been "missions" in the traditional sense of winning converts, for many Christians in this land have labored for world rehabilitation and social reconstruction. Following the holocaust of World War II, Protestants, Catholics, and Jews not only supported denominational programs designed to aid world recovery but also contributed time and money to national and international programs aimed at helping people and nations recover from the devastation of the war. American Protestants and Catholics rendered vital support to this movement through the Red Cross, CARE, Church World Service, Catholic Relief Services, Lutheran World Relief, the LDS Relief Society and Welfare Program, and many other similar agencies.

Paralleling the increase in religious pluralism and a renewed emphasis on the social gospel has been the movement to weaken denominational boundaries and unify Christians of various faiths. Some leaders of this ecumenical movement are striving to establish increased interdenominational cooperation, while others optimistically envision a merger of innumerable Christians into a vast world church.

One of the most powerful forces precipitating the current interest in the ecumenical movement has been the gradual erosion of differences dividing many Protestant congregations. In some Protestant circles, dogma is being deemphasized and interest in creeds and theology is being replaced with the conviction that no authority (Bible, creed, or theologian) should compel conformity of belief. Various influential preachers proclaim that Christian living is the primary essential of Christianity and conclude that Protestants and Catholics should not dissipate their strength through theological confrontations. Instead of emphasizing dogma, some suggest that Christians should exert their thoughts and energies toward improving society. Many contemporaries further contend that pooling energies and resources and uniting in a single religious community will enhance the quest to serve humanity.

Meanwhile, Protestants who are striving to preserve the historic Protestant faith tend to remain aloof from ecumenical programs designed to unify Christians. Many hold that such a movement leads to an abandonment of the classical faith and a compromise of religious convictions. Also, many orthodox do not believe that mergers would promote the worldwide expansion of the pure gospel of Christ nor effectively increase programs designed to foster Christian ideals.

While various barriers impede the progress of the ecumenical movement, many religious leaders in America have remained optimistic. Reviewing the significant action and encouraging dialogue of the 1950s and 1960s, many clergymen profess that a modern miracle is occurring and what appeared an impossible goal in the 1940s has become a realistic objective in the 1970s. Individuals, for example, point to the significant mergers of the past two decades as evidence that amazing developments are transpiring. In 1957, the Congregational Christian Churches (a union in 1931 of Congregational churches with a body called Christians) merged with the Evangelical and Reformed Church. This union was consummated in 1961 and the name United Church of Christ was adopted, thereby forming a church with a membership of approximately two million. In 1958 the United Presbyterian Church of North America and the Presbyterian Church in the USA combined, uniting over three million. In 1961, the American Unitarian Association and the Universalist Church of America became the Unitarian Universalist Association with a membership of 170,000. In 1962, four bodies of Lutherans (the American Evangelical Lutheran Church, the Augustana Evangelical Lutheran Church, the Finnish Evangelical Lutheran Church, and the United Lutheran Church of America) merged, adopting the name of the Lutheran Church of America; it has a membership of over three million.

While most members of churches recently united with other bodies have approved the marriages, the unions have not always reduced the number of denominations in America. Some congregations have not endorsed the program and have retained their traditional denominational ties so that in some communities a Congregational Church stands near a United Church of Christ and in other communities Universalists who have not merged with Unitarians continue to worship as independent congregations.

One of the energetic bodies currently striving to promote unity among Christians is the National Council of Churches of Christ in the United States of America. This body emerged in 1950 after the Federal Council of Churches combined with several other agencies. Representing twenty-six Protestant denominations and seven Eastern Orthodox bodies with membership of more than forty million, the National Council of Churches strives to promote cooperation among Christians in areas such as evangelism, research, missions, education, and social welfare.

The World Council of Churches is another agency that was formed to promote harmony among Christians. Meeting in Amsterdam in 1948, the First Assembly of this body stated that its major objective was to "hasten international reconciliation through its own members and through the cooperation of all Christian churches and of all men of good will." This international, interdenominational organization has also declared that it aims to state "the Christian understanding of the will of God" and to promote "its application to national and international policy."

Members of the World Council of Churches have learned that it is less difficult to state goals than to fulfill missions. Various controversial decisions adopted by this body have afflicted it with debilitating problems, and this wing of the ecumenical movement has failed to win the support of many orthodox Christians and of Protestants in some lands who have been offended by their actions.

Another characteristic of religion in modern America has been the rather constant increase not only in church membership but in the percentage of Americans who are affiliated with religious societies. This gradual rise of membership began about 1800 and has continued with few interruptions to the present, as indicated by the information included in Table 1.

After examining church membership statistics during the past two centuries, some authorities contend that there have been a number of long-term revivals in America, the latest occurring after World War II. Others insist that the figures reflect a long, continued upward trend for American religion. Meanwhile, others examine facts and figures that lead them to the conclusion that there has been an increase in the secularization of American life. Recently, another view suggests that one of the most distinguishing characteristics of religion in America has been its stability.[4]

Although major disagreements appear among scholars concerning religious trends in America, the different views expressed are not entirely incompatible. Paradoxes often exist so that some elements in American life might reflect increased secularization and other aspects of our culture might reveal an increased interest in religion.

Conflicting interpretations also arise because of disagreements concerning definitions of such terms as religion and revival. Religion, for example, has been defined as a system of beliefs, as an experience, an awareness, a feeling; as a practice or mode of conduct. Some definitions include combinations of these concepts.

Extreme caution should be employed in comparing early nineteenth- and twentieth-century church membership figures. During the past hundred years there have been significant changes in the definition and requirements for church membership. Prior to the Civil War, many congregations were an assembly of believers who endorsed a specific body of doctrine. Excommunication of wayward members was frequent. Individuals were constantly

Table 1
RATIO OF CHURCH MEMBERS TO POPULATION IN AMERICA

Percent	0	10	20	30	40	50	60	70
1650	▨▨▨▨ 14%							
1700	▨▨▨ 12%							
1776	▨▨ 8%							
1800	▨▨ 7%							
1810	▨▨ 9%							
1820	▨▨▨ 11%							
1830	▨▨▨ 13%							
1840	▨▨▨ 14%							
1850	▨▨▨▨ 16%							
1860	▨▨▨▨▨ 23%							
1870	▨▨▨▨ 18%							
1880	▨▨▨▨ 20%							
1890	▨▨▨▨ 22%							
1900	▨▨▨▨▨▨▨ 36%							
1910	▨▨▨▨▨▨▨▨ 43%							
1920	▨▨▨▨▨▨▨▨ 43%							
1930	▨▨▨▨▨▨▨▨▨ 47%							
1940	▨▨▨▨▨▨▨▨▨ 49%							
1950	▨▨▨▨▨▨▨▨▨▨ 57%							
1960	▨▨▨▨▨▨▨▨▨▨▨ 63.6%							
1967	▨▨▨▨▨▨▨▨▨▨▨ 64.4%							
1970	▨▨▨▨▨▨▨▨▨▨▨ 62.4%							

being removed from the fellowship in a society for failure to attend services, for lack of orthodoxy, for adultery or fornication, for drinking or excessive indulgence of alcoholic liquor, and for a variety of other "transgressions." Moreover, children were usually not enumerated on the membership records of the early American churches. In the twentieth century, however, subscription to the basic provisions of a historic creed is no longer a test of membership in many Christian societies. Heresy trials and excommunications have almost disappeared from the practices of many American congregations, and children are frequently included on membership rolls.

While direct comparisons of early nineteenth- and twentieth-century church membership figures are misleading, there is much evidence supporting the fact that organized religion was neglected in early America. Throughout the colonial period most congregations were small and in many sections of the land there was a shortage of meetinghouses and ministers. Most Americans lived on rural farmsteads where the scattered population, coupled with a pluralistic religious heritage, hindered many groups from organizing and providing satisfactory support for a minister.

Early in the nineteenth century, problems created by the American frontier environment were partially solved and the societies that developed effective missionary programs grew rapidly, becoming the dominant Protestant religions of the mid-nineteenth century. The Baptist farm preachers, the Methodist circuit riders, and itinerant Presbyterian ministers, for example, most effectively took organized religion to rural America; by 1850 approximately three-fourths of all Protestants belonged to one of these three denominations.

Although there appears to have been a decline of organized religion during the era of the Civil War, the decline was quickly arrested and the upward trend of church membership continued. After the rise of the cities and the advent of the automobile, most American families were brought within the shadows of a meetinghouse. Circuit riders dismounted, and many Baptist farm preachers became college-trained urban, suburban, or village pastors. Roman Catholics and Lutherans engaged in gigantic development programs, providing houses of worship and clergy for new immigrants. Meanwhile, the frenzied emotionalism that characterized many revivals during the second Great Awakening of the early nineteenth century subsided. Conversions continued, but the new converts of modern America were better educated and less prone to engage in physical demonstrations. Their personal commitments were channeled in new directions. Nevertheless, vast throngs stepped forward in churches, stadiums, and auditoriums and joined others in prayer and song, quietly and solemnly testifying to the world that they had gained a spiritual conviction that Jesus Christ is the redeemer of mankind.

While the role of the itinerant preacher changed and most American revivals were cloaked with new attire, many congregations welcomed into their fold people of various religious convictions, including those who did not desire to profess any formal pattern of belief. Membership in a religious community not only became acceptable in modern America, but in some circles religious affiliation was considered economically, socially, and politically desirable. Consequently, for the past 170 years the numbers uniting with many American churches have increased yearly.

There is also evidence that religion in America, especially during the past two decades, has been in a state of stability. Church attendance polls indicate that during the 1950s (see Table 2) participation in religious services reached

Table 2

CHURCH ATTENDANCE POLLS

Date	Percent of Adults Attending Church	Date	Percent of Adults Attending Church
1940	37	1962	46
1947	45	1963	46
1950	39	1964	45
1954	46	1965	44
1955	49	1966	44
1956	46	1967	45
1957	47	1968	43
1958	49	1969	42
1959	47	1970	42
1960	47	1971	40
1961	47	1972	40

a modern plateau; and while the percentage of Americans affiliated with churches continued to increase in the 1960s, the percent reporting church attendance declined. Another set of statistics supports this view of a contemporary state of stability, for as the 1960s gave way to the 1970s there seems to have been a minor decline in the percentage of church members in this land, a trend which interrupted the gradual upward flow of religious affiliation that had continued with only brief interruptions since 1800.[5]

There are other themes which emerge in a study of religious trends in modern America. Currently there is a new emphasis on the liturgy as a means of turning men toward God. Instead of debunking religious practices of the past, many theologians are studying rites prescribed for public worship in hopes of discovering unifying themes.

In recent years there has also been a black religious revolution in this country. Early in the century there was a major thrust among blacks to own and control their religious institutions. This movement led to an increase in membership of major Protestant faiths and the Roman Catholic Church, and precipitated the creation of many new denominations. Currently there is a trend to integrate white and black congregations; and a number of competent and dedicated black ministers are securing opportunities in what were formerly white congregations.

Although religious changes in America have been constant, the mosaic has continued. Pluralism, diversity, toleration, and separation of church and state have continued as dominant ecclesiastical characteristics of the United States, while religion has remained an important force in the history of this nation.

Part One
Basic Religious Contrasts:
Catholicism and Protestantism;
Orthodoxy and Liberalism

1

Roman Catholicism

One of the major claims of members of the Roman Catholic Church, the world's largest Christian Church, is that it is the one and only true religion. In explaining this principle of distinctiveness, members of this faith emphasize that Jesus of Nazareth founded his Church more than nineteen centuries ago in the land of Judea and conferred upon the leaders of this movement the power and jurisdiction to teach all mankind the beauties of the gospel of Christ. "As the Father has sent me," Christ instructed his apostles, "even so I send you."[1] Roman Catholics also teach that included among the conferred powers was the exclusive right of leadership, for they assert that Christ specifically said to one of his most beloved apostles,

> You are Peter, and on this rock I will build my church, and the powers of death shall not prevail against it. I will give you the keys of the kingdom of heaven; and whatever you bind on earth shall be bound in heaven, and whatever you loose on earth shall be loosed in heaven.[2]

Members of this religious community insist that the rock referred to in this controversial scripture was Peter and that this promise was partially fulfilled shortly after Christ's resurrection. On Pentecost Sunday in A.D. 33, they explain, Peter became the supreme shepherd of the new church; and the bishops, priests, and people were placed under the jurisdiction of this venerable leader. According to their tradition, Peter eventually went to Rome, ruled the church from this capital, and became a martyr during the persecution of Nero. Roman Catholics further testify that the bishops or popes of Rome are the only proper successors of Peter and that these spiritual leaders have continued to exercise this supreme jurisdiction.

In addition to claiming that Christ transferred the power of leadership through Peter to the bishops of Rome, the Roman Catholics also defend their conviction that their church is the only true religion. They assert that Roman Catholic bishops are the only religious leaders who have received authority in an unbroken line from Christ. The right of ordination, they say, is an exclusive power of the bishops, and the right to administer most sacraments is limited to the bishops and priests who have received this delegated authority. Most insist that influential leaders who have left the Roman Catholic fold have abandoned the rights which they enjoyed; while many individuals have sought to reestablish the universal church, Catholics maintain that the schismatic reformers have lost their authority and have merely created man-made institutions.

Another significant claim of members of the world's largest religious community is that their church is the only true "catholic church" in the sense that it is the only truly universal church. It is considered the only church which teaches all the doctrines unfolded by the Man of Galilee and the only worldwide church being, as they say, everywhere in the world. Sometimes members of this communion summarize their uniqueness by emphatically declaring that their church is the only faith founded by Christ and clothed with Christ's power and authority; the only pure apostolic church, meaning in part the only church whose uninterrupted history dates back to Pentecost Sunday; and the only true community established by Christ for the salvation of all mankind.[3]

Although orthodox Roman Catholics insist that their communion is the only church today that is clothed with Christ's power and authority and is traceable without interruption back to New Testament Christianity, many popular patterns of belief currently held by members of this faith were not crystallized until they had survived centuries of vehement debate. Since the early Christian church spread into a world in which there was a universal interest in religion, constant confrontations between the earliest generations of Christians and their pagan contemporaries erupted. The arguments stimulated Christian intellectuals to defend their faith, resulting in the production of innumerable apologies. As the years passed, however, Christians became alarmed because influential defenders of the faith had perpetuated a myriad of conflicting beliefs.

In the midst of internal doctrinal diversities and savage external persecution, a new emperor appeared who helped alter significantly the course of history. Early in the fourth century, Emperor Constantine issued an edict of toleration, making Christianity a legal religion within the Roman Empire. After extending toleration to Christians, the emperor labored to promote unity within the divided church and convoked the first ecumenical council. Constantine not only selected the site for this historic gathering but also issued invitations to the bishops, determined the agenda of the meeting, and presided over the imposing body. Approximately three hundred bishops and many others, both Christian and non-Christian, gathered at Nicaea in A.D. 325. At the request of the emperor, delegates discussed and debated several conflicting beliefs, including the concept of God. During the meetings, the controversial views of Arius (that there was a time when Jesus did not exist and that Jesus was a being separate and distinct from the Father) were condemned in favor of the position that Jesus was not made but is coeternal and of one divine essence with the Father.[4]

Although a precise definition of God was adopted at Nicaea, many rejected the verdict, and Christians continued to quarrel vehemently over the issue of the nature of the diety. As the fourth century drew to a close, however, other significant developments transformed the religious behavior patterns of vast numbers residing in the Roman Empire. Under the powerful jurisdiction of Theodosius the Great, Christian orthodoxy was again defined. At the Council of Constantinople (A.D. 381), another historic gathering influenced by a Roman emperor, delegates again endorsed the concept that God consists of three persons of one divine essence. Subsequently, Theodosius deposed Arian bishops and ordered all Arians to acknowledge the Nicene faith. In addition to establishing the Nicene faith as the norm of orthodoxy, Theodosius attempted to force all non-Christians to conform to the religion of the state. Every pagan form of public worship was forbidden— the performance of bloody sacrifices, the worship of images in temples, and the veneration of pagan shrines and images. Pagan temples and houses of worship were confiscated. Outspoken critics were silenced and paganism was reduced to a state from which it never fully recovered. Because of vigorous constraint, vast numbers within the empire adopted the religion of the state; and Christianity and the Nicene faith emerged as the dominant religion of the decaying Roman Empire.[5]

As Christian emperors expanded their political jurisdiction, Christianity was gradually imposed upon most of the inhabitants of Europe. Except for a few persecuted Jews and Spanish Moslems, most people residing in western Europe during the latter half of the Middle Ages were Roman Catholics.

During these triumphant centuries, many ecumenical councils were held in which dogmatic statements of belief were adopted. After the first two general councils defined the nature of God, four ecumenical councils considered the nature of Christ, after which Christians officially rejected the notion that there must be two distinct persons in Christ, the human and divine, but held instead that there were two natures in him, divine and human.

Although the first eight ecumenical councils were held in eastern Europe or Asia Minor, all other gatherings classified as general councils by Roman Catholics have been held in the West, and many important doctrinal definitions have been adopted during these meetings. At the Fourth Lateran Council of 1215, transubstantiation was declared an article of faith. During the

Seventeenth General Council of Basel-Ferrara-Florence (held between 1431 and 1445), the church officially endorsed as dogma the concept of purgatory and the belief that the Holy Ghost proceeds from the Father and the Son.

The most fruitful ecumenical council in issuing dogmatic definitions occurred during the era of the Reformation. At the Council of Trent (1545-1563) explicit definitions were adopted concerning justification, grace, original sin, the sources of religious truth, and the seven sacraments.

During the past century, two significant gatherings have been held in Rome. At the First General Council of the Vatican (1869-1870), the dogma of papal primacy and infallibility was defined; in more recent years, the Second Vatican Council (1962-1965) opened the door for major revisions in church policies and procedures. This council, for example, defined the nature of the church, granting bishops a larger role in church government and giving laymen a more active part in the liturgy. It pledged the church to promote unity among Christians, including the participation of Catholics in the ecumenical movement, and it extended to parents the right to choose freely the type of education they desired for their children. This body also authorized the use of vernacular languages in portions of the Mass and other sacraments, such as baptism and marriage; approved a communion of both bread and wine not only to clerics but also to the laity according to the discretion of bishops; reaffirmed a decision of Trent which recognized the validity of Protestant baptisms if such ordinances were performed correctly and with proper intent, and officially extended the sacrament of extreme unction (which is now called the sacrament of anointing with oil) to not only the dying but also to the sick.

Another memorable contribution of this Vatican council was the issuance of a decree on toleration. "It is an injustice," the delegates ruled, "done to the human persons, and to the order laid down for men by God, if a man is denied the free exercise of religion in society; saving a just public order." This decree was based on the conception that every man has "an inalienable personal right to determine his own religious attitudes within the limits of public order without any coercion on the part of civil authorities."[6]

The remarkable expansion of this faith on the American continent and the phenomenal numerical growth of Roman Catholicism in the New World is another memorable episode in the history of this church. Two-and-a-half decades before Martin Luther posted his Ninety-five Theses, Christopher Columbus planted the Spanish culture on the picturesque island that is today known as Santo Domingo and Haiti. Through conscientious and persistent labors, the Spanish soon earned the reputation of being the most successful explorers and colonizers of the New World. As ambitious conquistadors and zealous missionaries continuing a crusade which originated against the Moslems of Spain, they diffused their religious behavior patterns throughout

Latin America. Consequently, the faith of the new immigrants was effectively superimposed over the religions of the aborigines.

Roman Catholics were not only responsible for the initial European colonization of Latin America, but also for the first permanent European settlement in North America. As early as 1565 the Spanish established a permanent military post at St. Augustine, Florida; during the first decade of the seventeenth century, French Catholics initiated the successful colonization of Canada at Quebec and of the southwestern section of that which is today the United States at Santa Fe, New Mexico.

Even though the thirteen colonies were primarily settled by Protestants, two of the influential promoters of the English colonization of North America were Roman Catholics: George and Cecil Calvert, the first and second Lord Baltimore. After George Calvert had secured a liberal charter from the king, his heir directed the English colonization of Maryland at St. Mary's in 1634, and for more than half a century this colony was under the political control of benevolent Catholic rulers.

Cecil Calvert was also responsible for planting toleration on the American continent. As a member of a persecuted society, the second Lord Baltimore and many other English Catholics recognized the advantages that would accrue to them if the English government discontinued its attempt to maintain religious solidarity in that country. In addition to endorsing the principle of toleration, Cecil recognized that the establishment of toleration in Maryland was an economic and a political necessity. To profit from his business enterprise, it was necessary for Cecil to attract non-Catholics to his colony; and in order to prevent a revoking of his charter by the English monarch, this entrepreneur recognized the political expediency of extending toleration to Anglicans. From the inception of this colony's history, therefore, toleration was a practical reality.

As the years passed, Cecil Calvert learned of Catholic persecution in his colony and perceived that jealous Englishmen increasingly opposed his chartered rights. Subsequently, the second Lord Baltimore prepared and submitted to the colonial assembly an act which he anticipated would grant relief to Catholics of Maryland and would at the same time reduce the pressures in England which threatened his charter. Responding to the desires of their proprietor, the Maryland assembly enacted America's first toleration act in 1649. This important landmark along the trail of religious liberty extended toleration to all Trinitarian Christians residing in Maryland.[7]

Although Maryland was founded under the direction of Roman Catholics, at no time during the colonial period was a majority of the settlers in this colony members of this faith; few Catholics were attracted to the other English mainland colonies. In some of the thirteen colonies Catholicism was not regarded as a legal religion, and in all these colonies there were periods in which Catholics were not granted the legal right to vote or hold office. The rights of Catholics were also greatly curtailed in Maryland as well during the first half of the eighteenth century. After the Catholic proprietors lost jurisdiction over this colony, a penal age for members of this faith was inaugurated. Catholics were forbidden to hold public services, to proselyte, or to establish parochial schools in Maryland.[8] Since an unhealthy religious climate in the thirteen colonies discouraged Catholics from immigrating to this section of the New World, the Roman Catholic Church remained, numerically speaking, one of the smaller religious societies in the English colonies. In 1776 there were about fifty Catholic meetinghouses in the thirteen colonies.[9] Because the houses of worship were small and most Americans of that era lived on isolated farmsteads, few members of this church were in a position to attend services regularly. The faith of many of the immigrants languished.[10]

During the American Revolution, Roman Catholics secured some relief from oppression. France was an ally of America. Many patriots hoped to win the support of the Canadians. Americans of various religions fought together for a common cause, and George Washington emerged as one of the leading champions of religious liberty. Washington not only promoted religious harmony among his troops but ordered the cessation of Guy Fawkes celebrations, a popular anti-Catholic holiday. By his actions and by the laudable accomplishments of many other Americans (Deists, Baptists, Presbyterians, and Catholics) religious liberty emerged as a legal and theoretical reality in the young republic. [11]

The first substantial growth of Catholicism in this country began about 1830 as a result of a great influx of immigrants from Ireland and Germany. By the middle of the century, there were probably more than a million Roman Catholics residing in the new nation. Although in 1850 there were about 1,200 Catholic churches in the United States, representing an increase of 1,097 in three decades, the problem of providing members of this faith with facilities and spiritual leadership continued to be acute. [12]

Following the Civil War, especially at the turn of the century, the tidal wave of immigration reached unprecedented proportions. Never before in the history of mankind have so many people been uprooted. And the Roman Catholic Church benefited more than any other denomination from this tremendous immigration. During the fifty-year period from 1850 to 1890 the number of Catholics residing in the United States increased from about one-and-one-half million to more than six million and the number of churches increased from 1,200 to about 10,000. Early in this period the Roman Catholic Church emerged as the largest religious community in the United States. Another phenomenal increase in the membership of the Roman Catholic Church occurred between 1890 and 1906. During this brief sixteen-year period, membership doubled, with approximately fourteen million Roman Catholics in the United States reported in the religious census of 1906. Within another forty years, this church almost doubled its membership again, reporting a membership of twenty-seven million in 1946. In 1967 the Roman Catholic Church continued to retain its commanding numerical position among the American religions with a membership of nearly forty-seven million, indicating another approximate doubling of membership during these two decades.[13]

In addition to being the leading supporters of American parochial schools, Roman Catholics are also benevolent supporters of innumerable social services, including hospitals, orphanages, homes for senior citizens, and institutions for the blind, the deaf, the emotionally and/or socially maladjusted, the mentally retarded, and other handicapped individuals. Family counseling, child welfare, services for unmarried mothers, neighborhood center programs, and Indian programs are additional services rendered under the auspices of Catholic charities. In 1973, for example, 24,853,267 patients received treatment in 702 general hospitals supported by members of this faith. At the same time, 15,896 children received help in the 216 Catholic orphanages and infant asylums; and Catholics were supervising the needs of more than 19,000 children residing in foster homes.[14] In addition to these social services, members of this denomination assist in the rehabilitation of alcoholics partly through the support of Alcoholics Anonymous and Narcotics Anonymous.

Patterns of Roman Catholic Belief

Roman Catholics believe that the church of Jesus Christ is not merely a brotherhood of men united by bonds of grace, but is a viable institution of individuals with an authoritative leadership. This hierarchical society is sometimes compared to a pyramid. The pope, the bishop of Rome, stands at the head of this church. Next to the pope is the College of Cardinals, men who serve as advisers of the pope to head various administrative units, and, following the death of the Roman pontiff, to elect a new pope. The bishop of Rome is also aided by the Roman Curia, an official body of papal administrative officers. Immediately below the pope are the other bishops, who are appointed from Rome generally after recommendations from local leaders. Archbishops are in charge of the archdioceses and bishops are the ruling authority in the dioceses. Under the bishops are the local priests who possess the power of jurisdiction to the extent delegated to them by the bishops whom they are ordained to assist. The broad base of the pyramid consists of the baptized members for whose sake the entire organization exists.[15]

Although Roman Catholics are monotheistic, believing that there is only one God, they agree that there are three persons in God: God the Father, God the Son, and God the Holy Ghost. The three persons in the Trinity are considered equal, existing together from and to all eternity. The three divine persons, though really distinct, are referred to as one because they possess the same divine nature and are united in thought, will, and being. God the Father is the Creator. God was also incarnated and made man and God the Son is referred to as the Redeemer. Jesus Christ is one person in two natures, divine and human, truly God and truly man, two wills in perfect harmony. God the Holy Spirit is known as the Sanctifier who proceeds from the Father and Son. This dogma of the Trinity is classified as one of the greatest mysteries of the church. It is regarded as a truth that man cannot fully comprehend.

Roman Catholics further teach that God is an infinitely perfect spirit, an immaterial being without parts or bodily form, who is omniscient, omnipotent, and omnipresent.

In explaining God's omniscience, Catholic theologians state that God knows perfectly all things that have occurred in the past, all that currently takes place, and all that will exist both in the physical and moral order. Although Catholics generally say that all things "are naked and open to His eyes," this complete foreknowledge does not necessarily mean that God prevents man from exercising free will. Most Catholics insist that God knows all things including the future free actions of all men. He has extended to mankind the right to exercise independent judgment.[16]

Catholics further teach that God has dominion over everything he has created, but this omnipotence extends only to that which is possible and not contradictory. Catholic theologians assert that God cannot make, for example, a square circle, not because God's power is limited but because of the inherent limitation of the impossible or contradictory idea. God can, however, accomplish all that he wills to do.

According to members of this faith, God through his power and operation is present everywhere and is in all things. Although Catholics say that God has no precise form and is not limited spatially, he is considered to be the "source of the being and action in all places and things."[17]

The earliest known creations of God, according to Roman Catholic theology, were angels. Angels are referred to as spirits (without bodies) who serve and praise God. It is also believed that all these special creations were originally good, but by their own choice, some sinned; these fallen angels became devils. Catholics have not departed from the traditional belief that devils can inhabit human bodies and that priests have the authority and power to cast evil spirits out of afflicted bodies.

Although in the past most members of this denomination have interpreted many events as resulting from the actions of angels or devils, many now question some of the historic traditions of the church, concluding that where natural causes operate there are no angelic interventions. Many modern members further teach that angels and spirits have no precise form and never appear in human bodies. Although some theologians speculate that angels can appear in different forms, including human forms, many Catholics insist that angels do not have wings. The winged type of Christian angel is said by many contemporary theologians to be a derivation from the winged Greek goddess of Victory, Nike.[18]

Believing that angels are keenly interested in the welfare of mankind, members of this faith teach that these special creations of God pray (along with the saints) for mankind and use their power to aid those who seek their help. Another commonly held belief of Catholics is that every individual has a guardian angel.

Roman Catholics teach that two sources of religious truth are the Bible and tradition. The church is regarded as the only proper teacher and interpreter of the Bible and indicates which of the various ancient writings are inspired. Another historic teaching that is binding upon the membership is that God is the author of the scriptures because he was the originator of these writings. Many Catholics say God enlightened the mind of the authors of the Bible so that they penned precisely that which God desired to be written. Although the Council of Trent specified that God was the originator of the scriptures, some Catholic theologians contend that the authors of the Bible were merely secretaries acting as mechanical recorders. Inspiration means that God influenced the human writer so that the individual recorded correct concepts. God's inspiration, some theologians add, might also consist in directing a writer to approve that which someone else has recorded.[19]

While some Catholics hold that God has assured that an accurate transmission of his words is passed from one generation to another, in recent years an increasing number of Catholics have subscribed to the theory that the Bible contains myths, legends, and opinions of men. Errors of omission, addition, and mistranslation are considered to have significantly altered portions of the original recordings. Since none of the original manuscripts are available, some Catholics conclude that there is no way of knowing precisely what some of the authors originally wrote. Some scholars of this faith also insist that since the Bible was not written to teach others physical science, individuals should not consider this book as a scientific treatise.[20]

Unlike most Protestants, Roman Catholics declare that the Bible should not be regarded as the sole norm of faith. According to Catholics, the scriptures are susceptible to a variety of interpretations. Moreover, the Bible was not meant to be a constitution upon which God's church should be built. It does not contain everything important regarding the faith and practice of the Christian church. One example of a practice endorsed by most Christians which Catholics say is not explicit in the Bible was the change of the Sabbath from Saturday to the Lord's Day on Sunday in order to commemorate the resurrection of Jesus Christ.

Maintaining that the Bible is not complete and is difficult to understand, Catholics aver that another source is necessary to determine religious truth. That second source is tradition. As all important truths of the gospel were conveyed by Christ to the apostles, people can learn through tradition those things which were known by the apostles of old. By examining the writings of church fathers, the decisions of general councils and the decrees of popes,

Catholics believe that mankind can ascertain all essential truths not revealed in the Bible.

About the creation and the fall, Catholics agree that God created the world out of nothing. To them the word "create" means "to make out of nothing." Although they also hold that the souls of Adam and Eve were directly created by God, members are divided regarding the manner of this creation and the characteristics of Adam before the fall. Some hold the traditional view that the bodies of Adam and Eve were specially created by God. Some priests also teach that in their original state, Adam and Eve had perfect control of their passions, were free from disease, suffering, and death. If our first parents had not sinned, many suggest, they would have completed their temporal life without experiencing the dreaded separation from the body called death, and all mankind would have enjoyed the gifts which God had conveyed to our first parents, including the gift of grace or the sharing of the divine nature. Failing to obey God, probably committing the sin of pride, Adam and Eve fell. As a result of the fall, some contend, man became physically imperfect and became subject to disease and death.[21]

A popular modern restatement that conflicts with traditional views regarding Adam's place in history is that evolution was probably God's method of creation. Many contemporary Catholics also note that the church has not defined the gifts Adam possessed before the fall except to use the words "holiness" and "justice." Some theologians speculate that the first man might have been a primitive man who enjoyed fellowship with God. They add that Adam's special endowments might have been his possibilities rather than his perfections. The story of the fall, some liberal Catholics continue, is a myth or folklore informing us of man's estrangement from God. The sin of Adam might have been a refusal to obey God. As a consequence of Adam's transgression, some conclude, all men suffer death, and man's relationship with God is strained.[22]

In order that man might again be reconciled to God, Roman Catholics teach that the Son of God became human and then redeemed mankind. By his sacrifice on the cross Christ acquired for all worthy individuals deliverance from the evils of sin and from eternal death; and he placed man in a new relationship with God, a state of grace. The Council of Trent emphasized this concept by decreeing that only through Christ could the original sin be removed; only through baptism are the merits of Christ applied to adults and children.[23]

Many different theories explaining the deliverance of mankind from sin by the death of Christ have been advanced by Catholics during their long history. One of the early Christian theories of the atonement, known as the ransom theory, concentrated on the cross as a means by which God overcame the power of Satan. Since it was believed that Satan held sinful man in bondage or as a hostage, Christians speculated that a ransom was paid by God to the devil. As the years passed, however, some Christians concluded that the cruci-fixion had more of an effect than merely canceling the ransom price for man. It was argued that because of Christ's actions man was released from Satan's dominion. If one accepts the ransom theory, theologians reasoned, man's release from Satan could only have occurred through divine bargaining or deception.[24]

In the eleventh century, a medieval theologian named Anselm developed the substitutional theory, another view that at one time was widely held by Christians. Anselm rejected the notion of a redemption from the devil, claim-ing that the devil played no role in the work of the cross. The atonement, he suggested, was solely related to man's relationship to God. Because man by sinning disgraced God, God's honor had to be repaired. Justice demands that sins should be punished, Anselm said, and all must pay back the honor which they have stolen from God in accordance with the seriousness of the crime. Since man's sins were of such a serious nature, he could not provide a proper propitiation (appeasement or conciliation). God alone was in a position to make the required infinite satisfaction. According to this theory, the volun-tary suffering and death of Christ on Calvary was a positive act or gift which served as a payment for the offense of sin, the debt being paid not to the devil but to God. Consequently, the means was provided by which the sins of all men of all ages could be forgiven.[25]

In the thirteenth century, Thomas Aquinas again altered the pattern of Christian thinking by turning man's attention from the substitutional concept of the atonement to what is called the vicarious moral satisfaction theory. Thomas Aquinas rejected Anselm's view that the justice of God demanded Christ's death on the cross as a satisfaction for human sin. Our sovereign God, he suggested, is the fountain of justice. God is free to forgive anyone and everyone he desires. After agreeing with Anselm that the sins of man dis-honored God, Thomas explained the mode of redemption by suggesting that the action of Christ on Calvary not only vividly revealed to man the love of God but also incited man to love the Father of us all. It was this offering of love, he said, that led God to dispense his grace to mankind.[26]

Another medieval theologian, Abelard, advanced another theory which has served as the basis for perhaps more modern Protestant interpretations of the atonement than any other presentation. The central theme of the Abelardian view is that Christ reconciled man to God by revealing the love of God in His life, a life which was climaxed by His expressions of love on Calvary. Accord-ing to this theory, by setting a perfect example, Christ inspired mankind to trust and love God; and when a person internalizes these ideals and overcomes the barrier of sin, he is reconciled to God.[27]

Although many Catholics profess that there are elements of truth in Abelard's view of the atonement, most members of this church vehemently reject the liberal Protestant expression which considers the efficacy of

Christ's life and actions on Calvary solely in an exemplary and inspirational manner. Roman Catholics generally insist that the passion of Christ earned or acquired for man the deliverance from sin and the reunion of man with God. By Christ's atonement, they say, men may share anew the divine nature or regain the grace which was lost by the fall of man.

In contemporary Catholic and Protestant writings one finds various combinations of atonement ideas emphasized by medieval theologians. Many Catholics of the twentieth century reason that Christ's suffering and death provided a satisfaction for a debt which mankind was unable to pay. By offering his blood to God, many priests explain, Christ ransomed man from the slavery of sin. Catholics further emphasize that the crucifixion was a demonstration of God's love and that the cross impressed mankind with the horror of sin. The current emphasis also considers the atonement a work of divine mercy rather than a juridical placation of divine wrath.

The Roman Catholic Church is further distinguished by its distinct position regarding life beyond the grave. Although Protestants, Eastern Catholics, and Roman Catholics agree on a number of eschatological concepts, Roman Catholic teachings regarding purgatory, treasury of merits, indulgences, masses for the dead, and limbo are unique. No other major religious society in this country proclaims these concepts precisely as held by Roman Catholics (or some of the more recent offshoots of this faith).

In harmony, however, with popular Protestant thinking, Roman Catholics agree that death is the separation of the body and the soul. At the instant the soul parts from the body, Catholics explain, it is judged by God in what is known as the Particular or Private Judgment. At the end of the world, all mankind, the righteous and wicked, will be resurrected with the "bodies they now have." The resurrected bodies of the righteous will be distinguished by their agility (perfect dominion over the body), subtility (a spiritualized nature), impassibility (incapability of suffering) and clarity (rising in glory). Although some Roman Catholics continue to teach that the resurrected body will be a youthful body of flesh and bones and will include all of man's organs, others substitute this traditional view with the concept that the nature of the resurrected body is a mystery. In some way, many contemporaries teach, the transformed, perfected, spiritualized bodies will be identifiable and materially identical with the bodies of this life, but will not consist of flesh, bones, nor organs.[28]

Immediately after death, Roman Catholics continue, men enter one of three or four states of existence. Individuals who die without the least stain of sin will enter heaven and behold God, partaking of the beatific vision. The essential element in heaven, according to Catholics, is not only seeing God, but is being united in mind and heart with our Eternal Father. Although some members believe that heaven is a place, liberal Catholics conclude that heaven is essentially a state of mind.

Since Roman Catholics maintain that upon death few men are prepared to enter heaven, they believe that many who will eventually be united with God first enter an intermediate state called purgatory. Purgatory is regarded as a temporary place or condition for those who die and have not been severed from God by mortal sin but are not in a state of perfect purity, an essential prerequisite for a union with God. While in purgatory individuals make reparation or amends for unforgiven venial sins (less serious sins) or for mortal sins (more serious transgressions that merit eternal punishment) which have already been forgiven. Although no one knows the duration of this purification, it is believed that individuals remain in purgatory until they are free from guilt and punishment. Immediately after this cleansing, the souls are assumed into heaven. After the General Judgment, many Catholics allege, the "purifying fire" will discontinue and purgatory will cease to be a state of existence.[29]

Roman Catholics further teach that no one knows the nature of purgatorial punishment, except they agree that individuals in purgatory are denied the beatific vision. Although the souls detained in purgatory cannot lessen or shorten their own sufferings, Catholics teach that the punishment can be alleviated by men on earth through prayers, the sacrifice of the Mass, and indulgences. Some people, Catholics contend, have entered heaven with a surplus of credits which have been placed in a treasury of merits. By securing indulgences, individuals may draw from this treasury and apply the merits to souls in purgatory, thereby alleviating their suffering. Since they profess that after a person sins he must not only be forgiven but must also pay a penalty before he is purified, members of this church further explain that indulgences are instruments enabling individuals to secure for themselves or for the deceased a remission of temporal punishment arising from sins which have been forgiven through the sacrament of penance.

This remission is contingent upon compliance with the conditions stated in the indulgence and is classified according to the extent to which temporal punishment can be lessened. A plenary indulgence enables a person to secure a full remission of the punishment to which he might be liable for forgiven sins. A partial indulgence remits punishment only to the extent specified by the indulgence, such as sixty days or ten years, for instance. This would be the equivalent of performing penance for ten years, but even then there is no way of relating precisely the value of this action to alleviating cleansing in purgatory.[30]

Although there is no official position of this church regarding limbo, another proposed state of existence in the life beyond the grave, many Catholics believe that unbaptized infants are not qualified to enter heaven nor do they deserve the torment of hell. Since infants die in a state of original sin and are not in a state of grace, it is commonly believed they enter the Limbo of Children. It is further believed by many Catholics that since Adam's sin excluded all from heaven until Christ redeemed mankind, Old Testament prophets and worthy pagans proceeded to the Limbo of the Fathers. There they awaited the coming of the Savior and were released after his sacrifice.

The condition of the souls in limbo is another subject open for theological speculation. Most Catholics conclude that the souls in limbo do not suffer the torment of hell but are denied the beatific vision.

While many Catholics believe in the existence of limbo, some speculate that the contemporary emphasis on baptism of desire (the belief that in some mysterious manner all who perform an act of perfect love for God are baptized) might eliminate the need for such a state of existence. Until recently, Catholic theologians have generally limited baptism of desire to adults, for acts of faith, love, and desire seemed beyond the attributes of a small child. But some members currently reason that a child might benefit from the desires of parents, or of the church, or as a consequence of God's sincere desire to save the souls of men. Liberals emphasize that while the church has decreed that baptism is necessary to remove the original sin, this declaration does not preclude the possibility of the sin being removed by some other means. There is no official position of the church, liberals insist, regarding the fate of infants whose baptism is physically or morally impossible. In recent years, this reevaluation of a traditional belief has precipitated innumerable theories regarding possible means by which infants can enter heaven. It has prompted some priests to counsel aggrieved parents that their unbaptized infant might in some way secure everlasting salvation.[31]

While Catholics are not in agreement regarding limbo, it is the doctrine of the Roman Catholic Church that individuals who die in a state of mortal sin and without sanctifying grace will go to hell and be eternally separated from God. This church also teaches that there is no passage from heaven to hell and no possible way for one in hell to escape everlasting punishment. Some priests maintain that those sent to hell will be tortured by a literal fire that afflicts the soul and the resurrected body eternally, without diminishment or end. Other Catholics insist that the future punishment for sin is not necessarily physical torment. Possibly, some contend, the meaning of *damned* is that individuals are unfree and that the real punishment of hell is separation from God.[32]

Another identifying feature of the Roman Catholic faith is its position regarding the number of sacraments ordained by Christ. Roman Catholics insist that there are seven sacraments, no more and no less. Unlike most Protestants, Catholics further contend that sacraments are the channels or the means by which individuals receive sanctifying grace. They are sometimes viewed as pipes or funnels through which God channels his divine nature or his power that cleanses man. Salvation, Catholics continue, is the divinization of the soul. In order that the soul may enjoy the beatific vision, it must be transformed. This elevation is a gift of God and is accomplished by an infusion in man of supernatural powers and virtues called sanctifying grace. It is a change in man, not merely a change in God's attitude toward man. Grace is also considered a force in man which is continually nourished by God, enabling man to live on the level to which God raised him by sanctifying grace. This second kind of grace is called actual grace. Roman Catholics further maintain that if a proper intention is present, grace is conferred through the sacraments. The rite, however, becomes ineffective if one is willfully set against receiving the sacrament at the moment it is administered.[33]

After examining the Roman Catholic position regarding the consequences of the most important sacrament, baptism, it is not surprising that members of this religious community insist that this rite is necessary for salvation. According to Roman Catholics, baptism conveys to recipients a special power, the power of sanctifying grace, which removes the stain and guilt of original sin. Through baptism, individuals also receive the benefits of the atonement, secure a remission of personal sins and punishment due to mortal and venial sins and are admitted into the church.

Proper baptism, according to members of this faith, occurs when water flows across the head of the recipient accompanied with a proper prayer: "I baptize thee in the name of the Father, and of the Son, and of the Holy Ghost (or Holy Spirit)." Ordinarily a priest who is the pastor over the parents of the infant or the candidate who is joining the church should perform this rite, but in cases of necessity Catholics recommend that anyone (Protestant, non-Christian, agnostic, or atheist) may and should baptize.

Since baptism is considered essential for salvation, Catholics specify that God has made it relatively easy for individuals to receive this sacrament. If a person is not baptized by water, he might be baptized by laying down his life for the church. Such martyrs are considered baptized by blood. And in recent years, baptism of desire has gained a new emphasis. According to some Catholics, baptism of desire is a means by which individuals who intend to receive this sacrament satisfy the requirement by making an act of contrition or of perfect charity.

In this faith, two sponsors, a man and a woman who are not the father or mother of a child, act as spokesmen at infant baptisms. These sponsors or godparents assume a lifelong responsibility for the spiritual welfare of the child. As long as a local religious leader is assured that a child will be reared a Roman Catholic, any infant may be baptized by an ordained priest. In cases of necessity (such as danger of death), anyone, Christian or non-Christian, male or female, may baptize.

The complement and completion of baptism is called the sacrament of confirmation. According to Roman Catholics, confirmation conveys to recipients not only grace to be a more faithful Christian but also special powers emitted by the Holy Ghost. This sacrament consists of the imposition of the hands of the clergy and the anointing with oil on the forehead. Although bishops must consecrate the oil and ordinarily administer this sacrament, in

1947 the pope declared that under certain conditions authorized priests could administer this rite. A sponsor of the same sex as the candidate—but not the father, mother, husband, or wife of the recipient nor the same person who served as a godparent at baptism—must guarantee the character of the candidate and must promise to assist the person in continuing his pursuit of a Christian life. During the rite, the recipient must also take the name of another saint in addition to the name he received at baptism. Ordinarily, confirmation is not conferred until after a child has reached an age of reason and received first communion.

The most sacred and central service of this religion is the Mass. During this solemn ceremony, Catholics testify that Christ offers a perfect gift to God—himself. He makes, it is believed, the same sacrifice through the ministry of the priest that He made on the cross at Calvary, except that it is an unbloody immolation. Catholics seriously contend that Christ is truly the victim of the altar. Christ offers himself in the Mass to apply his redemption to mankind.

Another distinguishing feature of Roman Catholicism that differs from Protestant traditions is that during the Mass the sacrament of the Holy Eucharist becomes a reality, for they teach that when the bread and wine is consecrated it is changed into the body and blood of Christ. During this ceremony, Catholics believe, Jesus becomes present under the appearance of bread and wine. Although that which remains has all the appearance of bread and wine, it is taught that the substance of Christ totally replaces the annihilated substance of the bread and wine when the priest says, "This is my body" and "This is the chalice of my blood." Therefore, it is held that when communicants partake of the unleavened wheat bread (or both the bread and the wine) they receive literally the whole and entire body of Christ. Another sublime mystery of Catholicism is that during this sacrament Christ's glorified body remains in heaven and at the same time is truly present, whole and entire, on the altar. Roman Catholics further teach that the Mass contains a propitiatory sacrifice which is efficacious for both the living and the dead.

The sacrament of the Holy Eucharist is considered of such importance that members of this church must receive communion at least once a year or when in danger of death. Otherwise, many priests teach, members commit a mortal sin; and some priests insist that individuals are guilty of a serious sin if they do not participate in a Mass at least once a week, unless justified by a valid excuse. Ordinarily, however, communion is not given to infants. First communion usually takes place after a child has reached the age of accountability.

The sacrament designed to reconcile the sinner to God is penance. This rite consists of contrition, confession, and satisfaction of the penitent coupled with the absolution by a priest. Satisfaction is the completion of a prescribed reparation. In his absolution, for example, a priest will impose upon a person a penitential exercise, usually consisting of reciting certain prayers or performing specified good works. The confession usually takes place in a booth, called a confessional, which is divided into two compartments, one for the priest and one for the penitent. A small opening covered by a screen is located between the compartments which permits the flow of words but at the same time conceals the identity of the confessor. A member is also not required to confess to a priest in his parish, but all who have committed a mortal sin are required to confess at least once a year. All who have committed a serious or mortal sin (such as stealing about thirty dollars or more; excessive swearing; sexual sins of adultery, fornication, homosexuality, and masturbation; taking the name of God in vain; or failing to attend weekly Mass) should also receive penance before partaking of the Holy Eucharist. Venial or less serious sins may also be confessed to a priest but such declarations are not considered necessary. Through this sacrament, Roman Catholics believe that obedient members are blessed with a remission of sins and in many instances obtain a remission of the punishment arising from their more serious transgressions. If a member of this society does not confess annually, he cannot under normal conditions be buried with the blessings of the church.

Anointing the sick, formerly called extreme unction, is the sacrament which is confirmed on the sick or dying. It is believed by Roman Catholics that this sacrament heals the body and soul and remits sin. This rite is performed by a priest anointing the body of the afflicted with consecrated oil.

Two sacraments which all worthy members of the Roman Catholic Church do not necessarily receive are holy orders and marriage. Holy orders is the sacrament which according to Catholics conveys grace to a priest, giving him the power and authority to perform his priestly duties; and marriage is the sacrament which unites a man and a woman to assure the proper use of the procreative power and to draw spiritual strength from each other. Marriage is also deemed a conveyer of grace, blessing couples so that they might discharge their duties as parents more completely.

Members of this religious community must be married in the presence of a Roman Catholic priest and two Catholic witnesses. Otherwise, it is taught, individuals are not married and live in mortal sin. Only a bishop has the authority to authorize a mixed marriage, and such authorizations are granted only if the non-Catholic promises that the children resulting from the union will be reared as Catholics. Another characteristic of this faith is that although a priest must be present at a proper marriage of a member of this church (with few exceptions), the clergyman does not administer the sacrament of matrimony. Instead, the couple being married administer the sacrament to each other. Although a Catholic marriage is until death, such a valid marriage cannot be dissolved by human power or any change except death. The church, however, claims authority to declare that a marriage is not valid, thereby dissolving the marriage. Roman Catholics, in other words, do not secure divorces that break the bond of marriage but sometimes (not frequently) secure annulments or invalidations of their marriages.

Another distinguishing aspect of the Roman Catholic religion which divides it from most Protestant traditions is the belief that saints act as mediators and intercessors for men on earth. Catholics believe that saints become our advocates and protectors, interceding for us with Christ and through him with the Father. Mary, the Mother of Christ, is especially revered and venerated. During the past century and a half, the church has officially adopted two dogmas regarding Mary—the Dogma of the Immaculate Conception and the belief in the Assumption of the Virgin Mary. In 1854, Pope Pius IX proclaimed that from the moment of her conception, Mary was preserved free from original sin; in 1950 Pope Pius XII declared that immediately after Mary's death, her body was reunited with her soul and entered heaven.

Roman Catholics further believe that the church has power to set apart or bless many things which in turn excite righteous thoughts and encourage good works. Among the sacramentals in this church are the sign of the cross, the use of holy water, candles, ashes, palms, crucifixes, images of the saints, and rosaries.

Distinguishing Beliefs

There are many differences in the beliefs of Roman Catholics and teachings generally endorsed by orthodox Protestants. Included among these distinguishing Roman Catholic beliefs are the following doctrines and practices.

Roman Catholics teach that in addition to the Bible, tradition is a proper source of religious truth. Unlike Protestants, they also say that the church is the only proper teacher and interpreter of the Bible and that through the church, God has indicated which of the various ancient writings are inspired. Moreover, Roman Catholics teach that tradition is disclosed through the writings of church fathers, the decisions of general councils, and the decrees of popes.

While many Protestants hold that grace is God's forgiveness of man, Roman Catholics believe that grace is a gift of God which changes man and makes him like God. In order to become like God and enjoy the beatific vision, they explain, the soul must be transformed. This elevation is accomplished by the infusion into man of God and of supernatural powers and virtues called sanctifying grace. These cause a change in man. Grace is also considered a force continually nourished by God, enabling man to live on the level to which God raised him by sanctifying grace. This second kind of grace is called actual grace.

In addition to believing in a heaven and a hell (a popular Protestant view), Roman Catholics hold that the dead who have not been severed from God by mortal sin, but are not in a state of perfect purity, enter a place or condition called purgatory. They further believe that indulgences enable individuals to secure for themselves or the deceased a remission of punishment arising from sins. Most also believe that limbo is a place where unbaptized infants reside.

While Protestants teach that all who have been saved by God benefit from the atonement, Roman Catholics expand this view by saying that man benefits from the atonement by receiving the sacrament of baptism.

Roman Catholics further believe that sacraments are the channels or the means by which individuals receive sanctifying grace. A popular Protestant view is that sacraments are outward signs of an inward grace, and while Protestants generally teach that there are only two sacraments or ordinances ordained by Christ, Roman Catholics hold that there are seven sacraments: baptism, confirmation, Holy Eucharist, penance, annointing the sick, holy order, and marriage. Roman Catholics also believe in transubstantiation and that Christ is the victim of the altar.

Another distinguishing characteristic of Roman Catholicism is its assertion that the pope is the "Vicar of Christ on earth and the Visible Head of the Church," whose authority is supreme in matters of faith and discipline. Moreover, members of this church claim that the authority held by their religious leaders can be traced directly back to Christ and his apostles through the imposition of hands and prayer by those having this power.

Unlike Protestants, Roman Catholics also believe that it is proper to venerate saints and relics.

Miscellaneous Beliefs

The following beliefs of Roman Catholics harmonize with teachings generally accepted by orthodox Protestants.

The Roman Catholic Church affirms that God is an infinitely perfect spirit and is omnipotent, omniscient, and omnipresent. There is only one God, they teach, but there are three persons in God. God the Father is the creator. God the Son was incarnated, was made man, and is the redeemer. God the Holy Spirit is the sanctifier and proceeds from the Father and Son.

Roman Catholics also hold that angels are the earliest known creatures of God and are spirits who serve and praise God. All were created good, they say, but by their own choice some sinned and these fallen angels became devils.

Roman Catholics also assert that God created the world out of nothing, explaining that the word "create" means to make out of nothing.

The Roman Catholic Church further teaches that the souls of Adam and Eve were directly created by God and that the first sin is called the original sin. Because Adam stood as a representative of the human race, they say, there is a transmission of hereditary guilt from the first man to the entire human race.

According to Roman Catholics, God through Christ reconciled man to God. This reconciliation was effected by Christ through his shedding of blood on the cross. Christ thereby acquired for man deliverance from the evils of sin and from eternal death and placed man in a new relationship with God, a state of grace.

2

Eastern Orthodoxy

And when the day of Pentecost was fully come, they were all with one accord in one place. And suddenly there came a sound from heaven as of a rushing mighty wind, and it filled all the house where they were sitting. And there appeared unto them cloven tongues like as of fire, and it sat upon each of them. And they were all filled with the Holy Ghost. (Acts 2:1-4)

These descriptive words of Luke unfold to members of the Eastern Orthodox communion the historical origin of their church, for according to these Christians, the one and only true church was originally constituted on the memorable day of Pentecost. After the apostles had gathered at Jerusalem, the Holy Ghost descended with visible power upon them. On that occasion, these special witnesses of Christ preached, baptized, and then organized the believers into the first Christian community. Within a few years, other bodies of saints had been gathered in all the major centers of the Roman Empire, and eventually Christianity spread from these towns into many other parts of the Old World.

Although there was only one major body of Christians in Europe and the Near East during the early Middle Ages, it was characterized by striking diversity of belief and practice. There was also a lack of central leadership in the early Medieval Church, for no one person or group of religious leaders was universally recognized throughout the church as the supreme head. Meanwhile, political, cultural, and economic differences emerged, dividing Europe into an eastern and a western civilization. It is not surprising, therefore, that significant religious differences developed separating the Eastern and Western Christians and that the first major schism in the Medieval Church occurred when Christians living in these two sections of Europe failed to harmonize their differences.

The doctrinal dispute that ignited a disruption of the church and provided the occasion for a permanent separation was on two fundamental issues: the primacy of the pope and the procession of the Holy Ghost. Eastern Christians refused to acknowledge the western claim of universal supremacy of the bishop of Rome, contending that all bishops have equal authority. Moreover, they held that Roman Catholics erred when they altered an ancient creed with the insertion that the Holy Ghost proceeds from the Father and Son. The Holy Ghost proceeds from the Father alone, Eastern Christians contended. The theological estrangement led to bitter debates. In 1054 A.D. a papal legate arrogantly laid on a church altar a bull of excommunication against the patriarch of Constantinople. Although this event has been traditionally labeled as the date of the "great schism" and was a bitter episode in ecclesiastical history, it was not the first nor the last event in the long process of separation.[1]

Conscientious attempts at reconciliation were sought for generations by leaders of both churches, until finally the actions of insolent crusaders cemented the schism. During the fourth Crusade, the vengeance of embittered warriors was diverted from the Moslem enemy to Christians residing in Constantinople. In 1204 western Christians sacked the historic city, robbed churches, and returned to their homes with what many regarded as priceless sacred relics. The offending swords of these crusaders shattered all hope of reconciliation in that era of history, and doctrinal diversities have persisted, preventing a successful healing of the rupture.

While the East and West engaged in theological controversy, Eastern Christianity spread into Russia. During the reign of Vladimir (980-1015) Orthodoxy became the state church of Russia and remained so until 1917. At first the church was feebly superimposed on pagan religions, but in the fourteenth and fifteenth centuries the Orthodox faith effectively replaced the old religions throughout Russia. Then after the Turks captured Constantinople in 1453 the Russians assumed temporary leadership of Eastern Christianity, becoming in one respect the successors of Byzantium.

For many centuries Orthodoxy was almost purely an eastern religion, confined to eastern Europe and portions of Asia. During the past two centuries, however, there has been a major dispersal of this faith. As early as 1794 Russian Orthodoxy was carried by missionaries to Alaska, and during the last half of the eighteenth century Russians commenced missionary work in Japan and Korea and established churches in the continental United States. Meanwhile, Greeks were also establishing societies in various parts of the world. Greeks organized the first permanent Orthodox church in London in 1838 and gathered the first group of Orthodox Christians in the continental United States in New Orleans in 1864.

The most significant dispersal of Orthodoxy in modern times has taken place during this century. At the turn of the century the first truly substantial immigration of Greeks to America occurred. This tidal wave was followed by a great stream of Russian immigrants who fled their native land after the outbreak of the Bolshevik Revolution, and the Orthodox churches followed these immigrants. Between 1906 and 1956 this religion, which grew primarily through a steady stream of the uprooted, was one of the fastest growing faiths in the United States, increasing from an estimated membership of 130,000 to about 2,400,000 during this fifty-year period.[2] During the decade from 1956 to 1966, the growth was from 2,400,000 to 3,172,000, or an increase of 32 percent.[3] Since some local groups report family membership rather than enumerating every member, various historians estimate that Orthodox membership in the United States is closer to five million than the reported three million.

There is no single headquarters of this community of churches in the United States. Many of the churches, such as the Greek, Romanian, Serbian, and Syrian are organized along national lines and are connected with their respective national churches in Europe or Asia. However, most of these churches have been Americanized in the sense that English is being used both in the worship service and in the teaching and preaching of this faith.

The great dispersal of Orthodoxy through immigration has certainly not been confined to the United States, for in recent years there has been a significant growth in this community of churches in Canada, Australia, western Europe, and portions of Africa. Orthodoxy has, therefore, recently emerged as a worldwide movement.[4]

While Orthodoxy has been increasing in the western world, it has been declining rapidly in numbers and influence behind the iron curtain. A large percentage (possibly 85 percent) of this communion now live under Communist rule and are subject to rather severe religious restrictions.[5] In fact, Orthodoxy has been affected more by this political ideological revolution than any other denomination. As a result of legal limitations and the constant flood of atheistic propaganda imposed upon the masses, some Orthodox churches have almost been exterminated. But other churches have adjusted, have reorganized, or have entered a modern Christian underground. In spite of fifty years of persecution, organized religion in Communistic lands has not withered away.

Although Greece is the only country in the world today which is still officially Orthodox, Eastern Orthodoxy has remained one of the leading (numerically speaking) religions, with an estimated world membership of from 60 to 90 million practicing Orthodox Christians and from 120 to 150 million believers. Excluding Protestantism, which is a grouping of many Christian religions, Orthodoxy ranks second among Christian faiths and sixth among the world religions.[6]

There are four historic centers of the Eastern Orthodox church: Constantinople, Antioch, Alexandria, and Jerusalem. The Patriarch of Constantinople at this time is recognized as the first bishop among equals and has the primacy of honor. In addition to these four ancient patriarchates with their many geographical and ecclesiastical subdivisions, there are other major autonomous societies, including the Orthodox churches of Greece, Russia, Romania, Bulgaria, Poland, Czechoslovakia, Albania, Serbia, and Cyprus. Each of these societies maintains a separate and independent administrative structure and is directed by councils of bishops called synods. While they are free in their inner life and management, they are in full communion with each other and united in their liturgical life and traditional beliefs.

One of the important beliefs of Eastern Orthodoxy is that all bishops are theoretically successors of the apostle, Peter. They generally specify that Peter was given an honorary position among the apostles as head of the theologians. They further emphasize that while the jurisdiction of Peter and the other apostles was over the entire church, the bishop's jurisdiction was and should perpetually remain over a specified geographical region.

To substantiate their belief in the equality of bishops, Orthodox Christians frequently turn to the writings of church fathers, such as Ignatius of Antioch, who declared:

> Follow the bishop as Jesus Christ did the Father. . . . Nobody must do anything that has to do with the Church without the bishop's approval. . . . Where the bishop is present, there let the congregation gather, just as where Jesus Christ is, there is the Catholic Church. Without the bishop's supervision, no baptism or love feasts are permitted.[8]

Prior to the ninth century, Orthodox Christians maintain, bishops in the East and West were essentially independent of higher ecclesiastical authority, but gradually after that date the bishop of Rome began to assert himself over other bishops. In the eleventh century, they assert, the papacy was greatly strengthened by the Cluniac reform movement which sought to purify and unify the church under a central leader. For years the bishop of Rome (or pope of Rome) remained a successor of Peter, but after he endorsed programs that conflicted with traditional Christianity, such as advancing a view of primacy, his special position of honor was conveyed to others.[9]

When the Orthodox consider the controversial text in which Christ declared that his church would be built upon the rock (Matt. 16:18), they generally conclude that the rock is not Peter but Peter's faith. Peter's faith, they explain, made it possible for him to become the rock upon which the church was founded and in one respect all who share his faith are his successors and are eligible to return to God's presence. In support of this belief, Orthodox Christians again turn to the writings of early church fathers and note that a majority of them endorsed this interpretation.[10]

Similar to Roman Catholics but unlike most Protestants, Eastern Christians believe that there are two sources of religious truth, the Bible and tradition. The Bible, they maintain, was not meant to be a constitution upon which God's church should be built. Since this sacred work is not a complete description of the gospel of Christ and is susceptible to a variety of interpretations, they contend that another source, tradition, must be employed to determine religious truth. Some Orthodox even conclude that tradition is the sole source of gospel truth, claiming that scripture is one of the outward forms in which tradition is expressed.

Orthodox Christians further believe that tradition includes more than the faith that Jesus conveyed to the apostles. It includes such outward forms as the Nicene Creed, the decisions of the first seven ecumenical councils; definitions by local councils and letters prepared by bishops and approved by the church; the liturgy; canon law; and icons. The decisions of the first seven ecumenical councils (but not others regarded as general councils by Roman Catholics) are regarded as infallible, and other expressions of faith become infallible only when approved by the whole Orthodox community.[11]

There is an emphasis in this communion on the study of the writings of the church fathers. Some of the fathers are regarded as authoritative interpreters of the faith, but Orthodox Christians recognize that these expositors taught conflicting opinions in the areas of theological speculation, such as the fall, the atonement, and life beyond the grave. Moreover, they have not universally endorsed the decrees of councils such as the Council of Trent, which defined Roman Catholic beliefs on a variety of subjects. Therefore, there is no single authoritative document describing the basic beliefs of Orthodox Christians.[12]

There has been and currently is a major emphasis in this church on the doctrine of the Trinity. Orthodox Christians teach that God is a spirit, an immaterial being, and that he is omnipotent, omnipresent, and omniscient. They further explain that God is three persons of one essence, coeternal, Father, Son, and Holy Spirit. The Father is the creator of all things, visible and invisible. Christ was incarnate by the Holy Ghost and of the Virgin Mary, becoming man for our salvation; and the Holy Ghost was sent by Christ to guide His church.

Orthodox Christians also emphasize that their theology is a negative approach to God, for they insist that God is a mystery who cannot be comprehended by man. Positive statements about God, they say, must be offset by describing what God is not. As St. John of Damascus (ca 675-749) asserted, declarations specifying that God is "good, and just and wise . . . do not tell God's nature but only the qualities of His nature." Although "it is plain . . . that there is a God," the essence and nature of deity is "absolutely incomprehensible and unknowable." It is evident, he concluded, that God is incorporeal, formless, intangible, invisible, infinite, incognizable, and indefinable. "It is not within our capacity, therefore, to say anything about God or even to think of Him, beyond the things which have been divinely revealed to us."[13]

In addition to emphasizing the dogma of the Trinity and the incomprehensible nature of God, Eastern Orthodox Christians devote much attention to the sacraments. Recognizing the importance of the sacramental life among the membership of this church, Orthodox authors sometimes refer to their communion as "primarily a worshipping community."[14] As do Roman Catholics, they teach that there are seven major sacraments. They say these outward, visible signs convey inward spiritual grace to recipients. While Protestants teach that grace is an attitude of God, or God's graciousness, Eastern Christians, in harmony with Roman Catholic belief, assert that grace is divine power or the saving power of God by which men receive the benefits of the atonement. This grace is stored in the church, is administered through the sacraments, and is absolutely necessary for salvation. Some Orthodox theologians also claim that there are more than seven sacraments, adding that there are many other actions in the Church which possess sacramental characteristics, such as performing services for the burial of the dead, anointing a monarch, and blessing churches, icons, homes, fields, animals, cars, and the water on the day of Epiphany (the feast celebrating Christ's baptism).[15]

Through baptism, Eastern Christians maintain, recipients are cleansed of their personal sins and the original sin and become members of the earthly kingdom of God. This sacrament is performed by three-fold immersion. In some instances only part of the body is immersed (as in the case of infants), and water is poured over the body, once in the name of the Father, once in the name of the Son, and once in the name of the Holy Spirit. In infant baptism, two sponsors who are not the parents of the child confess the Orthodox faith on behalf of the infant and accept for the infant the offer of fellowship into the church.[16]

In addition to practicing three-fold immersion, there are other significant differences between the Orthodox and the Roman Catholic positions regarding the sacraments. Whereas Roman Catholic children are not confirmed until after they reach the age of accountability, infants of Orthodox parents and converts are confirmed or chrismated (a special sacramental ordinance) immediately after baptism.[17]

Although another difference in the two major Catholic churches is that young Orthodox children are invited to partake of Holy Communion, the two denominations agree that during this service Christ is crucified in an unbloody crucifixion. Christ is not only regarded as the literal victim of the sacrifice, but he is also considered the priest who invisibly performs this ceremonial act. This sacrifice is not regarded merely as commemorative, but is considered a true and literal sacrifice of the very body of Christ. During the liturgy (or Mass, as Roman Catholics would say), Orthodox Christians teach that the bread and wine are changed into the body and blood of Christ. After the bread and wine have been consecrated, Orthodox members receive both the leavened bread and wine. Roman Catholics usually receive a sacrament of one kind, a wafer of unleavened bread.[18]

There are also significant differences in the beliefs of members of the two Catholic communions regarding confession. In the Orthodox church the penitent stands next to a small desk during the confession and a priest stands by the side of the confessor. The priest is not regarded as a judge but as a counselor who strives to recover the spiritual health of the sinner. In most Orthodox churches, priests do not claim authority to forgive sins but petition the Lord to grant the penitent "assurance of repentance, pardon and remission of his sin, and absolve him from all his offenses, voluntary and involuntary."[19]

Marriage is another visible sign in which couples receive special blessings from God. Orthodox Christians, unlike Roman Catholics, permit divorce under certain conditions and also permit remarriage. Married men are permitted to become ordained priests and most parochial clergy are married, but bishops cannot be married for they are taken exclusively from the monastic clergy. Marriage to a baptized Christian of another faith is permitted if the nonmember promises to baptize the children of the marriage in the Orthodox church.

The sacrament of holy unction and the last rites are different services in this communion. While the sacrament of holy unction is administered to those who are physically or mentally ill and to those seeking purification, last rites is a service reserved for dying members.

Ordination is considered another of the seven sacraments. In addition to emphasizing apostolic succession, Orthodox Christians stress lay participation in the appointment of the clergy. During the ordination service, the congregation hails the new clergymen with the word, *axics,* signifying that the individual is worthy to be ordained. Then bishops lay their hands on the candidate's head, ordaining him in the name of the church.[20]

Orthodox Christians, like Roman Catholics, also emphasize veneration of icons, religious pictures, and saints. They also pray to saints, asking saints to pray for them, but they do not venerate three-dimensional statues. In every faithful Orthodox home a corner, usually in the bedroom, is dedicated for the family sanctuary. In this sanctuary are placed icons of Christ, Mary, and a patron saint, a cross, a prayer book, dried flowers of Good Friday, holy water, and other such religious objects. An icon is also placed in the eastern corner of the living room, and, according to custom, Orthodox guests who enter an Orthodox home venerate the icon by making the sign of the cross and bowing. Before entering the sanctuary of their church, Orthodox members approach a wall in the nave containing pictures. The worshipper first kisses the Christ icons, then the Mary icons, and then the icons of the angels and saints. He also venerates the icons by bowing and crossing himself.[21]

Mary is held in high esteem because she is the mother of God. Orthodox Christians believe that Mary was a virgin when she bore Christ and that she remained a virgin throughout her life. Most members of this society further believe that the original sin was not imputed to Mary (nor in the Augustinian sense to other people), and many conclude that after Mary's death, her body was taken into heaven, being made fully spiritual.[22]

Even though there is no dogma of the church regarding the fall, atonement, and life after death, many members do hold certain beliefs regarding these subjects. Most Orthodox members believe that our first parents rebelled against God, and because of their transgression all men are born into a state of moral and physical (meaning we shall suffer death) corruption. They further believe that as a consequence of the original sin, man's nature has assumed a corrupted form.

Most Orthodox Christians also speculate that through the atonement of Christ, man is able to regain the Holy Spirit. Although Christ's sacrifice is applicable to all, men do not benefit from this act until they are baptized and reborn. God, they explain, initiates the word of salvation by arousing the seeds of moral and spiritual powers remaining in man after the fall; man plays a vital role in the salvation experience by accepting this precious gift.[23]

When an Orthodox member considers life beyond the grave, he usually declares that death is the separation of the body and spirit. The spirit is partially judged at death and enters a state of happiness or misery. At the time of the general judgment, the body (defined usually as a spiritual body) will be resurrected, and men will be assigned to everlasting happiness or everlasting punishment. While some Orthodox members speculate that possibly the punishment of the wicked will not continue eternally, others insist that this view of universal salvation has been condemned by the church. Most agree that the Roman Catholic belief of purgatory, limbo, treasury of merits, and indulgences are doctrinal innovations and should not be endorsed by members of their communion.[24]

In the twentieth century, members of the Orthodox church recognize that modern confrontations are producing new challenges. While many behind the iron curtain are striving to combat the debilitating influence of communism, Orthodox Christians living in the free world are confronted with other problems. Theories advanced by Bible critics and modern scientists sometimes conflict with beliefs that have been popular for generations. The new ecumenical spirit is also creating tensions in the church. While some Orthodox are striving to advance a program designed to create Christian unity, others insist that in order to enthusiastically and effectively support such a program the Orthodox Christian will be forced to compromise on basic traditional beliefs and practices. The problem Orthodox immigrants have in adjusting to a new life in a new nation has also beset many families, but a great many have adjusted admirably to this challenge and have become respected, productive workers and loyal leaders in the lands that have given them new hope and opportunities.

Although the modern history of Orthodoxy contains sorrowful notes of religious persecution and economic oppression, these years of unparalleled change have not altered the major religious emphasis of this community of churches. The traditional emphasis on veneration of icons, daily worship, and the importance of the sacrament has not lessened. Eastern Orthodoxy has remained "primarily a worshipping community."

Distinguishing Beliefs

Although there are many parallels in the beliefs of Eastern Christians and Roman Catholics, there are also a number of differences that have prevented these two communions from reuniting. Included among the most distinguishing beliefs held by most members of the Eastern Orthodox family of churches that are not endorsed by Roman Catholics (and are generally not held by Protestants) are the following doctrines and practices.

While Eastern Christians agree with Roman Catholics by asserting that the authority of Christ was conveyed by Peter and the other apostles to the bishops, unlike Roman Catholics they claim that all bishops were and are today equal in authority. However, they explain, some bishops have obtained honorary positions on the basis of the location of their ecclesiastical jurisdiction.

They also teach that religious tradition must include more than the faith which Jesus conveyed to the apostles. It includes not only outward forms such as the Bible, the Nicene Creed, and decisions of the first seven ecumenical councils, but also definitions by local councils, the liturgy, canon law, and icons.

Eastern Christians further hold that the Holy Ghost proceeds from the Father alone.

Other differences in Eastern Orthodox and Roman Catholic theology relate to the sacraments. In the Eastern Orthodox church, baptism is performed by threefold immersion, and immediately after baptism, infants (or converts) are confirmed or chrismated, thereby receiving the gift of the Holy Spirit. According to members of this faith, by means of this sacrament members receive a portion of the royal priesthood and are granted the right to participate in the administration of other sacraments. Moreover, during the Orthodox communion services, leavened bread is placed in the wine and both elements are conveyed to the communicants who are served by a spoon from the chalice. Orthodox priests may celebrate only one liturgy on a given day.

Confession is also different in the two Catholic communities. During confession in the Eastern Church, the priest stands by the side of the confessor. The priest is not regarded as a judge but as a counselor who strives to recover the spiritual health of the sinner.

Three other differences in the practices of these churches are that Orthodox Christians stress lay participation in the appointment of the clergy, require celibacy among bishops only, and perform the rite of holy unction with the priest reading seven lessons prior to anointing the afflicted with oil.

Although there are many monastic communities in the Eastern Orthodox Church, there are no orders. Each monastery is a self-governing unit.

Other differences in these two religious communities pertain to beliefs held by Roman Catholics that are rejected by Eastern Christians. While Orthodox Christians emphasize veneration of icons, they do not approve of the veneration of three-dimensional statues. Most Eastern Christians (and Protestants) also reject the Roman Catholic beliefs concerning the immaculate conception of Mary, the assumption of Mary, purgatory, limbo, treasury of merits, and indulgences.

Miscellaneous Beliefs

Most Eastern Christians endorse many beliefs that are also held by Roman Catholics and most orthodox Protestants, such as a triune God, angels as special creations of God, the world being created out of nothing, Adam and Eve being created through the will of God, and death being the separation of the body and spirit. Moreover, they share with Roman Catholics (but not with most Protestants) the belief that grace is a divine power of God, that during the liturgy (or Mass) Christ is the victim of the sacrifice and is the priest who performs the ceremony, and that the bread and wine are changed to the body and blood of Christ.

3

Orthodox Protestantism

On 31 October 1517, twenty-five years after the effectual discovery of America, a resolute leader boldly posted *Ninety-five Theses* on the massive doors of the All Saints' Church in Wittenberg, Germany. Martin Luther's attack on the Roman Catholic practice of granting indulgences initiated a theological storm that rapidly spread through most sections of western Europe. While religious solidarity was maintained in nearly every European community, the Protestant Reformation rapidly transformed that section of the world from the land of the universal church to a region of multiple religious societies. Within a generation, half of Europe witnessed a profound religious change. Most of the northern German states and the Scandinavian countries endorsed Lutheranism. The reformed faith popularized by John Calvin spread from Geneva to many other communities in Switzerland and into Holland and Scotland. Meanwhile, Anglicanism became the established faith in England, and small groups of Anabaptists emerged as savagely oppressed minorities in a number of western European communities.

During the seventeenth and eighteenth centuries the major religions of western Europe were transplanted to North America. Initially most of the immigrants to the thirteen colonies sailed from England, the major exception being the Dutch who colonized the Hudson River Valley. Then in the eighteenth century the great bulk of emigration came from Scotland, northern Ireland, and Germany. Consequently, the Church of England, the Congregational faith, the Baptist denomination, the Society of Friends, the Presbyterian Church, the Lutheran communion, and the Dutch and German Reformed churches emerged as the dominant religions of early America. Throughout most of the colonial era, 95 percent of the church members were Protestants and the majority of these Christians could trace their historical roots back to John Calvin.

Most of the denominations of early America were also creedal religions, in that most members of American faiths endorsed the basic provisions included in the popular creeds of Christendom, such as the Lutheran Augsburg Confession, the Presbyterian Westminster Confession of Faith, and the Thirty-nine Articles of the Church of England. Hundreds of local articles of faith were also prepared by American clergy patterned after the confessional documents, especially the Westminster Confession. In order to become a full-fledged member of many congregations individuals were required to accept an exposition of faith as a proper expression of the teachings of Christ and his apostles.

Although a significant reorientation of Christian thinking has occurred among many Protestants and Catholics, the majority of members of contemporary American churches endorse most elements of the historic faith. During the 1960s a number of polls were conducted among ministers and laity to determine their basic patterns of belief. The most extensive survey that has ever been conducted in this land concerning a variety of beliefs reflecting traditional Protestant theology reported responses of 7,441 clergy throughout the nation.[1] Another questionnaire was submitted to approximately 3,000 laity residing in four metropolitan counties in northern California.[2] Other polls were conducted in this same decade among adults throughout the nation, among ministers of Utah, most of whom had attended theological schools and served parishioners in other states, and among Lutheran high school youth and ministers of the American Lutheran Church and the Lutheran Church—Missouri Synod.[3] These polls revealed a number of striking parallels, for the percentage of agreement on most theological issues tended to be similar among members and clergy of the respective denominations. Over 90 percent, for example, of the Southern Baptists, of Lutherans belonging to the Missouri Synod, and of members of churches classified as "small sects" (including members of the Holiness-Pentecostal movement) endorsed most elements of the classical Protestant theology. When ministers and laity of the American Baptist, American Lutheran, Disciples of Christ, and Presbyterian denominations considered these same questions, in which over 90 percent of the Southern Baptists and Lutherans of the Missouri Synod agreed, their responses generally varied from 50 to 75 percent agreement, the American Baptists and American Lutherans being slightly more conservative on most issues than the Disciples and Presbyterians. Meanwhile, most Episcopalians, Methodists, and Congregationalists indicated that they did not endorse most beliefs included in the polls which reflect the historic Protestant tradition. Of these three faiths, the greatest reorientation of Christian thinking had occurred among the Congregationalists (or members of the United Church of Christ), and the Methodists tended to be more liberal on most theological issues than the Episcopalians.

The Catholics who responded to the questionnaire circulated in northern

California were generally more conservative on most theological issues than the average Protestant. The Catholic laity, however, were not as orthodox in most respects as the Southern Baptists or the Lutherans of the Missouri Synod, but were slightly more conservative than the American Lutherans on subjects such as the virgin birth, the divinity of Christ, biblical miracles, the existence of Satan, the necessity of baptism, and children being born into the world already guilty of sin. The California poll further revealed that a significant reorientation of Catholic thinking had occurred in the area of requirements for salvation. Of the Catholics who responded to the questionnaire sent to residents of the Bay Area, only 51 percent specified that belief in Jesus Christ was "absolutely necessary" for salvation; 65 percent said that baptism was "absolutely necessary"; 39 percent indicated that participation in Christian sacraments, such as the holy communion, was "absolutely necessary"; and 28 percent recorded that membership in their particular faith was "absolutely necessary" for salvation. According to this same religious survey, 23 percent of the Catholics specified that "practicing artificial birth control" would definitely prevent salvation.[4] (See appendix.)

By assuming that the various religious polls conducted in the 1960s reflect fairly accurately the theological positions of most American clergy and laity, one could categorize the major American faiths according to theological moods—attempts to preserve the historic faith or interest in seeking modern reinterpretations of the "old time" religion. Although theological moods are most clearly observed in the area of doctrine, characteristics of orthodoxy and liberalism are also evident in traditions of worship and in church government. Some denominations, such as the Lutherans, are conservative in doctrine and worship, whereas Episcopalians are, generally speaking, liberal in their theology and conservative in their worship. The problem of determining theological profiles of denominations is further compounded because some groups are noted for their conservatism on some theological issues and their rejection of other aspects of their historic faith. This deviation from traditional beliefs is clearly evident among Calvinists, for most Protestants whose historical roots stem back to John Calvin no longer endorse man's total depravity and predestination as taught by Calvin. Nevertheless, there are basic differences in the moods of the various denominations. Data included in Table 3 indicate the relative positions concerning doctrine of many of the major denominations, Protestants and non-Protestants, in the United States, arranged according to their numerical strength in this country. "O" stands for orthodox, "L" for liberal. In some instances most members might be orthodox, but if there is a large liberal minority within the society, this fact is noted by the insertion of an "L" in parentheses. An "O" in parentheses indicates a large element of orthodoxy in a liberal communion. In cases where there are about equal numbers of orthodox and liberals in a denomination, this theological profile is indicated by an "M" meaning moderate.[5]

Table 3
THEOLOGICAL PROFILE OF AMERICAN RELIGIOUS SOCIETIES

Roman Catholic	0 (L)
Southern Baptist Convention	0
Methodist Church	L
Protestant Episcopal Church	L (0)
United Presbyterian Church in the USA	M
Lutheran Church, Missouri Synod	0
Lutheran Church in America	0 (L)
American Lutheran Church	0 (L)
Churches of Christ	0
The Church of Jesus Christ of Latter-day Saints	0
United Church of Christ	L
Christian Churches (Disciples of Christ)	M
American Baptist	0 (L)
Assemblies of God	0
Church of God in Christ	0
Seventh-day Adventists	0
Jehovah's Witnesses	0
Church of the Nazarene	0
Reformed Church of America	0
Unitarian Universalist Association	L
Society of Friends	L

The published results of the religious polls conducted in the 1960s and information circulated by the National Council of Churches not only indicate that most Americans are orthodox but also provide helpful guidelines in estimating the percentage of Americans who have retained the basic elements of their historic beliefs. In their *Yearbook* for 1972 the National Council of Churches published information on nearly 200 non-Catholic Christian bodies in the United States.[6] Approximately 80 percent of these American denominations (most of which are properly classified as Protestant) are known for their theological conservatism. Although there are liberals in orthodox churches, there are also conservatives in the moderate and liberal denominations. Probably about two-thirds of all American Protestants have retained most basic elements of their historic theology.

Information gathered by the National Council of Churches and twentieth-century census reports indicates that membership in denominations which are known for their orthodoxy has increased more rapidly during the past seven decades than communions which are known for their search for modern reinterpretations of Christian theology, as indicated by data included in Tables 4 through 7.[7]

Table 4
RELATIVE GROWTH OF SELECTED
RELIGIOUS SOCIETIES 1906-1956, 1956-1966

Religious Bodies	Membership 1906	1956	Percent of Growth	1966	Percent of Growth
Eastern Orthodox	129,606	2,396,906	1754.7%	3,172,163	32%
Churches of Christ	159,649	1,700,000	964.8%	2,350,000	32%
Latter-day Saints	256,647	1,372,640	430.9%	1,963,008	43%
Lutheran	2,112,494	7,286,589	244.4%	8,794,106	20%
Baptists	5,662,234	19,165,780	238.4%	23,812,119	29%
Protestant Episcopal	886,942	2,759,994	210.9%	3,410,657	23%
Roman Catholic	12,079,142	33,574,017	177.9%	46,246,175	35%
Presbyterian	1,830,555	3,858,709	110.7%	4,420,566	14%
Methodist	5,749,838	11,775,731	104.8%	13,287,081	13%
Disciples of Christ	982,701	1,897,736	93.1%	1,918,471	1%

Table 5

GROWTH DURING THE 1960S OF SELECTED RELIGIOUS SOCIETIES
WITH A MEMBERSHIP OF MORE THAN 10,000,000

Denomination	Increase from 1961-1970	1970 membership	Percent of Growth in 1960s
Roman Catholic	5,338,064	48,214,729	12.4%
Southern Baptist Convention	1,649,544	11,628,032	10.7%
United Methodist Church	-122,451	10,671,774	--1.1%

Protestant orthodoxy is sometimes associated with geographical sections of the United States. Most Protestants living in the South, for example, are known for their theological conservatism, and rural America is also sometimes associated with orthodoxy. But one needs to use caution when he connects theological concepts with geographical areas. Throughout this nation, in urban industrial centers, in farming communities, in the North, the South, the East, and the West, and in nearly all Protestant denominations one contacts Christians who endorse most traditional patterns of Protestant theology.

Although conservatives do not always agree on what should be included in a list of the essential elements of the Christian faith, there are a number of beliefs that are persistently proclaimed from orthodox pulpits and expressed

Table 6

GROWTH DURING THE 1960S OF SELECTED RELIGIOUS BODIES WITH A MEMBERSHIP OF FROM ONE MILLION TO TEN MILLION

Denomination	Increase from 1961-1970	1970 membership	Percent of Growth in 1960s
The Church of Jesus Christ of Latter-day Saints	477,756	2,073,146	30%
Greek Orthodox	375,000	1,875,000	25%
Lutheran Church, Missouri Synod	324,100	2,788,536	13%
American Lutheran Church	157,852	2,543,293	6.6%
Churches of Christ (from 1958-1968)	150,000	2,400,000	6.7%
Lutheran Church in America	37,647	3,106,844	1.1%
Episcopal Church	-32,044	3,285,826	-1%
American Baptist Conv.	-72,027	1,472,478	-4.5%
United Presbyterian, USA	-155,266	3,087,213	-4.8%

Table 7

GROWTH DURING THE 1960S OF SELECTED RELIGIOUS SOCIETIES WITH A MEMBERSHIP OF FROM 300,000 TO 1,000,000

Denomination	Increase from 1961-1970	1970 membership	Percent of Growth in 1960s
Reformed Church in America	137,396	367,606	59.6%
Jehovah Witnesses	115,789	388,920	42.5%
Salvation Army	69,102	326,934	27.0%
Seventh-day Adventists	81,267	420,419	24.6%
Church of the Nazarene	67,637	383,284	21.5%
American Baptist Convention	135,736	786,536	20.9%
Assemblies of God	100,710	625,027	19.6%
Russian Orthodox Greek Catholic Church	150,000	1,000,000	17.6%

in the writings of those seeking to preserve the classical faith. As early as 1520, Martin Luther set the theological tone of the Reformation by publishing three pamphlets in which he described his belief regarding authority, grace, the sacraments, and the source of religious truth. Since the basic views unfolded by Luther on these four subjects conflicted with the Roman Catholic position and were adopted by most subsequent Protestant reformers, these beliefs became and have remained the most distinguishing beliefs of orthodox Protestants.

One of these distinguishing Protestant doctrines is known as the priesthood of believers and was popularized by Luther in his tract, *Open Letter to the Christian Nobility of the German Nation.* In this work Luther contended that the congregation of faithful saints was a body of priests, all possessing the same authority. "Our baptism," he taught, "consecrates us all without exception," making us all priests. "Every one," he added, "who has been baptized may claim that he has already been consecrated priest, bishop, or pope." To support this conviction, Luther quoted from Peter and Revelation: "You are a royal priesthood and a realm of priests" (1 Peter 2:9), and "Thou hast made us priests and kings by thy blood" (Rev. 4:9).[8]

According to Luther's interpretation of the Bible, Christ shared all he possessed with all Christians and through faith all may become kings and priests with him. The New Testament Church emerged in Luther's theological framework as a kingdom of priests—a new and redeemed community. As a community of believers, Christians were to bear the burdens of one another, as Christ had done. This view was expanded to include the belief that all men were priests to each other.[9]

Although Luther considered all believers in Christ to be priests, he taught that all should not exercise the public office of the ministry. No one, he said, had the right to administer the sacraments nor serve as teachers of the Word of God publicly without the consent of members of the church. "Only by consent and command of the community," he specified, should an individual "claim for himself what belongs equally to all." Consequently, the congregation of priesthood bearers had the responsibility of selecting one of their numbers and commissioning him to exercise authority on behalf of others.[10]

"When a bishop consecrates," Luther explained, "he simply acts on behalf of the entire congregation, all of whom have the same authority." Suppose, he reasoned, a group of Christians settled in an isolated desert community without being accompanied by an ordained priest. These believers would have the authority to choose one from the congregation and endow him with the office of preaching, baptizing, administering the sacrament, and pronouncing absolution.[11]

Luther rejected not only the doctrine of apostolic succession but also the view of the Catholic church concerning ordination. Roman Catholics assert that priests receive the power to perform the sacraments through ordination, but Luther believed that one received the right to exercise the priesthood not through ordination, but through the call to serve. Luther did not regard ordination as an integral part of the priesthood. Ordination, in his view, was regarded as a public acknowledgement or confirmation of the call by a congregation. Luther further maintained that through selection by a congregation, ministers received a commission rather than a special power, a commission granting them the right to exercise the priesthood shared by all believers.[12]

Since the era of the Reformation, nearly all orthodox Protestants have endorsed the doctrine of the universal priesthood of believers. In contrast to the Catholic view of endowed authority, most Protestants endorse Luther's view of common authority and agree with him that Christ's authority was conferred upon the entire church and not merely upon the apostles. One major exception in this country to this endorsement by Protestants is the Episcopal faith, which holds to lineal succession.[13]

Many Protestants also include in definitions of priesthood of believers the concept that Christians should place themselves under the direct authority of God, including receiving, through the Holy Spirit, direct addresses from God. Many also teach that the doctrine of priesthood of believers does not mean that everyone is a priest but that everyone has the responsibility to make the message of the Bible their message and in that respect should be a priest to their neighbor. All, however, do not await the call by a congregation prior to exercising the priesthood. Periodically, enthusiastic revivalists emerge who insist that they have been commissioned by the Spirit to proclaim the gospel of Jesus Christ to all mankind.

A second doctrine popularized by Luther in 1520, that became the most distinguishing characteristic of orthodox Protestantism, was the concept of justification by faith alone or, in another term, salvation by grace alone. Luther endeavored to summarize succinctly the most essential aspects of his faith in his *Freedom of a Christian* and included in this treatise the belief that men are saved by the pure and free mercy of God, manifest to man through faith. Many medieval theologians considered the righteousness of God as "His demanding justice," but Luther concluded that God's righteousness is more than judging and is most clearly evident in his bestowal of faith and thereby salvation upon man through Jesus Christ. According to Luther, salvation is not earned. Man can never merit salvation by his own action. It is given, he explained, solely by the grace of God, for by God's grace some individuals are considered righteous and are made acceptable heirs of salvation.[14]

The popular orthodox Protestant doctrine of grace needs to be considered in light of the historic belief regarding the nature of man and the atonement of Christ. Many Protestants endorse the popular Roman Catholic explanation that Adam, who was created righteous and without sin, stood as a representative of the entire human race. After the fall, there was a transmission of hereditary guilt from the first man to all mankind. All men inherit the original sin and are born without grace, with a soul that is spiritually dark. All are blind of understanding in spiritual things and are prone to evil. All have further incurred divine wrath, and all are subject to death.

Even though most orthodox Protestants have retained the traditional belief that all men are sinners because of Adam's rebellion against God and man's hereditary connection with him, the religious surveys of the 1960s indicated that one of the most significant deviations from the classical faith among members of denominations known for their orthodoxy was in the area of the nature of man and the fall of Adam. Slightly more than 60 percent of the Lutherans and Baptists who responded to three different polls expressed a belief that man could not help doing evil or that man by himself was incapable of anything but sin. A small majority also noted that they had retained the belief that Adam's sin was imputed to all mankind.[15]

A popular contemporary description of the consequences of the fall and man's nature is a statement adopted in 1963 by the Southern Baptist Convention, the largest alliance of Protestant societies in the United States:

> Through the temptation of Satan man transgressed the command of God, and fell from his original innocence; whereby his posterity inherit a nature and an environment inclined toward sin, and as soon as they are capable of moral action become transgressors and are under condemnation.[16]

While orthodox Protestants insist that as a consequence of the transgression of Adam man is by nature a sinner and falls under the condemnation of God, they further proclaim that by His real suffering, Christ reconciled the world with God, redeeming all men from sin, death, and the power of the devil. Christ, they add, made satisfaction with his own blood, procuring for all sinners perfect righteousness, life, eternal bliss, and full acquittal of all who believe in him. Luther emphasized that Christ is our Redeemer "who suffered death in order that" man might be free from death, become His child, and be led to righteousness and eternal life.[17]

According to many contemporary orthodox Protestants, Christianity is a redemptive religion in that it offers to mankind salvation from sin and guilt. Many teach that the sinner needs to be forgiven of his transgressions and purified, or that man needs to be justified and sanctified. Justification is frequently defined as the act, state, or process of being accepted as righteous by God. It is also identified as the process by which God brings man back into a right relationship with Him. Sanctification is often referred to as the process of becoming clean and pure. Two other words frequently employed by Christians when they discuss salvation are *redemption* and *regeneration.* Redemption is used to identify the act that frees man from the bondage of sin, and regeneration is regarded by most Christians as the rebirth which takes place when one receives the grace of God.

While there is a basic agreement among Catholics and Protestants concerning the general definition of these four terms, there is a major difference among them concerning *how* man is justified and sanctified or how one is redeemed. The precise meaning of these concepts, therefore, differs considerably among Catholics and Protestants and among those who are orthodox and liberal.[18]

Orthodox Protestants generally agree that the transformation of man occurs by means of the atoning sacrifice of Christ and the regenerative and sanctifying influence of the Holy Spirit. They insist that the essence of Christianity has always been the belief that salvation from sin, guilt, and pollution comes through the "historical expiation" or the atonement wrought by Jesus Christ. And Protestants have traditionally emphasized that the term of salvation is simple acceptance of Christ as Lord and Savior.[19]

Many early reformers, including Luther and Calvin, did not make a sharp distinction between justification and sanctification. They considered justification not only as God's forgiving man and establishing a new relationship with him but also as the Holy Spirit's operating within man to produce a new holiness. Sanctification was man's obtaining forgiveness of sins and righteousness. As the years passed, other reformers, such as John Wesley, began emphasizing justification and sanctification in separate classifications. Wesley, early Pietist groups, and many leaders of the contemporary Holiness-Pentecostal movements developed a doctrine of Christian perfection, emphasizing that it was possible for individuals to obtain a kind of complete sanctification, or perfection, in this life.[20]

Although a comparison of beliefs of Protestants and Catholics concerning the fall and atonement reveals many parallels, a major difference centers on the concept of grace. Roman Catholics teach that grace is a gift of God that cleanses man and makes him like God. It is considered as infused power which imparts virtues to the soul, elevating the soul to a higher being. Catholics further believe that grace is dispensed through the institution that is clothed with the power of God. Men are justified, Catholics say, through faith and works, which include baptism and other sacraments. Since the sacraments are considered channels by which God dispenses grace, Roman Catholics teach that man begins to receive the grace of God and initially benefits from the atonement of Christ by receiving the sacrament of baptism and continues to receive grace through the instrumentality of other sacraments.[21]

In contrast to the Roman Catholic position, Luther popularized the concept that grace is God's forgiving man despite man's rebelliousness.[22] This definition is currently held by many Protestants; and in harmony with Luther's basic teachings, many orthodox assert that God's freely given redemptive love is bestowed directly upon mankind without the need of an institution.

Another essential ingredient of classical Protestant theology is that faith is the channel employed by God to notify man of his new relationship to diety. Faith is considered as the "lively apprehension of grace made known and received."[23] Southern Baptists recently described the process of salvation as held by most orthodox Protestants by declaring:

> Only the grace of God can bring man into His holy fellowship and enable man to fulfill the creative purpose of God. . . . Salvation involves the redemption of the whole man, and is offered freely to all who accept Jesus Christ as Lord and Savior, who by His own blood obtained eternal redemption for the believer.[24]

While the Medieval Church considered salvation in light of the grace of God coupled with the most worthy actions of men, Luther insisted that works were not the means of salvation but were the fruits of faith. "The Christian who is consecrated by his faith does good works," Luther explained, "but the works do not make him holier or more Christian, for that is the work of faith alone. And if a man were not first a believer and a Christian, all his works would amount to nothing and would be truly wicked and damnable sins."[25]

Modern orthodox theologians continue to emphasize that men are not saved by their works but through grace alone. Nevertheless, works are not neglected, for many Protestants currently emphasize that works, not of a ritualistic nature but of an ethical character, are necessary for salvation. Works are sometimes referred to as necessary evidences of faith. In conclusion, many orthodox insist that a genuine Christian is not only one who seeks to imitate the example set by Christ, but is also a person who enters into a living, personal relationship with Christ and "receives and rests upon Christ for salvation from guilt and corruption of sin."[26]

Although Protestants traditionally have endorsed this view of justification by faith alone, they have been divided into two basic camps regarding man's role in the salvation experience. The Calvinistic wing has emphasized that man plays no essential role in the salvation experience, while the Arminian wing has insisted that while God proffers grace to mankind, only those who embrace this gift will be saved. During the colonial period most church members were Calvinists, holding to the concept of unconditional election or predestination, but in twentieth-century America most orthodox Protestants teach that man is a free agent who plays a vital role in the salvation experience. A popular belief is that the free will of man enables him to accept or reject Jesus as his Lord and Savior.

In harmony with his view concerning the priesthood of believers and justification by faith, Luther adopted a definition of the church that did not include endowed authority or the institution as a sacramental agent, but emphasized the concept of the assembly of believers. According to the German reformer, the church was a community of believers in which the gospel was preached in its purity and the sacraments properly administered. He emphasized certain sacraments as essential, not for the receiving of grace but for the apprehension of faith and for proper worship. Faith, he taught, was apprehended by hearing the word and by receiving the Lord's Supper. Preaching was considered a vital part of the service during which communicants received the sacramental emblems. Luther further emphasized that there was no benefit from this rite unless faith was manifest in the recipient.[27]

Although conflicting views concerning the sacraments have served as one of the major sources precipitating divisions among Protestants, nearly all orthodox Protestants endorse a number of concepts popularized by Luther in 1520 in his *Pagan Servitude of the Church,* commonly translated as the *Babylonian Captivity of the Church.* Luther described baptism and the Lord's Supper as two sacraments ordained by Christ, rejected the view that during the Mass Christ was the victim of the altar, denied that the bread was changed into the body of Christ, and recommended that communicants receive both sacramental elements, the bread and the wine.[28]

In addition to popularizing the doctrines of priesthood of believers, justification by faith alone, and two sacraments, Luther unfolded in his Reformation treatises another concept that became a distinguishing characteristic of historic Protestantism—the scripture as the sole norm or standard of faith. Luther contended that tradition was an unreliable source for Christian belief and conduct, for he reasoned that popes, fathers, and councils had issued innumerable, conflicting decisions. After rejecting the belief that the Roman pontiff could not err in matters of faith and that the universal church alone could properly interpret the Bible, Luther advocated that scripture should be regarded as the sole authority for religious truth, that all essential aspects of the Christian faith were included in that work, and that the Bible should be interpreted by the community of believers. Christians, Luther explained, were to rely on the Spirit of God rather than the church or the pope to guide them along the path of truth and righteousness.[29]

One concept concerning the scriptures that is popular among many orthodox Protestants and is sometimes referred to as a fundamentalist doctrine is the belief in the verbal, plenary inspiration of the Bible. Although fundamentalism better represents a mood or attitude than an organization, an interdenominational, militant crusade emerged at the turn of the century which was known as the fundamentalist movement. Many concepts enunciated by the fundamentalists in the early twentieth century are currently regarded as essential aspects of the Protestant faith by many Americans, especially individuals residing in the South.

The fundamentalist movement originated in the northeastern metropolitan areas of this land in response to an increased reorientation of Christian thinking among members of various denominations.[30] After liberalism became a dominant force in some congregations, many ministers and lay members sought to preserve various theological concepts that had been popular among Protestants since the sixteenth century.

A variety of fruitful seeds of this crusade were planted during a series of Bible conferences in this country, some of the most celebrated being held in Niagara in 1886, 1895, 1901, and 1914. As the years passed, one of the influential vehicles employed by those seeking to preserve the historic faith was the publication in 1909 of twelve pamphlets entitled "The Fundamentals." This work, which was widely circulated, included articles written by a variety of Americans and was financed by two lay brothers, Lyman and Milton Stewart, founders and leading stockholders in the Union Oil Company of Los Angeles. Eventually, the crusade created such a storm and led to strife within so many communities that fundamentalism was turned by some into a term of reproach and the movement dissolved. Most beliefs, however, which leaders of this crusade sought to preserve are being perpetuated by various groups in modern America. Many articles which originally appeared in *The Fundamentalist* have been revised and republished and are currently available in the book *The Fundamentals for Today.* [31]

A variety of ideas concerning the inspiration of the Bible that were advanced in the turn-of-the-century Bible conferences were concepts promulgated by three Princeton professors: Charles Hodge, Archibald Alexander Hodge, and Benjamin B. Warfield. Basing their belief on doctrinal traditions popular among many Lutherans and Calvinists of the sixteenth and seventeenth centuries, these scholars concluded that God would not reveal his will through a fallible work, emphasizing that when originally written, the Bible was verbally inspired and inerrant in all its parts. [32]

Defining their attitude concerning the Bible, fundamentalists persisted in saying that "inspiration" conveyed the concept that the scriptures are God's breath, for, they declared, God "breathed out" or spoke through the mouth of a prophet. "Plenary inspiration" was referred to as the belief that all the scriptures are inspired, plenary denoting full or complete. Many Protestants today also declare that in all its parts the Bible was inspired, for they assert there is no section of the scriptures that was not breathed out by God.

The word "verbal" was also a term that was frequently discussed by fundamentalists. Verbal inspiration was defined as God putting words into the mouths of the prophets. According to one noted preacher, W. B. Riley, the words recorded by the prophets were the very words of God, for God employed the human tongue and pen to express himself. His will, Riley added, was revealed through the lives and lines of many men "who spake as they were moved by the Holy Ghost." Multitudinous were the penmen and various were their styles of writing, but the oneness of purpose they expressed informs us "that a single entity lies back of it all; . . . Jehovah thought, while Moses, the Prophets, and Apostles wrote." [33]

Another explanation of the meaning of verbal inspiration was prepared by Dr. Lewis Sperry Chafer, the president of the Evangelical Theological College of Dallas, Texas. "In their original form," President Chafer explained, the scriptures "were as perfect as any and all of his works, and were expressed with infinite accuracy which was and could be secured only through divine control of the precise words in each and every case." [34]

Although fundamentalists held that the Bible was "verbally inspired," most rejected the mechanical theory of the activity of the Holy Spirit. Leaders of this movement did not believe that the authors of the Bible were in reality little more than stenographers. They insisted that their belief denied the presence of error in the Bible. As explained by J. Gresham Machen, the Holy Spirit "so informed the minds of the Biblical writers that they were kept from falling into the errors that mar all other books." [35]

Admitting that God had not revealed in all cases the precise method in which he revealed his will to man, fundamentalists suggested that "it might have been as varied as the persons to whom the message came." Nevertheless, they insisted that "in no case was the human agency, as to its limitation of vocabulary, restriction in literary style, or misunderstanding of facts, allowed to lessen the absolute, final, and divine character of the message." [36]

Leaders of this movement did recognize, however, that the scriptures were originally written in Hebrew, Aramaic, or Greek, that all the original versions have been lost, and that current versions of the Bible were translations of other translations and of records that were copied and recopied. Consequently, W. B. Riley asserted that to claim "inerrancy for the King James Version, or even for the Revised Version, is to clothe with the claim of verbal inspiration a company of men who would almost quit their graves to repudiate such equality with prophet and apostle." [37]

While considering the subject of the transmission of the Bible, fundamentalists admitted that some errors and variations crept into the text through mistakes of copyists and translators. Nevertheless, they insisted that such errors were comparatively few and the imperfections were generally speaking not significant alterations. Such a recognition did not detract from their "unqualified allegiance to the doctrine of Verbal Inspiration." [38]

The basic beliefs concerning verbal, plenary inspiration of the Bible as advanced by fundamentalists are evident today in the writings and sermons of members of various American denominations. Many Lutherans, Baptists, and members of the Church of Christ and various Reformed bodies hold this concept as a fundamental Christian belief.

Many Lutherans, Baptists, and members of other religious communities who are striving to preserve the historic tradition have rejected verbal inspiration. Many orthodox Christians insist that verbal inspiration makes the authors merely stenographers who have lost their free will and ability of self-expression. Some contend that ideas can be expressed by employing different words and when God conveyed his thoughts to the prophets, they in turn expressed accurately the revelations in their language, employing individualistic styles.

Orthodox Protestants, however, are generally known for retaining a belief in plenary inspiration. Individuals who are seeking to preserve classical Protestantism tend to agree that the entire Bible is the written word of God. Rejecting the view that the Old Testament is merely an advisory authority, they insist on the divine authority of the Old and New Testaments, saying that all the Bible and only the Bible is the word of God. Moreover, they usually assert that the Bible authors are trustworthy teachers of doctrine and reliable historians, narrating historical facts and recording events in an orderly, accurate, dependable manner. They also tend to endorse the judgment of early church leaders who decided the books that should be included in the Old and New Testaments and maintain that God guided them to protect the writings of the prophets. Most reason that if God declared that which the people should know, then he also must have provided the means whereby the words would be preserved and transmitted accurately to mankind. Consequently, in harmony with views popularized by fundamentalists in the early twentieth century, many contemporary Protestants state that only minor mistranslations appear in the modern versions of the Bible.[39]

Many American clergy in recent years have rejected the traditional belief in the inerrancy of the Bible. But when nearly 900 Lutheran ministers belonging to the Missouri Synod were asked if they believed the Bible to be the "inspired and inerrant Word of God not only in matters of faith but also in historical, geographical, and other secular matters," 76 percent responded that they "agreed" or "definitely agreed" with the statement. Less than 34 percent of the ministers of other faiths (American Baptists, Lutherans, Presbyterians, Episcopalians, and Methodists), however, indicated an agreement with this belief.[40]

In addition to emphasizing the verbal, plenary inspiration of the Bible, fundamentalists of the early twentieth century proclaimed a variety of other doctrines that are popular among many orthodox Protestants of today. Frequently fundamentalists issued doctrinal statements that included the following nine articles of faith.[41]

> I. We believe in the scriptures of the Old and New Testaments as verbally inspired of God, and inerrant in the original writings, and that they are of supreme and final authority in faith and life.
> II. We believe in one God, eternally existing in three persons, Father, Son, and Holy Spirit.
> III. We believe that Jesus Christ was begotten by the Holy Spirit, and born of the Virgin Mary, and is true God and true man.
> IV. We believe that man was created in image of God, that he sinned and thereby incurred not only physical death but also that spiri-

tual death which is separation from God; and that all human beings are born with a sinful nature, and in the case of those who reach moral responsibility, become sinners in thought, word, and deed.

V. We believe that the Lord Jesus Christ died for our sins according to the scriptures as a representative and substitutionary sacrifice; and that all that believe in Him are justified on the grounds of His shed blood.

VI. We believe in the resurrection of the crucified body of our Lord, in His ascension into heaven, and in His present life there for us, as High Priest and Advocate.

VII. We believe in "that blessed hope," the personal, pre-millennial and imminent return of our Lord and Savior Jesus Christ.

VIII. We believe that all who receive by faith the Lord Jesus Christ are born again of the Holy Spirit and thereby become children of God.

IX. We believe in the bodily resurrection of the just and the unjust, the everlasting, conscious punishment of the lost.

Although many orthodox Protestants of today agree that elements of the popular fundamentalist doctrinal statements harmonize with their convictions (such as the belief in the Trinity, the virgin birth of Christ, the substitutionary atonement, and salvation through faith), several doctrines included in the formal fundamentalist declarations would not be endorsed by many contemporary Protestants who are known for their theological conservatism. In addition to the concept of "verbal inspiration," many orthodox reject the fundamentalist view concerning the "personal, pre-millennial and imminent return of Jesus Christ."

In considering eschatology (the doctrine of the final world events, including the second coming of Christ, the resurrection, and judgment), most conservative Protestants of modern America profess that at the end of the world Christ will not come to inaugurate a millennium but to judge the dead. The Savior's first act, some specify, will be to resurrect the bodies of all men, after which the public judgment will commence. When orthodox consider the doctrine of the resurrection of the body and of hell, many depart from beliefs that were popular among Protestants of colonial America. Some who are orthodox in most respects emphasize a belief in a spiritual resurrection that includes man's total personality but precludes a physical body of flesh and bones. Some also deny that hell is a place where men suffer everlasting physical punishment in the traditional sense of the term. While conservatives adopt conflicting views concerning life beyond the grave, most teach that the unrighteous will be consigned to a place of everlasting punishment and the righteous will dwell forever in heaven with the Lord.

Fundamentalists popularized a number of beliefs representing the historic faith that were not included in the formal fundamentalist doctrinal statements; many of these tenets are generally held by orthodox Protestants of modern America. Conservative Protestants, for example, are known for their description of the trinitarian God as a spirit, an immaterial being without form or bodily parts, and of a God who is omnipotent, omniscient, and omnipresent. Most have also retained the popular traditional belief concerning angels and devils. Orthodox Christians assert that God made a great multitude of finite spirits called angels. All were created good, but a part sinned and fell, becoming evil spirits who exert their power over the minds and bodies of men.

Even though most orthodox Protestants reject evolution as God's method of creation and insist that Adam was specially created by a divine act of God, some conservatives have reevaluated their faith concerning the creation. In some orthodox circles, individuals disagree about how God created man. A few who classify themselves as orthodox in most respects reject the "immediate-creation theory." Some reason that science traces the biological ancestry of Adam back to dust or a small organism while the Bible traces his spiritual ancestry back to God. Like the fundamentalists, many conservative Protestants are also divided over the issue of the period of time involved in the creation of the world. Some conclude that God created the world out of nothing in six literal days of twenty-four hours each, while most hold that the world was created out of nothing during six long eras of eons.[42]

Summarizing classical Protestantism, many authors describe the centrality of the word of God in the faith and practice of these Christians. Jesus Christ is considered the head of the Church and is known as the word of God made flesh. The word of God is also expressed in the Bible, especially the redemptive message of free grace made possible through the atonement of Jesus Christ. The preached word is considered the attempt by the church to keep the word relevant in the lives of Christians; and the enacted word is referred to as reliving "the drama of God's encounter with man."[43]

The Historical Roots of Contemporary Theology

4

During the late nineteenth and early twentieth centuries a major reorientation of religious thinking took place among Americans of various faiths. Following the Civil War, this emerging nation proved to be a fertile field for the transplanting of liberal religious thoughts that had emerged in Europe, especially Germany. As Americans made great advancements in their educational systems, an increasing percentage of the population was exposed to newly discovered scientific facts and theories. Remarkable technological developments, conspicuous medical discoveries, and other noteworthy scientific advancements focused man's attention on the capabilities of the human race. In some respects, man's dependence on the influence of God and faith in the Bible seemed to shift to a dependence on medical science and scholarly conclusions; and a radical change occurred in the beliefs of many citizens of the modern nation. After rejecting aspects of the classical theology, many individuals endorsed that which they considered "a new dynamic faith" or patterns of belief that were deemed more compatible with the thinking of twentieth-century man and were judged as relevant and meaningful to each succeeding generation.

The transformation of the religious convictions of many Americans is partly evidenced by an examination of the impact of Darwinism on American Christian thought. The introduction and popularization of evolution in mid-nineteenth-century America created a violent storm that has not yet fully subsided. This scientific theory included the concept that man's physical body evolved from lower forms, thereby challenging the traditional belief in Adam's special creation. After many Americans adopted Darwin's basic premises and then embraced later refinements and alterations of evolution, they turned their attention toward a reevaluation of the Genesis account of the creation. Many concluded that the Bible was not intended to be a scientific treatise. Some suggested that while Genesis informed man that God was the creator, scientists were unfolding the mysteries concerning the method of creation.

While Christians were reconstructing their belief concerning man's origin, some reexamined the traditional dogma of the fall, which in turn had provided a basis for the classical view of man's nature and the need for an atonement. Many evolutionists reasoned that since the creation account should not be interpreted literally, the doctrine of the fall should be reexamined. Moreover, the belief that man literally inherited from Adam the original sin or an evil disposition was deemed incompatible with modern thought. Many also asked the question that if the fall were not a reality in the traditional sense of the term, what then was the real meaning of the atonement? What was the redemption? What was Christ's reparation?

The concept of evolution carried with it the ideas of appealing to facts, verifying concepts, the inevitability of change, and the survival of the fittest. Such views were regarded by some theologians, such as the French Jesuit evolutionist Teilhard de Chardin (1881-1955), as shattering to the traditional Christian emphasis on a static theology.[1]

After initiating a critical examination of classical Protestantism, many modern theologians agreed that only those beliefs (with few exceptions) which, in their opinion, survived the scrutiny of modern scientific investigation should be retained. In addition to preserving only those which were regarded as the "fittest" beliefs, many contemporary theologians announced that doctrines should evolve, suggesting that every generation should seek new expressions of Christian thought.

The reinterpretation of classical Protestantism was also advanced by the American popularization of biblical criticism. In an attempt to determine the precise meaning of biblical passages, a scientific approach was applied to the study of the Bible, including the incorporation of modern techniques of historical and literary criticism. Since many recognized that errors due to faulty translation appeared in the Bible, there was an attempt to determine the purest text available (known as the study of lower or textual criticism). Scholars also sought a deeper understanding of the Bible by attempting to determine what the original authors intended to say (a study known as higher criticism). To accomplish this, the scholars strove to place biblical writings in their historic and linguistic settings, seeking answers to such questions as who wrote the works of the Bible and when the various passages were written.

While men were critically examining the Bible, others were studying patterns of belief held by non-Christians throughout the ages. This study revealed that striking parallels existed in the beliefs of Christians and members of other world religions. Many accounts of a creation, of a deluge, of a dispersal, and of a messiah were located in the traditions of various faiths.

The Dead Sea scrolls provided further evidence that aspects of the gospel as taught by Jesus of Nazareth were known by others before the Savior's birth in mortality.

The impact of the new scientific thinking, the emphasis on reason as a means of determining religious truth, the general conclusions of Bible critics, and the discoveries of scholars in the field of comparative religions proved devastating to classical Christian and Jewish thought. Most Americans who were susceptible to the trends in modern thought altered considerably their attitude toward the Bible, a work that had served Protestants, Catholics, and Jews as the constitution upon which their beliefs had been based. After rejecting the traditional belief in miracles and prophecies, various contemporary theologians popularized a new definition for prophecy. Instead of holding that it was a prediction of future events, many contended that prophecy was a prophet's comments on the times in which he lived. These comments were sometimes viewed as interpretations of God's historical dealings with man.

Various contemporary theologians also concluded that many Old Testament narratives were myths or legends. Most liberal Bible scholars gave their definition of myth as a story which conveys an eternal truth. Most further held that the myth might or might not have as its origin a historical event. When modern Bible scholars reexamined the first five books of the Old Testament, they generally rejected the traditional belief that these works were written by Moses. Many substituted the Mosaic authorship of the Pentateuch with the view that it was the product of various authors. Numerous scholars further contended that much of Genesis was a compilation of myths inherited by the Hebrews from other cultural traditions.

After applying modern scientific, literary, and historical tools to a study of the entire Bible, William Newton Clarke (1841-1912), a Baptist clergyman and professor and a spokesman for a new theology, described the complexity involved in interpreting this scripture: [2]

> The fact is that [an] absolutely perfect understanding of what a writer meant by a written page can never be obtained. Even the more external matters cannot be managed to perfection. Perfect translation is impossible. The meaning of words and the structure of sentences can never be so determined that there shall be no ambiguity whatever, and the historical setting can never be perfectly reproduced in the reader's mind. But even farther beyond reach is the inner work of interpretation. One man cannot perfectly take another's point of view and think his thought after him: least of all can this be done when the other speaks out of another age and training, thinking his thought in a world of personal experience which to the student does not exist.

Higher criticism not only conveyed to Clarke the problems involved in formulating or defending a theology based upon statements included in the Bible but also led him to believe that all or portions of many biblical books should not be classified as historical and that individuals are "not required to agree to every statement" included in the Old and New Testaments.[3] Sounding an opinion that became popular among liberals of twentieth-century America, Clarke added that higher criticism led him to believe that "Christians need not attribute to the God of Christ all the acts and passions that Israelites attributed to the God of Israel, or approve the moral judgments that were recorded in days of inferior moral light."[4] Furthermore, Clarke rejected the practice of using "proof-texts" to support a particular theological system and contended that he was not bound to incorporate into his pattern of religious belief all statements appearing in modern versions of the Bible.[5]

Although many liberals of modern America rejected the Bible as revelation (as traditionally defined by Protestants), advocates of a new theology did not propose eliminating that work as a primary source of religious truth. William Adams Brown (1865-1943), a Presbyterian theologian who became professor of systematic theology at Union Theological Seminary, aptly described a popular liberal view of the Bible when he stated his reasons for retaining the work as the major source for man's religious convictions. "It is the most ancient, direct and reliable source for our knowledge of the historic Christ," he remarked, and "it is the most effective means for the awakening and stimulating [of a genuine] Christian life."[6] Brown also described why he believed the scriptures "deserve a unique position in the church as inspired and authoritative writings." "Through its living message to the needs and longings of the present," he explained, "[the Bible] lifts men, through communion with the historic Jesus, to faith in the living God from whom he came."[7]

The most drastic alterations of Christian beliefs occurred when men adopted the tools of modern thinking to an examination of the New Testament. Concentrating their reorientation on the central source of the classical Christian faith, a number of scholars endeavored to identify what they regarded as New Testament errors, legends and nonhistorical narratives, and they sought to expose incorrect theological interpretations of the person and mission of Jesus.

In a lucidly written summary of nineteenth-century critical investigations of the life of the Nazarene, Albert Schweitzer noted in his *Quest of the Historical Jesus* (1906, English translation 1910) that prior to the publication of David Strauss's *Life of Jesus* (1835) rationalists eliminated nearly all narratives that could not be explained in natural terms. Only those accounts in the Gospels that contained no supernatural elements were considered as historical possibilities. Although Strauss agreed with other critics that supernatural accounts were probably not historical realities, the German scholar emphasized that biographers should not avoid the miraculous elements of the

Gospels but should determine the source of what he called New Testament myths or legends. He suggested that an understanding of the origin of these myths would provide authors with an invaluable guide for the reconstruction of the life of Jesus.[8] Adopting a Hegelian method, the supernatural became the thesis (one proposition), the rational was the antithesis (a counter proposition), and the mythological was the synthesis (the combination of the thesis and antithesis to produce a higher state of knowledge).[9] With the advent of Strauss (1808-1874), critics began an intense analysis of what they regarded as the mythical elements of the Gospels, and the gates were thrown open for a modern flood of interpretations concerning the meaning of the New Testament miracles.

After he identified what he considered the myths of the Gospels (which included most biographical accounts relating events prior to the baptism of Jesus, John the Baptist's claim to revelation on the Messianic dignity of Jesus, the temptation, the "Sea-Stories and Fish-Stories," the raising of the dead, most healings, stories of Jesus' feeding the multitudes, the resurrection of Jesus and his ascension, and many other accounts that were regarded as "beyond credibility"), Strauss sought to explain the meaning of these narratives. For example, he taught that Jesus decided that he was the Messiah, the anointed one predicted by the Old Testament prophets. The basis for this unusual claim of Jesus, Strauss reasoned, was a combination of the strong Jewish expectation of the Messiah coupled with the appearance of an exceptionally impressive personality. After Jesus arrived at the conclusion that he was the Messiah, Strauss continued, he was willing to follow the example of earlier prophets, thereby preparing himself for "oppression, condemnation, and execution."[10]

David Strauss further contended that after the disciples of Jesus had endorsed his Messianic role, they agreed that the Nazarene should be viewed by later generations as a person mightier than any of the Old Testament prophets. According to Strauss, since the lives of the Old Testament prophets had been embellished with various legends, it is not surprising that the disciples continued this tradition of manufacturing myths. Therefore, Strauss concluded that to provide proof of the Messiah's prophetic dignity, the disciples of Jesus clothed the Nazarene with a variety of supernatural feats which were patterned after but were even more miraculous than the legends recorded in the Old Testament.[11]

Although Strauss's basic interpretations of what he considered the New Testament myths were regarded by most subsequent critics as unscientific, this German scholar set a pattern of interpretation that continued into the twentieth century. One of the popular currents of modern religious thought is interpreting the so-called New Testament myths in order that man might comprehend more fully the genuine Christian faith.

While contemporary theologians are known for their general rejection of the Bible's supernatural narratives as historical realities, they are also distinguished by their highly provocative but conflicting interpretations of what they classify as the Biblical myths and legends. After Albert Schweitzer reviewed the innumerable conflicting interpretations of the life of Jesus as advanced by nineteenth-century critics, the noted humanitarian observed that as a concrete historical personality Jesus had remained a stranger and an unresolved mystery. While Schweitzer believed that Jesus' life had been colored by various romantic myths, he urged others not to concentrate on controversial theological implications of the Savior's teachings but to follow the spiritual example of the Nazarene.[12] "Jesus is meaningful to our world," Schweitzer observed, "because a mighty spiritual force streams forth" from him.[13] Although we cannot know Jesus through a completely objective, scientific analysis of his life, he concluded, the mystery of Jesus' personality will be revealed to others as they live in harmony with the moral teachings unfolded by the Nazarene.[14]

Albert Schweitzer's religious convictions concerning the importance of losing one's life in the service of others echoed another popular liberal thought that passed from the nineteenth to the twentieth century. Contemporary theologians continue to assert that religion has a strong social and ethical character. Most liberals insist that one of the most important dimensions of religion is that of being concerned for the welfare of others and of rendering service to all mankind.

One of the most popular patterns of thinking today among liberal ministers and laity is known as existentialism. Since there has been a tremendous variety of ideas expressed by proponents of existentialism, it is most difficult to state briefly the nature of this system of thought. Existentialism is sometimes described as a reaction against the main philosophical emphases of the nineteenth century. Most philosophers of that era maintained that philosophers should study the essence of things—they should abstract what all things of a certain class have in common. With Plato, they affirmed that the "form" or idea of a table preceded the existence of any particular table. Existentialists affirmed the opposite of this form of thought, for instead of saying that "essence precedes existence" as the nineteenth-century philosophers had held, they generally taught that "existence precedes essence." Many existentialists who believe in God (theists) assert that after man evolved from lower forms, man examined the world in which he lived and began asking questions. Why a tree? Why man? Why me? What is the meaning of life? Friedrich Wilhelm Nietzsche (1844-1900), a distinguished German philosopher, reasoned that if you know the *why of life* you can learn the *how of life*. Many existentialists conclude that as man encountered problems, he turned to God and began formulating beliefs or doctrines. In harmony with Darwinian theory, existentialists generally state that doctrines have evolved. Many further teach that man has constantly been engaged in a quest for the real meaning of life and as a consequence has periodically reconstructed his patterns of faith.

Existentialists also often dwell on the concept of *existence*. According to the Danish theologian Soren Kierkegaard (1813-55), existence means "man's peculiar predicament as a creature of God." Although Kierkegaard held that man is absolutely dependent upon God for his being, he insisted that man is also an individual, "a center of self-awareness and of decision." Man, he taught, is free to choose and shape himself by his decisions.[15]

In harmony with the basic philosophy of Kierkegaard, many existentialists currently teach that a Christian is a certain kind of individual, one who considers alternatives, who chooses, decides, and above all commits himself. The spectator can be said to exist but the term *existence*, in the view of Kierkegaard and many contemporary theologians, does not properly belong to inactive things. Existence refers to a quality in the individual, his conscious participation in an act. Existentialists, therefore, emphasize being committed to a cause, being active, being involved. Many further teach that faith is not belief in a creed or doctrine; faith is a decision to commit oneself to God, which in part is accomplished through genuine service to mankind.

While one group of contemporary theologians concentrated on commitment, another wing of the liberal tradition decided that the emphasis of religion should be on feeling, experience, or self-awareness. This definition which was advanced throughout the nineteenth century has continued to be another popular substitute for endorsements of the historic creeds of Christendom.

One of the influential German philosophers who stressed that religion should be viewed essentially as contemplative or as an intuition was Friedrich Schleiermacher (1768-1832). After concluding that an incomprehensible God could not be understood in the same sense that men grasp knowledge in the field of science, Schleiermacher reasoned that religion should not be based on rationalism as held by most Deists nor should it be reduced merely to moral activities directed by man's belief in God. For Schleiermacher, religion was basically a God-determined feeling or a "quality of self-consciousness." Although he did not completely withdraw religion from the realm of knowing and doing into a single arena of pious feelings, the heart of his theology was man's dependence on God.[16] Man becomes aware of God, Schleiermacher explained, when man is moved by God. This human feeling was, in his opinion, a God-determined feeling. God, he asserted, "unifies for us all our ambivalent relationships with things and people" and provides direction to life in the sense that we can "understand it as continuous with nature and history." According to Schleiermacher, God was this principle of harmony and unity that was waiting to direct man; and religion was this feeling, this encounter with God, this "consciousness of the unity of all things in the Infinite." Before man encounters God, he added, man must "first discover humanity, and this he can do only in love and through love."[17]

In addition to emphasizing the experience of the God-consciousness, Schleiermacher stressed a theory of Christ's redemption that was similar to the moral influence theory that became popular in liberal circles in twentieth-century America. This German theologian decided that Christ's redemptive act was his calling of men into fellowship. Expressed in other terms, the redemption was Christ's exemplary life which stimulates observers to recognize their dependence upon God. According to Schleiermacher's scheme of thinking, the church provided a structure and fellowship where individuals who were attracted to the God-consciousness could find support and stimulation.[18]

While Schleiermacher suggested that men find God by looking into themselves, some who followed the path which he blazed turned the thrust of their theology toward a social gospel. Such was the case of Albert Ritschl (1822-1889). Acknowledging that Schleiermacher was his predecessor in unfolding the method of religion, Ritschl placed ethics on a plane equal with that of the religious experience. Agreeing with many other liberals that theological speculation was not a valid source of knowledge about God, this prominent figure in German Protestant theology insisted that religious thought was essentially practical and moral.[19]

As Ritschl revealed his basic theological pattern, he proclaimed many concepts that became popular among liberals living in twentieth-century America. Many, for example, who are currently known for their reinterpretation of classical Protestantism agree with Ritschl's definition of sin. Rejecting an association of sin with a universal inheritance or a historic Adam, Ritschl held that sin is the product of individual action, such as selfishness and ignorance.[20] The sins of man, he continued, separate man from God and the Christian faith offers mankind a redemption from his sins. This redemption includes justification (the forgiveness of sins and removal of guilt) and reconciliation. As he unfolded his concept of reconciliation Ritschl explained that renewal occurs when "man's mistrust of God" is replaced by his "positive assent" to God's purposes. And the redemptive power of Christ, he added, is Christ's ability to help man overcome sin, such as inspiring individuals to be motivated by love.[21]

After considering the differences in Christianity and other world religions, Ritschl decided that the distinguishing characteristic of Christianity was that it was a "monotheistic form of faith" in which everything refers "to the redemption wrought by Christ" or to the concept of a "redeemed community of Christ." Explaining this definition, Ritschl asserted that Christian theology emanates from the Holy Spirit and includes an indispensable combination of the doctrine of redemption and a system of morality. It is, he added, a "completely spiritual and ethical religion" which involves the impulse to "act from a motive of love." Ritschl was especially critical of forms of piety that neglected problems confronting mankind; instead of relegating the church to a secondary position of importance as Schleiermacher had done, he raised the church to a preeminent position, paralleling the spiritual experience. For Ritschl the historic church played a vital role in helping men overcome sin by inspiring them to be motivated by love.[22]

Various mainstreams of nineteenth-century liberal thinking penetrated the twentieth century, providing a basis for various modern religious beliefs. In addition to a reevaluation of the Bible as a historical record, an emphasis on interpreting the "myths" of the Bible, a concentration on existentialism, a belief in religion as a feeling or experience, reinterpretations of classical Protestant beliefs concerning the origin of man's sins and Christianity as a redemptive religion, there were other sources which provided a background for the beliefs of many Americans of today. For example, many liberals today teach that the views of Scheiermacher and Ritschl encouraged people to anchor their faith in the historic Jesus. This focus on the person of Jesus became one of the forces which led to the twentieth-century emphasis on the centrality of Jesus Christ in Christian theology.

Another legacy of the nineteenth-century liberal tradition was the feeling that religion should inspire a profound moral concern for others. As previously mentioned, Schleiermacher's theology suggested that experience should precede religious beliefs and that Christians should gain a feeling of absolute dependence upon God. This feeling, he added, should lead men to fellowship with others of similar experience. And Ritschl taught that humanity should be organized so that man will act on the principle of pure love, a love patterned after the example and teachings of Jesus Christ. These nineteenth-century concepts helped stimulate a continuation and a resurgence of twentieth-century Christian-motivated social action programs.[23]

Although twentieth-century theology stems back to the previous century, many modern theologians do not merely echo the most influential religious thinkers of the past. A number of distinguished theologians of this century have developed new and unique expressions of the Christian faith which have become popular in congregations throughout the world.

5

Contemporary Theology

The reorientation of classical Protestantism in modern America has become so complex that the average individual is overwhelmed when he seeks to understand the popular modern descriptions of the Christian faith. Most of the celebrated contemporary theologians are philosophers who couch their beliefs in a jargon that is sometimes incomprehensible to the masses. Many theologians have also altered traditional definitions of words and terms frequently used by preachers in the past; this increases the problem of comprehending the new theology. Expressions, for example, such as original sin, virgin birth, the fall, the atonement, the ascension of Christ, descending to hell, the resurrection, revelation, angels, and devils, frequently take on new meaning when incorporated in the sermons and writings of modern preachers.

The names of the most distinguished theologians of the twentieth century are also much better known than are the religious systems which they have developed. Two of the most distinguished contemporary theologians lived in Switzerland: Emil Brunner (1889-1966) of Zurich and Karl Barth (1886-1968) of Basel. Two other famous religious philosophers of the modern world were Germans, Rudolf Bultmann (1884 -   ) and Dietrich Bonhoeffer (1906-45). Another celebrated German, Paul Tillich (1886-1965), migrated to the United States where he continued to gain international recognition for his penetrating analysis of the Christian faith. Two well-known theologians of the modern age who were born in the United States were the brothers Reinhold (1892-1971) and Helmut Richard (1894-1962) Niebuhr. All of these men, reared in the liberal tradition, developed divergent and complex theological systems.

The pattern of belief of some Americans who currently endorse a modern reinterpretation of the classical faith is best reflected by examining the teachings of the most influential religious thinkers of the twentieth century. Consequently, an examination of the writings of some contemporary philosophers provides, in part, the flavor of faith of one segment of modern Protestantism.

In the twentieth century, an existential approach to the meaning of what liberals classified as New Testament myths or legends was undertaken by an influential and highly controversial German theologian, Ruldolf Bultmann. Like many of his contemporaries, Bultmann attempted to interpret the central meaning of the Christian faith for those of his generation. For example, he contended that miracles, those "wonder tales contained in the gospels," were mostly legendary, or at least had legendary embellishments. He also asserted that while the tragedy of Jesus' crucifixion was a historical reality, the death of the Nazarene should not be regarded as an atonement for the sins of mankind.[1]

One of Bultmann's most disputed statements was that dead men do not rise. While considering the "legend of the empty tomb" and reports of the appearance of the resurrected body of Jesus, Bultmann declared that "an historical fact which involves a resurrection from the dead is utterly inconceivable!" For Bultmann, the New Testament resurrection narratives were simply embellishments of primitive traditions. When he assessed Paul's testimony of the resurrection, the German theologian reasoned that Paul's attempt to prove such a miracle "by adducing a list of eye-witnesses" guarantees only that the apostle preached the concept, not that the event occurred.[2]

Although most of Bultmann's interpretations of the Bible were condemned vehemently by conservatives and were in some respects considered too conservative by some liberals, he is well known for his desire to demythologize the New Testament. Demythologizing did not mean eliminating what he regarded as the New Testament myths, but interpreting them existentially or in terms of understanding human existence.[3]

Bultmann was convinced that the major value of the Bible was not the reported miracles or proofs of the resurrection, but rather it was the *kerygma*, the "proclamation of what God has done for man in Jesus Christ." (*Kerygma* is a word derived from the Greek verb meaning "to proclaim.") According to Bultmann, this New Testament proclamation "of the event of God in Jesus Christ" emphasized the principle of repentance and the promise of the Holy Spirit to all who were transformed. *Kerygma,* he felt, should be considered existentially as a call to a new life. Bultmann did not believe that he was "dissolving the Christian faith in the acids of demythologizing," as his critics charged, but that he was reducing the mythological elements to a secondary status and was recovering for modern man the essential aspects of Christianity.[4]

One of the major premises advanced by Bultmann was that the history in the New Testament is basically mythical in character. He described this history as one set in motion and controlled by supernatural powers, a scene of supernatural activity of God and his angels opposed to Satan and his demons. According to Bultmann's analysis, the supernatural forces continually intervene in the affairs of man, depriving man of control of his own life. Evil spirits, for example, are reported to take possession of the bodies of men and thereby direct their thoughts and actions.[5]

For Bultmann this mythical, Biblical view of the history of mankind cannot be accepted by modern man. For preachers to pretend that contemporaries would endorse such supernaturalism, he reasoned, is both "senseless and impossible." In his opinion, this New Testament pattern is "simply the cosmology of a prescientific age."[6]

When Bultmann turned to a description of Jesus he concluded that the Nazarene was a concrete figure of history whose life was clothed with many mythical events. In his view the New Testament provides us the beliefs of the early Christian community, rather than a genuine biography of Jesus. Consequently, he held that the Gospels provide practically no information on the actual life and personality of Jesus. Bultmann also held the personal opinion that Jesus did not claim to be the Messiah; and he concluded that it is impossible for modern biographers such as Strauss to interpret myths accurately enough to portray the historical character of the Nazarene.[7]

Bultmann further concluded that the discovery of the historical Jesus was not an essential aspect of the Christian faith nor was such a factual biography necessary to comprehend the genuine message of Christianity. When individuals read the New Testament they should not be concerned with the historicity of the narratives but should continually ask existential questions, such as, how do the New Testament proclamations help me understand human existence, including my relationship to others?[8]

As Bultmann applied his pattern of thinking to the biblical writings, he proclaimed that the New Testament informs us that man is not only a fallen being but that the fall is total. He also suggested that man's bondage leads to "self-glorying and self-assertion" which is in direct contrast to man's authentic life of "self-commitment." Man can become aware of his plight when he learns that he is not what he should be nor what he would like to be. Such an awareness is essential to genuine human existence and is not a possession man can command at will.[9]

Another concept emphasized by this German theologian was that the authentic life "becomes possible only when man is delivered from himself." This deliverance occurs, he reasoned, when the love of God intervenes "as a power which embraces and sustains" man, "even in his fallen, self-assertive state." In one respect, this gift from God was regarded by Bultmann as a forgiveness of sin, but not as a release from punishment. It was the conviction of Bultmann that this forgiveness by God "delivers man from himself and makes him free to devote his life to the service of others." It is also an act of

God through which man becomes capable of "faith and love, of self-com-mitment," and of an "authentic life."[10]

Some of the New Testament eschatological elements, such as the Second Coming, were interpreted by this controversial philosopher as meaning that every individual is faced with imminent death, the end of human existence. According to this view, man learns from the Bible the urgency of making decisions, accepting responsibilities, and awakening to the fact that the end is near.

Turning to the atonement and resurrection, Bultmann held that to believe in the cross was not to endorse some theory of the atonement but was to become reconciled to God and to one's true being. This reconciliation occurs when one decides to turn from the world to God. Such commitment begins a new life and is, in reality, the resurrection implied in the New Testament. Moreover, Bultmann taught that in the resurrection a sinner rises from selfish-ness and from being self-centered to his authentic existence, the life of love and service.[11]

Bultmann's eschatological interpretations were applied to many other por-tions of the Bible. Creation myths, for example, are not treatises on how man and the world came into being but unfold the concept of man's dependent status. Myths of evil spirits tormenting man demonstrate "man's awareness of the tyranny of the world over his life." Although this tyranny might appear as the result of demonic powers, for Bultmann it arises from man's decisions to be "for the world and against God."[12]

Although many contemporary theologians reject Bultmann's interpreta-tions of biblical narrative and many critics assert that his demythologizing has created more problems than it has resolved, other liberals of the twentieth century hold that the demythologizing (and existential) interpretation of the Bible is one of the most promising trends of our time. Many liberals who do not endorse all of Bultmann's conclusions hold that this theologian's major contribution was the introduction of a thought-provoking and practical inter-pretation of the Bible. Some speculate theologians will be occupied for gen-erations in uncovering the meaning of New Testament narratives in such a way that the message will be considered applicable to modern man. Some of his admirers further insist that while this reinterpretation of the Bible occurs, Bultmann will have kept the "Christian faith a living issue in the contem-porary world."[13]

The flavor of contemporary theology is further expressed in the writings of Karl Barth, the most prolific writer of the modern theologians. Born in Basel, Switzerland, this son of a Protestant minister was trained in the liberal German theological tradition. After his ordination in the Swiss Evangelical Reformed Church, he served as minister in Switzerland and then became a professor, eventually teaching at several universities in Germany. When he refused to sign an oath of allegiance to Adolf Hitler, Barth was removed from his professional status and one year later was arrested and deported to Switzerland. For the next twenty years, from 1935 to 1956, he was professor of theology at the University of Basel and after his retirement from that institution continued to lecture occasionally and write profusely until his death on 9 December 1968.

Following World War I, Barth decided that religion had become an accommodation to science, and that during this harmonization, man's beliefs had been channeled from religion's biblical base into philosophical idealism. Barth further determined that because ministers failed to espouse that which was essential and authoritative, a vacuum had been created in the churches. Consequently, he sought to rediscover the church's message to mankind and resolved to provide a biblical basis for a new theology.[14]

While Barth was reconstructing Christian beliefs on the basis of his interpretation of the word of God, he continued to endorse many conclusions of biblical critics and retain other features of the liberal theological tradition. Unlike many other contemporary theologians, however, Barth constantly cited biblical references in support of his convictions and often couched his new theology in a biblical or classical Christian language. For instance, in his description of the virgin birth, Barth asserted that men should believe that Jesus was conceived by the Holy Spirit and born of the Virgin Mary. This traditional belief did not mean that "the Holy Spirit is so to speak the Father of Jesus Christ," nor is it informing man of "an unusual procreation and an unusual birth." Instead, this declaration reveals the reality of the incarnation, that God became man, that Jesus Christ is indeed true man, but that he is not just a man but he is God himself. "When we say," Barth explained, "born of Mary the Virgin," we mean that "God gives Himself an earthly human origin," that Jesus comes both from God and from a human being.[15]

Since Barth did not endorse many supernatural elements in the Bible as historical realities, rejected the classical view of the fall of Adam and of the virgin birth of Christ, and denied many other doctrines traditionally held by Protestants, many conservatives have branded Barth as a liberal; but after examining the heart of Barthian theology, many liberals classify him as a conservative. Nevertheless, he certainly did not retreat to Christian fundamentalism, and some men classify his theology as standing somewhere between liberalism and orthodoxy. His voluminous writings reflect a combination of liberal Protestant ideas flavored with classical expressions and beliefs. This new theology, which is sometimes referred to as neo-orthodoxy, proved compatible with the thinking of many Protestants who rejected some features of the old-time religion but believed that contemporary theologians generally departed too far from the historic faith.

One of the themes echoed by this Swiss theologian was God's search for man. Barth urged others to read the Bible in light of God's message to mankind. As individuals study the word of God and contemplate its message,

Barth articulated, believers should let God speak to them through the messages proclaimed in the Old and the New Testaments.

In addition to holding that the Bible was the only reliable source of human knowledge about God, Barth insisted that the focus of the scriptures was on God. As he compared modern theology with his study of the Bible, Barth contended that while many of his contemporaries concentrated on man, the Bible does not extol the virtues of man "but the virtues of him who" called man "out of darkness into his marvelous light!"[16]

In his writings, Barth often explained his views of God. Rejecting the liberal reliance on reason, Barth argued that neither Jesus nor the New Testament authors attempted to prove the existence of God. According to Barth, there is no need to prove this reality. In one sense God is unprovable for he is inconceivable and cannot be defined nor grasped by man's mentality. Barth insisted that God is the Father, the Son, and the Holy Spirit and, while explaining the mystery of the triune God, proposed that God has three ways or modes of being. [17]

Karl Barth not only provided a biblical flavor to his new theology, but he also concentrated on the sinful nature of man and the need for man's regeneration. As some admirers have observed, Barth put original sin and justification back into Protestant theology. Although Barth emphasized that man was a sinful creature, he did not return to the traditional position of a universal imputation of sin but, like many of his contemporaries, advocated that man separates himself from God of his own volition. Man's sin, he taught, is his enmity toward the grace of God. This estrangement makes man incapable of cooperating with God except through the power of the Holy Spirit.

As Barth continued to unfold his basic pattern of thought, he insisted that God does not desire that man should perish. Therefore, God liberates man from sin. "God does this," Barth continued, "not in spite of His righteousness, but it is God's very righteousness that He, the Holy One, steps in for us the unholy." God wills to save us, and he does save us. He makes man righteous, meaning "setting right." He intervenes and actually takes our punishment upon himself. God, therefore, reconciles man, redeems man, and transfers man to another status so that God no longer regards him as a sinner but as a righteous individual or "one who does right before God."[18]

Instead of using the word atonement, Barth employed a word meaning reconciliation, a "restoration of fellowship." Barth did not endorse a popular orthodox view that the atonement was penal satisfaction, that the reconciliation was the satisfaction of God, but that it was the "completed justification of man." God reconciles man; he converts man so that man turns from himself toward God. The heart of his view concerning reconciliation was that there was an exchange or a "change of places" between God and man. This was a two-way exchange, involving the action of "God's self-humiliation in assuming sinful flesh in Jesus Christ" and the "story of man's exaltation in righteousness in Jesus Christ." In other words, "God humbles himself to live with man in his sin so that man may be exalted to live with God in his righteousness."[19]

Although Barth's popularity seems to be declining, his influence has remained strong; and even though many Americans do not agree with all of Barth's conclusions, many believe that one of his greatest contributions was to divert liberalism back toward orthodoxy and toward a biblical basis for determining religious truth.

One of the most renowned American spokesmen for the liberal tradition was Reinhold Niebuhr. Born in Wright City, Missouri on 21 June 1892, this offspring of a scholarly German preacher graduated from the Divinity School of Yale University, after which he was ordained into the ministry of the Evangelical and Reformed Church. For thirteen years Niebuhr served a Detroit congregation of industrial workers. In 1928 he joined the faculty at Union Theological Seminary where he served as professor of applied Christianity and, prior to World War II, while teaching in New York City, became an active socialist.[20] However, partly as a result of witnessing international events and reading the attacks of Barth on Nazism and the writings of critics of Marxism, Niebuhr recalled that he awakened from his "Socialist slumber."[21]

In 1932 one of Niebuhr's most controversial ideas appeared in his celebrated *Moral Man and Immoral Society.* Although individuals are sinful, Niebuhr observed, society is even more corrupt. Man, he explained, "is endowed by nature with both selfish and unselfish impulses," which includes "a measure of sympathy and consideration" for others who are like him. Most people tend to "accept the moral opinions of their society" and seem to possess a sense of obligation toward that which they define as good. "As individuals," he articulated, "men believe that they ought to love and serve each other and establish justice between each other." Yet, he continued, one of the paradoxes of society is that large groups, such as races, classes, nations, large corporations, and labor unions, to which individuals belong are less likely to be moral than are the individuals. Groups tend to grasp for themselves "whatever their power can command. . . . In every human group there is less reason to guide and to check impulse, less capacity for self-transcendence, less ability to comprehend the needs of others and therefore more unrestrained egoism than the individuals, who compose the group, reveal in their personal relationships." Consequently, Niebuhr concluded that "civilization has become a device for delegating the vices of individuals to larger and larger communities."[22]

Throughout his preaching and teaching career, Reinhold Niebuhr expressed a deep concern for social issues and emphasized that religion provided mankind with the foundation that enabled human personalities to function in society. By emphasizing a personal God and man's relationship to deity,

Niebuhr suggested that religion should teach individuals the key values of human personality. This philosopher reasoned that while modern society had a tendency to depersonalize the individual, religion should make society more humane and should concentrate on resolving problems confronting modern man. Since individuals live in a social matrix, Niebuhr added, man cannot be fully understood nor helped except within a social system.[23] In harmony with this pattern of thinking, Niebuhr continued to devote his energies toward resolving critical issues which challenged his generation; and as a consequence of his writings and actions, his admirers credit him with channeling American theology from an idealistic to a realistic course.

Although it is perplexing to summarize patterns of liberal Protestant thought, some dominant characteristics emerge. Liberals are less interested than conservatives in most doctrinal questions described in the historic confessions of faith. The liberal emphasis is more on the love of God and of our neighbors than on the precise meaning of traditional Christian doctrines. And like the deism of the Revolutionary generation, it is much easier to identify those beliefs that are generally endorsed by conservatives but rejected by liberals than it is to describe the positive doctrinal assertions of modern theologians. In addition to denying the traditional view of special creation, the fall of Adam, the substitutionary atonement of Christ, the virgin birth, and most supernatural biblical narratives, liberals reject the classical view of life beyond the grave, including a resurrection of a physical body, a heaven for regenerated Christians, and a hell of everlasting punishment for all unregenerates. Also, in light of the modern emphasis on the immanence of God, some liberals do not perceive the need for angels who serve as messengers for God. Moreover, most contemporary theologians deny that there are devils who torment individuals and inhabit the bodies of mankind.[24]

Unlike deistic philosophy, however, liberal Protestantism should not be viewed primarily as a rejection of classical beliefs. Nevertheless, most contemporary theologians ignore many theological issues which are often included in the sermons and writings of orthodox apologists. Modern theologians are not concerned, for example, about the precise mode or form of the sacraments and do not search for texts in the Bible to prove theological positions which conservatives hold as basic Christian doctrines.

One area of thought in which there seems to be a significant semblance of harmony in the beliefs of liberals and orthodox Protestants is the subject of a triune God. Most liberals agree that there is one and only one God, who is a spirit. They agree with orthodox Protestants who say that God is three in one, Father, Son, and Holy Ghost, but rather than use the term "persons," many liberals explain the mystery of the trinity by saying that God is three modes of revelation, three reflections, or three ways of being.

Liberals also emphasize that God is omnipotent, omniscient, transcendent, and immanent. Some say that omnipotence includes the concept that God is the source of all being and power and that everything is under his general control. Yet they insist that man has his free will, but this free will does not imply that man can control the actions of God unless God permits it. Many teach that God's foreknowledge means that he can predict man's actions, but this prediction of man's choices is generally considered a knowledge of probability, not of certainty. In explaining God's transcendence, many liberals insist that God is far more than any of his creations, that he continues to act creatively, and that he is other than ourselves or the material universe. Some say that since God far transcends the world, deity should not be identified too closely with the physical world which he has created. Many indicate that the immanence of God means in part that God continues to sustain and comfort man, and that through His Spirit man can feel His love and goodness, thereby gaining a glimpse of God.[25]

There is also a focus among many liberals on the incarnation (that God was definitely present in Jesus of Nazareth) and on Jesus Christ as the authoritative guide for belief and practice. The word, many teach, is revealed to man by means of Jesus' teachings, his pattern of thought, and his exemplary conduct. This concept of the centrality of Jesus Christ in Christian thinking and action includes the proclamation that Jesus lived as man should live. His life was a perfect example of love and of complete dependence on his Father. Many contemporary theologians state that this "new content of conviction" should serve as a powerful stimulus for men to become concerned about the welfare of others.[26]

While orthodox Protestants generally teach that the Bible is the word of God and is the sole norm of faith, most liberal Protestants prefer to state that the Bible contains the word of God and should be considered as but one of the essential standards of faith. By saying that the Bible contains rather than is the word of God, contemporaries reflect their belief that the Bible contains not only historical narratives and religious truth but also includes within its covers nonhistorical narratives, myths, and unacceptable religious opinions. Concerning the inspiration of the Bible, modern theologians assert that biblical criticism seriously challenges endorsement of both verbal and plenary inspiration. A popular liberal and orthodox view is that portions of the Bible reflect that God's ideas were conveyed to man and man recorded them in his own language, while many fundamentalists say that the Bible is the very word of God (the ideas are of God and the language is God's language). But the orthodox and liberals tend to depart when liberals insist that the writings of Paul and many other key biblical authors contain inspired truths as well as incorrect religious opinions. A very small percentage of liberal Protestants proceed one step further by insisting that all parts of the Bible are solely the results of man's thoughts recorded in the language of the authors. These latter preachers insist that biblical authors were only naturally inspired as was Shakespeare and other influential literary artists.

Liberalism has refashioned other classical beliefs as well. A popular substitute for the traditional view of the fall and atonement is the concept that sin separates man from God, and that man, with the help of deity, may overcome this sin and be reconciled to God. Many liberals explain that man sins solely of his own volition and this sin creates a great gulf between man and his creator. Therefore, God became man and this man Jesus set the perfect example, providing humanity with a guide that enables individuals to overcome the barrier between themselves and God. Sometimes reconciliation is used interchangeably with the word atonement. Many contemporaries teach that Jesus reconciles man not necessarily by His actions on Calvary but by his total life of genuine love and service. Some add that the ultimate act in the life of Jesus was the example he set on the cross: while others were trying to kill him, Jesus forgave them. By this demonstration of love Jesus broke the hearts of his enemies; some turned to him, accepted his plea to live a life of love, and were, with the help of the Holy Spirit, reconciled to God.

Another popular belief endorsed not only by many liberals but also by many who classify themselves as basically orthodox is that heaven and hell are not places but states of mind. Many Protestants currently teach that hell is separation from God and heaven is communion with God.

While theologians are formulating modern expressions of traditional Christian beliefs, they are also addressing themselves to many issues that provide another reflection of the complexity of the new theology. Many theologians are currently asking, "How can one best determine religious truth?" Holding that the Bible is a product of human experience expressed in human language, liberals are trying to determine what they can classify as biblical truths. Furthermore, they are seeking a relationship between the Bible as a source of truth, and modern scientific discoveries and human reason, experience, and feeling as guides for determining valid religious understanding.

Since Jesus is regarded as the paramount figure in Christian thinking, liberals are also asking questions such as "Who is Jesus?" "What is the meaning of two natures in one person?" "How can one distinguish between Jesus as a concrete historical figure and the possible myths surrounding the life of the Nazarene which were formulated by the early Christian community?" or "Is it really important to reconstruct the genuine life and mission of Jesus?" Moreover, modern pastors are currently asking, "How does God move in history?" "And what do the messages of the Bible, including the life of Jesus, mean to people living in the modern world?"

Many contemporaries concentrate their thoughts on Christian ethics by asking, "What is the meaning of Christian love?" "What are sacrifice and justice to a Christian?" "How can Christ help man in the process of making decisions?" "How can one determine proper behavior?" and "Are inward feeling and man's concept of love a proper guide for determining moral behavior?"

In addition to seeking answers regarding authority and the Bible, the meaning and message of Jesus, God and the world, and Christian ethics, liberal theologians of twentieth-century America are asking themselves questions concerning the role of the church in society, the purpose of life, and the nature of things when life on this earth terminates. Liberal theologians make no claim to simplify the Christian faith but aim to provide mankind with new dimensions of thought and with new stimulation for Christian action. In short, contemporary theologians are trying to determine and then explain for modern man the essence of Christianity.[27]

Part Two
Transplanted Protestant Faiths

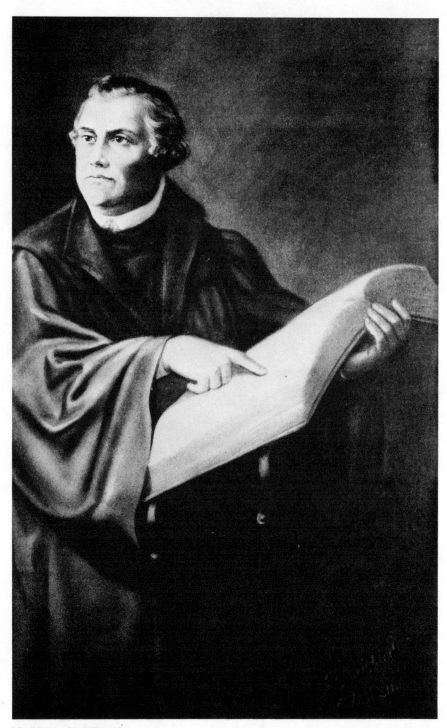

MARTIN LUTHER

6

Lutheranism

An individual who played a major role in significantly altering the course of human events was the initiator of the Reformation, Martin Luther. Born in the heart of Germany at Eisleben, Saxony, in 1483, this resolute leader lived during an era when conditions were favorable for a religious upheaval; and his ambition, determination, and faith led him to found what is generally known as the oldest and largest Protestant denomination in the world.

The fact that the Reformation struck so suddenly in so many different parts of Europe is evidence that a deep path leading to this religious revolt had been carved. Undoubtedly there were many complex underlying forces which set the stage for this reorientation of Christian thinking and practice. The spirit of inquiry and the humanistic spirit of the Renaissance emphasized the study of man and his accomplishments and prompted many to seek a new relationship with God. The invention of printing with movable type caused a multiplication of the number of books and a more rapid circulation of ideas; and the translations of the Bible into the vernacular enabled increased numbers to become acquainted with the messages contained therein. Nationalism increased and was coupled with a popularization of mercantilism. Mercantilists concluded that wealth in the form of specie was necessary in order to develop a powerful nation, and that wealth could be secured by exporting more goods and importing less. Since the dominant church sometimes impeded this growth of wealth by channelling money from various states to Rome, economy-minded politicians recognized the advantages of nationalizing the church, thereby diverting the pope's wealth to the treasuries of the state. Moreover, in the fifteenth century many Europeans recognized the apparent abuses in the universal church, became increasingly critical of the clergy, and determined that the church had incorporated into its theology various doctrinal innovations that did not harmonize with biblical teachings.

Two additional underlying forces that helped precipitate the Reformation were the peasants' desperate hope for a better world, and an apparent lack of religious zeal among many people. Some loved their country more than they could the religion prescribed in their community. The stage was set for a shattering confrontation between resolute reformers and supporters of the established church.

Martin Luther's devout interest in religion was manifest while he was in his early twenties. Shortly after gaining distinction as a student at the University of Erfurt and receiving a master's degree in 1505, he abandoned his intended interest in the profession of law, forsook his father's desires, and entered a monastery of the Augustinian order at Erfurt.

During his initial years in the monastery, Luther seemed so preoccupied with his own sins that he failed to become alarmed with the abuses which were visible in the church. His celebrated journey to Rome occurred in 1510-1511, and, although this excursion undoubtedly made him aware of the worldliness of many clergymen, this recognition was not the major turning point in his religious career.

Shortly after his appointment as professor of theology at Wittenberg, Luther concluded that salvation comes not through the sacraments, not through the works of man, and not through the church, but is a gift of God which comes to man through hearing and studying the word of God. He decided that this grace manifest through faith justifies man before God. Since such a view could not be suppressed in the mind of an impatient, outspoken critic such as Martin Luther, an irrepressible conflict was approaching between a courageous leader and a powerful church.

Luther was motivated to action after John Tetzel commenced issuing indulgences in more liberal terms than generally offered the people. On the eve of All Saints' Day, 31 October 1517, Luther made public his objections to Tetzel's actions by posting the *Ninety-five Theses* on the massive doors of the All Saints' Church, undoubtedly without realizing the repercussions it would have on the history of mankind. There is no divine authority, Luther announced in these propositions, for preaching that the soul flies out of purgatory immediately after the coins clink into the money chest. His tone remained critical when he insisted that God only can remit sins; he also proclaimed that Christians who conscientiously repent do not need letters of indulgence. Individuals should be taught that people who give to the poor or lend to the needy are engaged in more righteous deeds than are those who purchase indulgences. And he concluded that if the pope had authority to eliminate punishment for those who contributed to worthy projects, why didn't he, for the sake of love and justice, release everyone from purgatory?[1]

After the theses had been printed and circulated throughout Germany, the theological storm erupted, and Luther was instructed to state precisely his position regarding these propositions. When the German monk was interviewed in 1518 by Cardinal Cajetan, the papal legate reminded Luther of a papal decree which had defined the church's position concerning the treasury of merits. This pronouncement had specified that there was a treasury of the surplus merits of Christ, of the Blessed Virgin, and of the saints which was at the disposal of popes for the releasing of the faithful from temporal punishment arising from sins. Believing that the orthodox position concerning this treasury was not in harmony with biblical injunctions, Luther retorted that the pope was not an authority superior to scripture. One year later John Eck, another skilled theologian, arrogantly trapped Luther into confessing that he believed councils could and did err. On that occasion, Luther publicly insisted that, for the sake of scripture, Christians should reject as a source of religious truth the decisions of popes and councils.[2]

During the year following his confrontation with Eck, Luther set the theological tone of this religious revolt in his three famous Reformation treatises. It was during that memorable period that Luther popularized his belief concerning priesthood of believers, justification by the grace of God, two sacraments, and the Bible as the sole standard of faith. Since Luther refused to recant, and continued to preach doctrines which conflicted with the recognized beliefs of the universal church, Pope Leo I excommunicated the Saxon rebel. When Luther burned this bull of excommunication at Wittenberg on 10 December 1520, he severed all connections with the pope and the Roman Catholic Church.

Luther was granted a final opportunity to recant before the Diet meeting at Worms in 1521. Instead of retreating, however, Luther reiterated his belief that popes and councils had contradicted each other and he also stated that he could not accept their authority in matters of doctrine. "My conscience," he declared, "is captive to the Word of God. I cannot and I will not recant. . . . To go against conscience is neither right nor safe. . . . Here I stand," he concluded. "I cannot do otherwise."[3] After being condemned by the emperor and branded a heretic, Luther secured protection from Frederick, Elector of Saxony, and, while living for ten months in a secluded castle, worked diligently on a translation of the New Testament from Greek into German.

After translating the New Testament, the next project Luther undertook was to organize a new religious community. This work began in March 1522 at Wittenberg. By reforming the Mass and preparing a new religious service, Luther continued to direct the course of the Reformation. Since he emphasized a degree of spiritual freedom in the emerging Holy Evangelical Catholic Church of Saxony, Luther did not require all his followers to adopt his new liturgy. Nevertheless, he precipitated various schisms by insisting that Christ was actually present during the Lord's Supper. He also prepared a *Shorter Catechism,* which was a brief analysis of the principal doctrines he espoused, and a *Larger Catechism* intended primarily for ministers. Luther's basic teachings were incorporated into the Augsburg Confession. This early exposition of faith, drafted by Philip Melanchthon from articles prepared by Luther, was acknowledged by many political leaders in Germany. Before his death in 1546, Luther also completed a translation of the Bible; spread his religious convictions through constant preaching; married Katharine Von Bera, a former nun; became the father of six children; reared several orphaned children; introduced congregational singing; and wrote a number of hymns that have remained popular, including "A Mighty Fortress Is Our God," sometimes referred to as "the battle hymn of the Reformation."

From Germany, Lutheranism spread into many other parts of western Europe. Eventually many members of this faith, especially German and Scandinavian emigrants, settled along the eastern coast of the modern United States. As early as 1619, Lutherans from Denmark celebrated Christmas on Hudson Bay, but these colonists failed to remain in this hostile environment and a few survivors eventually returned to Copenhagen. A few years later, other Lutherans joined the Dutch settlers who established their homes at Fort Orange, near Albany, and on Manhattan Island. Many Lutherans who colonized New Netherlands, however, were compelled to attend services of the Dutch Reformed Church and were prevented from worshipping regularly until after the English occupation in 1664. Meanwhile, the first Lutherans to worship on a permanent basis in America were emigrants from Sweden who founded a settlement in 1638 near the Delaware River at the present site of Wilmington. As new colonies were planted and toleration for Trinitarian Protestants became a reality throughout the English mainland colonies, Lutheranism gained a foothold in other sections of America. By 1776 there were more than 220 Lutheran congregations in this land, a high percentage located in the Middle Colonies and western Virginia.

One of the major problems encountered by the early American Lutherans was the dire shortage of meetinghouses and ministers. Few ministers accompanied the early immigrants and most of the settlers scattered into the wilderness. Living on isolated farmsteads, most Lutherans failed to unite for religious worship, and a high percentage of former European Lutherans remained without meetinghouses throughout the eighteenth century. This problem created a serious challenge to colonial religious leaders, such as Henry M. Muhlenberg, sometimes known (because of his strenuous efforts to unite members of his faith) as the father of American Lutheranism.

Throughout the nineteenth century, Lutheran ministers labored diligently to provide members of their faith with spiritual leadership and places for worship. The problem was compounded by the explosive expansion of the American population across the continent and the continual arrival of poverty-stricken immigrants along the eastern seaboard. As the nineteenth century drew to a close, more of the uprooted arriving in the United States were of Lutheran heritage than any other Protestant faith. Although this tidal wave of emigration from Lutheran lands to the United States was not as significant as the movement of people from Catholic countries, the Lutheran Church benefited more, numerically speaking, from the late nineteenth- and early twentieth-century migrations than did members of any other Protestant faith. After the major problems of shortages of ministers and meetinghouses had been largely solved, Lutheranism emerged in the twentieth century as one of the major Protestant denominations in America.

While Lutherans were striving to provide organized religion for individuals of Lutheran heritage, leaders of the denomination concentrated on promoting unity among their ranks. Various factors, however, contributed toward dividing the Lutherans in America into a number of bodies. Lutherans from various European nations settled in different parts of the new nation, formed different organizations, and were kept apart by contrasting languages and cultures. Problems of transportation and communication also made it difficult for them to work together under one general body.

Another major force which kept Lutherans from uniting was the conflict of their beliefs. Two major kinds of Lutheranism were transplanted to this nation, pietistic Lutheranism and confessional Lutheranism. Pietistic Lutheranism was a form of belief and practice which emphasized experience in the Christian life and championed the importance of Christian action. After being transplanted to colonial America, this emphasis was popularized in the early nineteenth century by Samuel Simon Schmucker (1799-1873). Schmucker rejected not only the traditional view of the real presence of the body and blood of Christ as held by Martin Luther, but also the traditional Lutheran position concerning private confession and the necessity (for all who are granted the opportunity) of baptism for salvation.[4]

Prior to the Civil War, the movement led by Schmucker and other pietistic Lutherans became one of the most formidable forces in the Lutheran Church in America. Many endorsed only those which they considered to be the essential features of the Augsburg Confession. Denying the real presence of Christ during the Lord's Supper, many Lutherans advocated that Christ was spiritually received during this sacrament. Rejecting an emphasis on the necessity of baptism for salvation, many insisted that faith alone was essential. Moreover, many denied that man inherited the original sin. They also rejected the traditional belief that man was naturally depraved because of the fall. Many substituted a public confession for a private confession, regarded exorcism as a superstitious rite, and eliminated much of the ritual in the ceremony accompanying the Lord's Supper.

The other major form of Lutheranism that was transplanted to America was confessional Lutheranism, a revival of what many referred to as the traditional form of faith. In the nineteenth century, confessional Lutheranism emerged as a major reaction to the rationalism which was dominating the Lutheran Church in Europe. Proponents of this movement advocated returning to the theology of the confessional period in Lutheran history.[5]

As waves of immigrants arrived in the United States during the latter half of the nineteenth century, confessional Lutheranism became increasingly popular among the American members of this faith. Endowed with a deep appreciation of their religious heritage, these new immigrants vigorously disapproved the pattern of Lutheran church life which had become popular in the early republic. As the twentieth century was ushered in, the more conservative form of Lutheranism became the dominant influence among the members. Although during the past several decades the number of Lutherans in America espousing a reinterpretation of classical Protestantism has increased, most Lutherans in contemporary America are known for their orthodoxy, professing beliefs that represent in nearly all instances concepts popularized by Martin Luther.

Members of this communion have, however, made successful efforts to unite. Linguistic and cultural differences gradually dissipated. Transportation and communication barriers disappeared, and a common religious heritage and recognition of similarities of belief helped many members of this faith to crystallize their organizations. Throughout the past seven decades, there have been many significant realignments and mergers. Whereas there were at one time about 150 Lutheran bodies in the United States, today approximately 95 percent of all Lutherans belong to one of three major bodies: (1) The American Lutheran Church (a moderate body constituted in 1960 by the consolidation of the American Lutheran Church, members who primarily were of German background; the Evangelical Lutheran Church of Norwegian heritage; and the United Evangelical Lutheran Church consisting of many Danish immigrants), (2) the Lutheran Church in America (the most liberal body, which was formed about 1962 by the merging of the United Lutheran Church in America, the Augustana Evangelical Lutheran Church, the American Evangelical Lutheran Church and the Finnish Evangelical Lutheran Church), and (3) the most orthodox contemporary major group of Lutherans, the Lutheran Church—Missouri Synod (organized in 1847).

Although most American Lutherans hold that the congregation is the supreme authority in church matters, most congregations have united under synods for mutual assistance and to promote programs that could not be supported effectively by small, independent congregations. In some instances, however, these synods have exercised considerable authority in directing the affairs of local churches.

While about one-third of all Protestants in the world are classified as Lutherans, members of this faith currently constitute the third largest Protestant community in the United States next to Baptists and Methodists. Since World War II Lutherans have also engaged in effective evangelistic activities in this country, and have attracted many who are not of German or Scandinavian descent, thereby changing, in part, the complexion of many congregations.

All of the major bodies are also currently known for their emphasis on social welfare programs, world relief agencies, religious film production, aid to immigrants, counseling services to those in need, and various educational programs. Lutherans are among the Protestant leaders in this country who support colleges, theological schools, and parochial elementary schools. Throughout America, children, widows, senior citizens, the handicapped, and others desiring assistance benefit from programs sponsored by people whose religious heritage can be traced back to the successful instigator of the Reformation, Martin Luther.

Distinguishing Beliefs

The following beliefs reflect the historic tradition of the Lutheran Church and are currently held by most Lutherans but generally not by other Protestants.

Lutherans teach that baptism is necessary for salvation for all who are granted the opportunity. They claim, however, that the disposition of those who have not been baptized is unknown. Some emphasize that since only unbelief condemns, unbaptized infants will not be damned nor will they go to limbo. Some also reason that the necessity of baptism is not absolute. Ordinarily, many teach, Christ bestows his grace through baptism.

Another distinctive Lutheran belief is that in the sacrament of Holy Communion, the resurrected Christ imparts himself (his body and blood) to communicants. Although Lutherans reject transubstantiation (the changing of the elements), they believe that communicants receive bread and wine as the body and blood of Christ. They further hold that only worthy believers (interpreted by many as those having faith, who recognize they are sinners, and who believe they receive the body and blood of Christ) benefit from this sacrament. Nonregular communion is viewed as a sign of spiritual laxity by most members of this church.

According to Lutheran practice, preceding each celebration of the Lord's Supper is a public or private confession and the absolution one receives through this confession is considered part of the sacrament of Holy Communion. Lutheran ministers absolve sins not because they claim special powers but because of their belief in Christ's action. God has commanded, they teach, that ministers may announce to the confessors that their sins are forgiven them through Christ's forgiveness. All sins, they further hold, should be confessed, for small sins, they say, become serious when they are regarded as small. Some Lutheran ministers have departed from absolution as traditionally practiced and say that confession should take the form of pastoral counseling.

Another characteristic Lutheran practice is that ordinarily when a youth reaches the age of fourteen he participates in a special service called confirmation. This rite, which is different from most confirmation services that take place in Protestant churches, is normally preceded by two to four years of instruction.

Miscellaneous Beliefs

In addition to the beliefs listed above which are doctrines not accepted by most other Protestants, most Lutherans endorse the classical Protestant belief concerning the Bible as the sole norm of faith, the Godhead, angels, the fall, the atonement, life beyond the grave, and priesthood of believers. Lutherans also continue to emphasize the concept of justification by grace through faith.

Moreover, Lutherans believe that marriage, confirmation, and ordination of the clergy are rites of the church but are not sacraments; for God, they say, has not promised divine grace through these rites.

Transplanted Calvinistic Faiths: Presbyterian, Congregational, and Reformed Churches

7

While chapter one of the Reformation is sometimes launched by a consideration of the accomplishments of Martin Luther, chapter two frequently begins with a biographical sketch of another highly influential leader, John Calvin. Four of the eight largest Protestant churches in colonial America (excluding the Calvinist Baptists) were of Calvinistic origin, and approximately half of all active church members living in the English mainland settlements would fall under this same classification. Although the percentage of Calvinists has declined since the birth of this nation, throughout the history of this country many Americans have belonged to religious communities whose historical roots can be traced back to John Calvin, including the Presbyterian Church, the Congregational societies (most having united with other denominations, forming the United Church of Christ), the Dutch Reformed Church (which evolved in the United States into the Reformed Church in America and the Christian Reformed Church), the German Reformed Church (which became part of the Evangelical and Reformed Church and then merged with the Congregational Christian churches in forming the United Church of Christ), the French Reformed Church (Huguenots who tended to be assimilated into other faiths) and the Free Magyar Reformed Church in America (whose roots stem back to Calvin by way of Hungary). Although many members of these denominations have revised a few of the basic teachings unfolded by John Calvin, most have remained orthodox and generally endorse the Heidelberg Catechism, the Belgic Confession, and the Canons of the Synod of Dort as proper expressions of the biblical faith.

Although John Calvin was of French heritage and was twenty-six years younger than Luther, in a number of respects his early life resembled that of the celebrated German reformer. Born on 10 July 1509 in Noyon, a city located about fifty-eight miles northeast of Paris, Calvin gained distinction as

JOHN CALVIN

a student, but his early formal education was even more comprehensive than that received by Luther. After concentrating on theology and graduating in law, Calvin studied humanities, including exceptional training in Greek and Hebrew. Like Luther, a major turning point in Calvin's life occurred shortly after he concluded that men are saved solely by the grace of God. Calvin's sudden conversion probably occurred sometime during the years 1532 to 1534, but no French political leader rescued this critic, as Duke Frederick aided Luther. After a brief imprisonment in Noyon, the young reformer fled into Switzerland where the reaction against the traditional faith had fragmented into various forms of Protestantism.

Like Luther, Calvin popularized his beliefs by publishing influential works which described and then defended his religious convictions. Calvin's most celebrated apology was the *Institutes of the Christian Religion* which originally appeared in Basel in March 1536, when Calvin was in his mid-twenties. This book, one of the most influential works published not only during the era of the Reformation but during the history of mankind, enabled the brilliant Frenchman to become one of the world's foremost religious leaders. Although revised editions of the *Institutes* continued to be printed until 1559, the original work contained the basic beliefs of this theologian and was acknowledged by many as the most comprehensive and systematic popular presentation of Reformation theology that had been included under one cover.

Many beliefs popularized by John Calvin harmonized with Martin Luther's teachings. Calvin's indebtedness to the German reformer was apparent when he employed in his first edition of the *Institutes* references from Luther's *Catechism* and *Babylonian Captivity of the Church.* In addition to agreeing with Luther's basic position concerning God's sovereignty, the imputation of the original sin to all mankind, man's depravity, limited atonement, and the idea that good works are the fruit of faith rather than a means of salvation, Calvin also endorsed the major theological concepts in the three Reformation treatises of 1520: priesthood of believers, two sacraments, justification by faith alone, and the Bible as the sole source for religious truths.

Although the two famous reformers shared many religious convictions, Calvin did not attempt to employ the writings of Luther as an authoritative source. He disagreed with Luther on a few key issues. For example, Luther decided that if a practice was not mentioned and was not specifically forbidden in the Bible, it might be adopted by Christians. Meanwhile, Calvin believed that a pattern of religious behavior should not be endorsed by Christians unless it was sanctioned by the Bible. Consequently, more ritual appeared in the worship of many Lutherans than in most Calvinistic congregations.

Two specific differences in the basic theologies of Luther and Calvin centered on their views concerning the sacraments of baptism and the Lord's

Supper. While Luther insisted that baptism was necessary for salvation, Calvin argued that if faith alone was essential then baptism could not be regarded as necessary. That does not mean that Calvin did not encourage his followers to be baptized. Like Luther, Calvin suggested that infants should be baptized, in part as a sign and seal of the covenant of grace.

Calvinists held that circumcision had been instituted as a sign of the covenant that God would bless the faithful children of Abraham. Circumcision, they continued, was replaced by baptism, so parents should have their infants baptized as a sign that God would bless the children of the elect as he had agreed to bless the descendants of Abraham. Children as well as their believing parents are included in this covenant of grace and hence are entitled to that sacrament.

The second major difference in the theologies of Calvin and Luther pertained to the nature of the Lord's Supper. While Calvin shared the Lutheran view that Christ was not sacrificed during the Mass and that the priest did not change the bread and wine into the body and blood of Christ, he rejected the German's view that the body and blood of Christ were present, were truly distributed, and were partaken of by the communicants. Calvin also rejected the position advocated by Huldreich Zwingli, the Swiss reformer, who taught that the Lord's Supper was taken purely in remembrance of the body and blood of Christ. Taking a position that stood between the view of Luther's real presence and Zwingli's memorial, Calvin suggested that during the Lord's Supper Christ's body remained in heaven but his spirit engulfed the bread and wine so that faithful communicants received Christ spiritually.[1]

Included among the teachings of John Calvin was a description of church government which, in the view of the French reformer, was patterned after New Testament Christianity. He suggested that Christian leaders who directed the affairs of local churches should not only receive an internal call from God but should receive the approbation of the people. The name Presbyterian evolved from these elected elders who were called *presbyteros* in Greek. Presbyterian churches today are still governed by a representative system which includes four ascending judicial bodies who administer the affairs of the church, including sessions (composed of a minister and ruling elders of one congregation), presbyteries (consisting of representatives, ministers, and lay elders from the local churches, who have power of supervising ministers and many activities of the congregations, including examining, ordaining, and installing ministers), synods (another representative body which supervises the presbyteries), and the general assembly (the highest judicial and legislative body which is also composed of clerical and lay delegates).

After an unostentatious beginning as lecturer on the Bible and a temporary banishment, Calvin was invited to return to Geneva and eventually gained full control of the Reformation in that community. With the support of political leaders, he launched a successful revolution in religion, education, and government. By providing the church with a trained ministry, encouraging religious education among the people through regular Bible study in their homes, and by establishing a city of refuge for many oppressed in Europe, Calvin transformed this small Swiss village into what became known as the "City of God." According to one of Calvin's distinguished disciples, John Knox, Geneva became the most perfect school of life on earth since the days of the apostles.

After Calvin's death, his views were summarized into what became known as the five points of Calvinism. Although some scholars insist that the famous "five points" are not an adequate representation of Calvin's thought, they did become a capsule summary of the Calvinism that was transplanted to colonial America. These concepts amplify Calvin's view of God's complete sovereignty, including the doctrines of total depravity, unconditional election or predestination, limited atonement, irresistibility of grace, and perseverance of the saints.

A second-generation Calvinist who disagreed with some of the principal teachings of the Geneva reformer was the controversial Dutch theologian James Arminius (1560-1609). According to Arminian theology, man was endowed with a free will which enabled him to accept or reject the gift of salvation. However, salvation depended not upon man's will to be saved, for we are not free to perform righteous acts unless assisted by the grace of God.[2] In explaining this doctrine, many followers of Arminius proclaimed that God offers salvation to all men, but only those who accept this gift will be saved. Therefore man cooperates with God in the salvation experience.

The disciples of Arminius immortalized his name by developing their own five points in contrast to the five points of Calvinism. The orthodox Calvinistic concept that man was totally depraved was replaced with the view that (1) even though man inherited the original sin and was depraved, this depravity was not total, for man was endowed with free will which included the capacity to accept or reject the gift of salvation. The popular Calvinistic view of predestination was replaced by the doctrine that (2) the eternal decree of salvation refers to those who shall believe and persevere in the faith, implying that because of God's foreknowledge he has predicted but not decreed the final fate of man. The Calvinist concept of limited atonement for only the elect was substituted with the belief that (3) Christ's atonement was sufficient for all men, but only the faithful benefit from the act. And finally, irresistibility of grace and perseverance of the saints were denied in favor of the view that (4) men can reject the call by God and (5) man can fall or fail to persevere to the end.

From Geneva the religious convictions of John Calvin spread throughout western Europe. Eventually, the reformed faith became the national religion of the Netherlands and, under the leadership of John Knox, penetrated Scotland. In 1560 the Scottish Parliament abolished Catholicism and created a national church with a presbyterian system of government and confession of faith patterned after the teachings of John Calvin.

Calvinism not only became the established religion in the Netherlands and Scotland but also spread into England, Germany, Hungary, France, and other European nations. During the Puritan revolution in England, a Calvinist declaration of faith was drafted by a group of religious leaders gathered in Westminster Abbey. This creed, known as the Westminster Confession of Faith (1647), was adopted as a proper expression of Christian belief by a vast majority of the Presbyterians; prior to the mid-nineteenth century, the theology expressed in this exposition of faith was also accepted by most Congregationalists. Moreover, with a few exceptions (such as the doctrine of baptism), this description of Christian belief served as a basis for many Calvinist Baptist creeds, such as the Philadelphia Confession of Faith in 1742.

One of the major differences in the early beliefs of the English and Scottish Calvinists pertained to the proper form of church government. Many English Calvinists rejected the presbyterian system of government in favor of the belief that every congregation should be autonomous. According to Congregational polity, every local religious society should be given the responsibility of selecting its ministers, preparing a confession of faith, and directing its affairs without outside controls.

Early in the seventeenth century, Congregationalism was transplanted to America by the Separatists and Puritans. One of the most celebrated groups in early American history was the Pilgrims. These Separatists had withdrawn from the Church of England, worshipped contrary to the laws of England, and fled to the Netherlands, the only country where they knew they would be tolerated. Although toleration was extended to these English Calvinists, many were not satisfied with their new homeland. As they experienced assimilation into the Dutch culture, they complained of economic hardships. For these and other reasons, the Pilgrims decided to migrate to America. After a disquieting voyage on the historic *Mayflower,* they settled in Plymouth, Massachusetts, in December 1620. There these Pilgrim Separatists established America's first Congregational Church.

Shortly after the Pilgrims arrived in America, Puritans who had been struggling in England to purify the established church from within commenced colonizing Salem, Boston, and many other communities north of Plymouth. After arriving in the new world, Puritan leaders adopted the reforms which they had been clamoring for in England, and established a church which was similar to that in Plymouth. While their local churches were called churches of Christ, eventually they, including the church in Plymouth, became known as the Congregational Church.

By employing the state as an active agent to promote their ideals, the Puritans of Massachusetts Bay acted in harmony with the popular beliefs of that age and welded a tight chain of religious uniformity around their society.

As in Plymouth, only one religion was allowed to emerge in this colony. Then, by means of an expansion from Massachusetts into Connecticut, the "Bible Commonwealth" was extended to include the settlements at and near New Haven and along the Connecticut River. Throughout New England, except for Rhode Island, Congregationalism was the dominant religion during the colonial era. Though the number of churches outside of New England was few, Congregationalism was still the largest religious body in the English mainland colonies. In the mid-eighteenth century approximately one-third of all active church members living along the eastern seacoast were affiliated with this faith.[3]

While English Calvinists were establishing churches in New England, Dutch Calvinists penetrated the Hudson River Valley and settled Manhattan and portions of Long Island. Prior to the English occupation of New Netherlands in 1664, the reformed faith was the only legal religion in what is today New York. For years after the English seized this province, the Dutch Reformed church remained a powerful influence in that section of the new world.

Presbyterianism followed Congregationalism and the Dutch Reformed faith to America. In the early eighteenth century, the great bulk of emigration to the English mainland colonies was from Germany, Scotland, and northern Ireland. Many of these immigrants were Calvinists who poured into the middle colonies, especially western Pennsylvania. Others migrated into western Maryland and Virginia and many located their homes in the Carolinas.

Colonial Presbyterians encountered many of the same problems which confronted the Lutherans and most early American Christians. After arriving in the new world, many Presbyterians scattered into the frontier and were unsuccessful in forming congregations. Lacking trained ministers and houses of worship, many Presbyterian settlers lost contact with organized religion. Historians have estimated that as many as 200,000 to 250,000 Scots and Ulster-Scots migrated to the English mainland colonies; although a high percentage of these emigrants were Presbyterians, in 1776 less than 15,000 had been gathered into religious communities.[4]

One of the most famous colonial Presbyterian leaders was Reverend Francis Makemie, known as the father of American Presbyterianism. In addition to preaching from New York to Georgia, Makemie helped establish the first presbytery in America in 1705. When this representative body gathered in Philadelphia, the American Presbyterian Church was organized. Twelve years later this body was divided into three presbyteries and a synod was formed, with its first meeting also being held in Philadelphia.

As Americans expanded west, Presbyterians and Congregationalists agreed not to compete under specified conditions. By the Plan of Union of 1801, many congregations in western America voted for a minister, selecting a spiritual leader from one of these two communions. During the first three decades of the nineteenth century, however, most people hired Presbyterian preachers, and subsequently many pioneers changed religious affiliations. Therefore, the Plan of Union curtailed the expansion of Congregationalism. As a consequence of continued immigration from Scotland and northern Ireland and more effective missionary programs than those sponsored by other Calvinist faiths, Presbyterianism grew much more rapidly in nineteenth-century America than did any other religious society whose historical roots stemmed back to the Geneva reformer.

Although prior to the late nineteenth century most Americans of Calvinistic heritage endorsed the five points of Calvinism, throughout the history of this family of churches some members have questioned the harsh implications of the doctrine of predestination. While orthodox Calvinists were emphasizing that God's sovereignty meant that God's will and not man's will would be done, a few echoed Arminian expressions that man played a vital role in the salvation experience. This controversy over the nature of man's agency was one of the major issues of debate in colonial America and the early republic. Before the Civil War most Calvinists were aligned against the so-called Arminian societies (such as the Freewill Baptists, Episcopalians, Quakers, Methodists, Disciples, etc.); but after Appomattox, the controversy became a major source of conflict among Congregationalists, Presbyterians, and members of other reformed churches.

By the early twentieth century most Americans of Calvinistic heritage had rejected the traditional view of predestination in favor of the concept of man's agency. Although there is a vocal conservative minority in the United Church of Christ, most members of this denomination are currently known for their rejection of predestination and for their general acceptance of a contemporary theology. Meanwhile, Presbyterians are divided on many theological issues. Members of the United Presbyterian Church in the USA, currently the largest American body of Presbyterians, generally believe that man cooperates with God in the salvation experience. Slightly more than half might be classified as orthodox on most theological issues and approximately half endorse beliefs which reflect a reinterpretation of the classical Protestant theology. Nearly all members of this body have also endorsed the "Confession of 1967," an exposition of faith which conveys, in the language of contemporary Americans, many of the ideas included in the Westminster Confession.

Although major modifications have occurred in the patterns of belief of most former Congregationalists and many Presbyterians, other Christians of Calvinistic heritage have made an attempt to preserve the doctrines described in their historic creeds. Many Presbyterians living in the South and most members of the Christian Reformed Church are currently known for their strict adherence to the basic concepts popularized by John Calvin, the influential founder of the reformed faiths. [5]

Distinguishing Beliefs

Prior to the twentieth century, one of the most distinguishing beliefs of the Presbyterians and most members of other reformed churches was acceptance of what were called the five points of Calvinism. These five doctrines which reflect the historic tradition of this movement are as follows:

First, *total depravity* is the belief that since all men inherit the original sin, man can perform no completely righteous acts in the eyes of God until his regeneration or conversion. Man is not considered totally bad but there is nothing in man that has not been infected by the power of sin. According to this dogma, man can perform no good deeds in the eyes of God until after his election or regeneration.

Second, *unconditional election* or *predestination* is the doctrine that by the decree of God some men and angels are predestined to everlasting life and others foreordained to everlasting death. The number is so certain that it cannot be increased nor diminished. The elected are redeemed by Christ and others are ordained to dishonor and wrath for their sin. Few American Presbyterians, however, have believed in double predestination as taught by Calvin, that God elected some men to heaven and others to hell. Most have held, as Luther taught, that God elects men to heaven but does not condemn men to hell. Today, most Presbyterians believe that man has the free will to accept or reject the gift of salvation when it is offered by God.

Third, *limited atonement* is the belief that while Christ died for the sins of all the world, only the elect or believers in Christ benefit (in terms of salvation) from his sacrifice.

Fourth, *irresistibility of grace* is another belief representing the historic tradition of the Presbyterian Church. According to this tenet, man cannot resist the gift of salvation offered by God. Some Presbyterians currently teach that man cannot resist responding positively if he truly perceives the grace of God in Christ. Man, some say, has the power to reject the gift but he cannot resist it.

Fifth, *perseverance of the saints* is the doctrine that if a man is truly converted he will not fall. Many Presbyterians of contemporary America teach that a man might waver and sin but he will not fall completely. It is sometimes asserted that if he appears to have fallen, he must not have been saved originally.

Two other beliefs of Presbyterians that represent their distinct historical tradition relate to the practices of observance of the Lord's Supper and confirmation. While Presbyterians and other members of Reformed churches reject the Roman Catholic view of transubstantiation and the Lutheran concept of the presence of the total risen Christ, they also deny another popular belief that the Lord's Supper is merely a memorial. Members of this faith teach that communicants experience Christ spiritually during this sacrament. While Christ's body is in heaven, they generally affirm, his spirit is spiritually present with the bread and wine. Communicants, many explain, receive of Christ's very being for their spiritual nourishment and growth in grace.

Presbyterians also believe that confirmation is a service in which a person acknowledges what was done at his baptism. In some Presbyterian churches pastors confirm members by the laying on of hands. In other churches members stand before the congregation, between the minister and ruling elders, and the minister reads words of admission and service.

Miscellaneous Beliefs

Nearly all Presbyterians and members of other reformed churches believe in the Trinity and incarnation. Orthodox Presbyterians also endorse the classical Protestant belief concerning the Bible as the sole norm of faith, angels, the fall, the atonement, life beyond the grave, and a priesthood of believers. Liberal Presbyterians (and most Congregationalists), meanwhile, reject many of the historical beliefs and endorse popular modern reinterpretations of the traditional religion.

8

The Episcopal Church
in the United States

Prior to the mid-1780s, the religious community called the Episcopal Church in the United States or the Protestant Episcopal Church was known as the Church of England. Following the war for independence, however, Anglican leaders in the new nation reorganized this religious body, and the Protestant Episcopal Church became the self-governing American branch of the Anglican communion. The preface to the Episcopalian Book of Common Prayer clearly identifies the relationship of the two religious communities: "This Church is far from intending to depart from the Church of England in any essential point of doctrine, discipline, or worship; or further than local circumstances require."

In some respects there are many beginnings in the history of this denomination, including the emergence of Christianity in England, the English Reformation, the transplanting of Anglicanism to colonial America, and the reorganization following the American Revolution. One of the major problems encountered by historians in regard to this church is that of determining the precise role of King Henry VIII in the rise of the Church of England. Some authors describe this reformation without mentioning the actions of this controversial ruler. Many reputable writers concentrate on the English rather than the Roman nature of the Medieval Church in that land and emphasize the role of the English clergy in refashioning this church during the sixteenth century. The traditional approach, however, of describing the underlying forces of the English Reformation and then explaining the annulment issue has remained popular; and in light of the almost absolute power exercised by the Tudor monarchs, it seems appropriate to mention Henry VIII's participation in England's religious revolt.

As on the Continent, there were many forces underlying the English

Reformation, and in many respects the factors precipitating the religious upheaval in England resembled the political, economic, and social factors which led to the religious reorientation in continental Europe. Nationalism and a belief in mercantilism were especially strong in England, and an anti-clerical attitude was visible among many inhabitants of that land. But while the earliest leaders of the Reformation on the continent were Catholic clergy or students of theology, the ecclesiastical reform in England was launched by a political leader.

What is frequently referred to as the occasion rather than the cause of the English Reformation was Henry VIII's desire to secure an annulment of his marriage to Catherine and to marry his mistress Anne Boleyn. Torn by love and fearing a possible future revolt in England if he failed to provide his people with a male heir, Henry sought a special dispensation from Pope Clement, permitting him to sever his marital relations with his wife. After seeking an annulment for six years, Henry began living with Anne Boleyn. In January, 1533, Anne was with child; and toward the end of that month Henry and Anne were secretly married. The ensuing May, Thomas Cranmer, Archbishop of Canterbury, declared Henry's marriage to Catherine null and void, and acknowledged the marriage with his former mistress.

Meanwhile, Henry had prepared the ground for nationalizing the universal church. In 1532 the clergy were forced to accept Henry as their supreme legislator, and bills were introduced in Parliament providing for the ordination of clergy to the office of bishop solely by English authorities. One year later, Henry responded to his excommunication from the Roman Catholic Church by instructing the English clergy to teach that papal claims of power were human usurpations offensive to God. According to these decrees, the pope had no more authority in England than any other foreign bishop.

During the Parliamentary sessions of 1534 the momentous break with Rome was secured. This body, which was controlled by the monarch, recognized the English sovereign as head of the church in England and made provisions to transfer into the treasury of the state ecclesiastical revenue which previously crossed the English Channel. The government also officially repudiated all papal claims of rights and powers.

The reign of Henry VIII saw not only change in the hierarchy of the church but other significant innovations as well. Under the direction of Henry's leading advisor, Thomas Cromwell, the monasteries and all religious orders were suppressed. After the confiscated property reverted to the state, portions were sold to English nobles. Consequently, many aristocrats were tied economically to the reform movement. Meanwhile, the Old and New Testament were published in the vernacular and the clergy were instructed to encourage parishioners to read the English Bible.

The religious life of most people in England was not immediately altered by the inauguration of this reformation. Most Christians, recognizing few changes in the established faith, continued to worship in the traditional pattern. Parliament, in issuing official pronouncements concerning the doctrines and ritual of the English church, defended many traditional beliefs, such as transubstantiation, veneration of images and saints, prayers for the dead, and the seven sacraments. Although some statements were ambiguous, the pro-Catholic element was the dominant characteristic of the national church. The Church of England appeared similar to the Roman Catholic faith, but was headed by a popular king rather than a pope. Moreover, most priests accepted the reorganization without major opposition; and the clergy in Parliament, acting in harmony with the desires of the king, continued to direct the reform movement in England.

The Reformation which had erupted during the reign of Henry VIII was turned in a new direction after his death. In compliance with Henry's will, the young son of Jane Seymour (Henry's third wife, who died in childbirth) ascended to the throne. Since this delicate youth, Edward VI, was nine years old when he began his short reign, he permitted his Protestant friends to rule the land. Between 1547 and 1553, the beliefs of the Church of England were defined in favor of the Protestant theological position then being popularized on the Continent. The Mass was replaced by a communion service, transforming what had been a literal sacrifice of Christ into a commemorative act. Transubstantiation, purgatory, indulgences, and veneration of images and relics were declared innovations repugnant to the word of God. Numerous ceremonies and practices employing the use of holy water, ashes, and alms were eliminated, and the veneration of the cross was ordered to be discontinued. Pilgrimages were forbidden. English replaced Latin in church services. Extreme unction and all other rites employing oil were eliminated, and confession to priests was no longer deemed necessary.

The impact of Continental Protestantism on the Church of England is best summarized in the Forty-two Articles of Religion. This creed, prepared by Thomas Cranmer, was the first comprehensive statement of faith for the church and bears a striking resemblance to the creeds and doctrines proclaimed by reformers in Germany and Switzerland. Although it is impossible to determine the extent of the conversion of the English people to Protestant theology at this time, still the Church of England was protestantized before the death of the boy king.

Even though there was a reestablishment of Roman Catholicism in England during the reign of Mary, the counter-reformation was not enduring. When Elizabeth, daughter of Anne Boleyn, was crowned in 1558, England saw the inauguration of another dispensation. This talented leader skillfully undertook to settle the religious issue and direct the church along a road which neither led back to Rome nor to the Protestantism that had emerged on the Continent.

Twenty-three years after Elizabeth had become queen, she endorsed an

Articles of Religion for the national church. The Thirty-nine Articles were similar to the Forty-two Articles which had been enacted during Edward's reign and were approved by the religious leaders of the church, by Parliament, and by the "supreme governor." These articles provided the people with a norm of faith which was Lutheran and Calvinistic in tone. There was, however, an apparent ambiguity in some statements that was possibly designed to allow diversity on controversial theological issues. The creed was explicit on most issues endorsed by Lutherans and Calvinists but was generally vague when describing doctrines that divided these two wings of Protestantism. Although Elizabeth would not permit dissenting groups to organize, throughout her reign this influential queen permitted a wide latitude of belief in the established church—a distinguishing characteristic of the Church of England which has continued to this day.

The Anglican communion has not only been known for its theological pluralism, but has often been referred to as the compromise church. As observers have witnessed Anglican services, they have recognized Catholic elements in the patterns of worship. But on closer examination Anglican beliefs appear as popular Protestant tenets, with these major exceptions: the Anglican (and Episcopalian) endorsement of the Catholic view of apostolic succession, and emphasis on the sacraments. Consequently, this communion has been called a halfway house, a church which stands between Catholicism and Protestantism, Catholic in worship and Protestant in belief.

Since the first permanent English settlers in the New World were faithful members of the Church of England, the Anglican settlers of Jamestown organized America's first enduring Protestant church. This religious community was the only legal religion in Virginia for approximately seventy years. It was not until after the passage of the English Toleration Act of 1689 (which provided toleration for all Trinitarian Christians) that there was any significant growth of dissent in the Old Dominion: and religious pluralism did not become a noticeable characteristic of this colony until after 1740.

Although the majority of early immigrants to the English colonies founded before 1640 were members of the Anglican communion, the Church of England was not constituted in most of these early settlements. Upon arriving in the new world, Puritans established their Zion in the wilderness and many other settlers neglected to unite under the banner of the Anglican church. In the mid-seventeenth century, the Church of England was an organized body in only two American colonies, Virginia and Maryland. Although a variety of faiths had been transplanted to America, there was only one major body of Christians in each settlement located along the eastern seacoast. Congregationalists were established in Massachusetts, Connecticut, and New Hampshire; Baptists had organized in Rhode Island; members of reformed churches (Dutch and English) were worshipping in New York; and Swedish Lutherans had gathered in New Sweden. Meanwhile, Roman Catholic solidarity prevailed throughout New Spain and New France. Only in Maryland was there diversification of organized religion, with Anglicans and Roman Catholics worshipping independently.

A significant change occurred, however, in the American religious mosaic following the mid-seventeenth century. Since toleration was planted at the inception of all the mainland colonies founded or occupied by the English after 1660 (which included New York, New Jersey, Pennsylvania, Delaware, the Carolinas, and Georgia), Anglicans joined other Protestants in developing the wilderness, and members of this communion erected many churches near edifices built by other Christians. By 1750 the Church of England was represented in all thirteen colonies and had become the tax-supported religion in all the South and in New York City. In the mid-eighteenth century, Anglicans had erected more churches in the English mainland colonies than had any other religious body (except the Congregational faith). Half of these churches were located in Virginia and Maryland and the other half were about evenly distributed in the other provinces, with the principal exceptions being the few Anglican congregations in Georgia and New Hampshire.[2]

Like many other religious groups, most Anglicans who colonized North America became unchurched. In Virginia, for example, a high percentage of the immigrants settled on isolated farmsteads, and during most of the colonial era there was a dire shortage of ministers and meetinghouses in the Old Dominion. Moreover, most Virginian parishes were so large that the ministers could not effectively care for the spiritual needs of the farmers who were under their jurisdiction. Problems created by the frontier environment plagued this denomination throughout the colonial period, so that even though many inhabitants of Virginia and other provinces were of Anglican heritage, most immigrants of this faith loosened their ties with that church in England.

During the American Revolution the Church of England in the New World was almost destroyed. Although most Anglican clergy and laity did not actively support the loyalist cause, this religious society was branded as the "Tory Church." Half of the clergy of this denomination lived in Virginia and Maryland and few ministers in these two colonies were active Tories, but most of the one-third of Anglican clergy living in the North remained loyal to England. Consequently, Anglican ministers and churches became marked targets for patriot attacks, and many clergy of this faith fled to Canada or England. After the war, the Anglican community was directed by only half as many clergymen as presided over parishes in 1776.[3]

Another ecclesiastical consequence of the American Revolution was the disestablishment of the Church of England in the South and in New York City. Since the postwar society was no longer aided by public taxation and because this church lost much valuable property, an economic crisis gripped this religious community. The Confederation era was truly a critical period for the American Anglican communion.

In the midst of an apparent tragedy, Reverend William White directed a reorganization of the Church of England in this land. At a general convention held in Philadelphia in 1784, the name of this denomination was changed to the Protestant Episcopal Church, thereby eliminating one objectionable feature of the religion, the word *England*. Other conventions followed, the most important being the General Convention of 1789. In Philadelphia, the same community where Americans drafted a new national constitution, Episcopalians framed a constitution, a set of canons, and a Book of Common Prayer. A triennial general convention consisting of representatives of the churches, clergy, and laymen became the supreme governing body of the church. In 1808, the bishops became an upper house of the legislative convention while other clergy and laymen united to form a lower house, thereby establishing an ecclesiastical polity paralleling American state and national governments. Meanwhile, in 1801, the Episcopalians adopted a confession of faith which was almost identical with the Thirty-nine Articles of the Church of England.

During the era of reorganization, Reverend Samuel Seabury from Connecticut and Reverend William White traveled to the British Isles where they received episcopal consecration, after which White became the recognized leader of most Episcopalians. Although major transformations later occurred to make this religion more compatible with the American way of life, this faith had suffered from such a devastating stroke that for many years Episcopalians labored to recover from the decline precipitated by the American frontier environment and the war for independence. One evidence of the nature of the crises which had plagued this church is that in 1800 there were only 12,000 members.[4]

Since Anglicans continued to migrate to America, many immigrants of English ancestry united with the Episcopalian Church. Throughout the past century and a half the Protestant Episcopal Church has remained about the seventh or eighth largest religious community in the United States (based on an enumeration of all bodies of Baptists, Methodists, Lutherans, and Presbyterians under four general groupings). In recent years, however, leaders of this church have witnessed an increase in theological liberalism, a relatively slow growth in membership, and a financial crisis based on the lack of contributions.

The Episcopal church has retained the pluralism which has characterized the Church of England. In contemporary America there are three theological emphases in the Protestant Episcopal Church. One movement resembles the High Church of England and is characterized by an emphasis on sacramental worship. Another wing tends to concentrate on preaching the word, and like the Low Church of England has the sermon as a focus during the Sunday

WILLIAM WHITE

service. Whereas the architectural features of a high church will emphasize the altar, in a low church the pulpit will be the center of attention. The third major wing of this religious community is what is sometimes referred to as a broad church approach to the gospel of Christ. Liberals within this movement emphasize ethics and strongly support social action programs. A focal point of these Episcopalians is the lectern.

Although there are different emphases in the Episcopal churches in America, members of this denomination have not separated into distinct communions such as the High and Low church, as occurred in England. In some sections of the country, however, this church takes on an appearance different from that emphasized in other parts; and in some communities the character of a congregation seems to change as new ministers commence serving the people. Such pluralism is not perplexing to members of this communion; Episcopalians have learned to live with diversity, for it has long been one of the distinguishing characteristics of their religious heritage.

Distinguishing Beliefs[5]

One of the most distinguishing characteristics of the Episcopal Church is their emphasis on and their belief concerning the sacraments. According to members of this communion, sacraments are visible signs and effectual means by which God's grace works in man and by which man's faith is strengthened. Although some consider these channels of grace necessary to salvation, they do not hold that unbaptized infants will be damned. Members of this church also affirm that Christ ordained two sacraments: baptism and the Lord's Supper. Other important Episcopal rites of sacramental character (involving an outward sign and an inward grace) are confirmation, penance, ordination, matrimony, and unction of the sick.

Epsicopalians teach that baptism is a sign of profession of Christ and a renunciation of evil. Through baptism by pouring or immersion in the name of the triune God, candidates are incorporated into the church which is the mystical body of Christ, a fellowship of Christians guided, taught and strengthened by the Spirit of God. Through baptism faith is confirmed and grace increased. God is invoked to convey to the recipient a remission of sins by spiritual regeneration.

During this sacrament, a candidate is given a Christian name, and following his cleansing by water, the ceremony of signing the candidate's forehead with the cross occurs. This rite symbolizes a Christian's campaign against "sin, the world, and the devil," and his dedication to Christ.

In cases of infant baptism, the promises of faith and obedience are taken in the child's name by sponsors or godparents. Sponsors promise that the infant will receive a proper Christian education and will be encouraged to live a Christian life and eventually be confirmed. In one sense, the entire church is a sponsor.

Episcopalians also teach that the sacrament of the Lord's Supper is more than a memorial. Worthy communicants receive the bread and wine in remembrance of Christ and are nourished and strengthened by the spiritual body and blood of Christ. Although the substance of the bread and wine are not changed, the real and spiritual presence of the living Christ is at every Holy Communion. While Episcopalians disagree on the precise meaning of this mystery, they insist that Christ is really present at the Eucharist celebration.

Members of this faith further believe that baptism is a necessary qualification for receiving the Eucharist and that one must normally be confirmed or ready for confirmation before partaking of the Lord's Supper.

According to Episcopalians, confirmation is the gift of the strengthening power of the Holy Spirit, administered by bishops through the laying on of hands. Worthy members are promised increased gifts of grace, wisdom, understanding, and true godliness. In confirmation, a person baptized in infancy takes upon himself the vows made on his behalf by sponsors.

Another Episcopal rite is called the sacrament of penance or absolution. Episcopalians teach that confessions are properly made in private or in public services. They say that the penitent receive absolution from God through the priest's declarations. Members, therefore, receive assurances from the minister that they are absolved from sin and restored by God to membership in the body of Christ. In private confession, the penitent kneels before a priest at an appointed place, prays, confesses, receives counsel and then the priest, without assigning elaborate penances, declares that by the authority of Christ committed to him, "I absolve thee from thy sins."

According to Episcopalians, holy orders is ordination of the clergy through the laying on of hands by bishops, and there are three orders of ministers in this church: bishops, priests (elders or presbyters) and deacons. One of the most distinctive beliefs of this Protestant church is that only bishops possess the power of ordination and that their authority has come down in an unbroken line from the apostles. They further assert that only properly ordained ministers may preach publicly and administer the sacraments (except for baptism which nonordained Christians may administer).

It is also the belief of Episcopalians that through marriage men and women are joined together to live in faithfulness, to remain in perfect love and peace together, and to live according to God's commands. The ministers in holy matrimony are the contracting persons, for the bride and groom marry themselves by their covenants. The church solemnizes the marriage by pronouncing the blessing upon it.

In this religious community, divorces are not granted, but annulments of marriages are granted when circumstances warrant, and these "divorced" individuals may remarry.

Another Episcopal sacrament is called unction of the sick or the anointing or laying on of hands of the sick. Episcopal bishops and priests have the authority to anoint the sick with oil blessed for that purpose by a bishop, beseeching God to eradicate the pain and sickness of the body. Coupled with the prayer to restore to health is a prayer to release the afflicted from sin.

There are a variety of "religious" orders of monks and nuns in this communion who take vows of poverty, chastity, and obedience. Some primarily engage in spiritual contemplation, praying, and works of mercy. Living in communal societies, they participate in some manual activities.

Miscellaneous Beliefs

Episcopalians worship the Holy Trinity and believe in the incarnation, asserting that God became man. Jesus, they say, is truly divine and truly human, one person who is God and man. Many further teach that God is not only the creator of the heavens and earth but by his actions continually sustains the world.

Episcopalians also subscribe to a number of historical creeds, including the Nicene Creed, Apostles' Creed and Athanasian Creed. Some, however, profess that these documents have been framed in a symbolic language and, consequently, many have adopted contemporary interpretations of classical expressions of faith.

9

Methodism

One of the world's most energetic revivalists, whose eminence as an evangelist and reformer has been secured, is often honored as the founder of Methodism. Few men of the eighteenth century left such a visible mark of their achievements. Throughout the Christian world, among people of various religious persuasions, John Wesley is respected as a conscientious leader who influenced others to seek the light of Christ and to live according to that light.[1]

The life of John Wesley spanned the eighteenth century (from 1703 to 1791); throughout most of these eighty-eight years, religion was a primary preoccupation of his thoughts and actions. He was reared in a deeply religious environment, probably influenced more by his mother, Susanna, than by his father, Reverend Samuel Wesley, an Anglican minister who served in Epworth, Lincolnshire, England. Although Susanna lacked worldly wealth, she mastered Greek, Latin, and French, and developed an unusual capacity to express herself in speech and writing. Being endowed with natural beauty and a keen intellect, and personifying Christian ideals of integrity and love, Susanna Wesley became one of the outstanding women of her generation. This conscientious wife of a scholar and theologian was the mother of nineteen children, most of them dying in infancy. John was her second son and fifteenth child; her last child, Charles, another distinguished religious leader, aided John in establishing one of the world's largest religious societies.

Although John Wesley lacked material wealth, he succeeded in securing a good education, including instruction at one of the most prestigious schools in England. Shortly after completing the requirements for his first degree at Oxford, he was elected to a fellowship and appointed tutor and lecturer in Greek. Meanwhile, in 1725, he was ordained a deacon by the Bishop of Oxford and three years later a priest. After his ordinations, Wesley joined a group his brother Charles founded at Oxford that was designed to enrich the spiritual life of all members. Eventually John became the acknowledged leader of this small society in which individuals pledged to engage in regular Bible study and discussion, to partake of the sacrament of Holy Communion weekly, and to be involved in humanitarian activities, including visits to prisoners. Because these members disciplined themselves methodically, they were sometimes called "Methodists," and as another mark of opprobrium they were dubbed members of a "Holy Club" and were referred to as the "Bible Moths" and "the Enthusiasts."

During a visit to London in 1735, John Wesley was invited to be chaplain of the English community in Savannah, Georgia, and to labor as a missionary to the Indians. Accepting this call, Wesley journeyed to America and, after reviewing the religious situation existing among the whites of Georgia, directed the thrust of his mission to serving the immigrants. Wesley, however, was not a popular minister. His strictness and emphasis on sacramental observance annoyed many settlers. Friction developed and Wesley returned to England after serving less than two years, concluding that his experience in America was an utter failure.

Upon his return to his native land, Wesley reexamined his religious status and decided that he lacked spiritual vitality. He remembered when the German Moravians endeavored to show him "a more excellent way" during his voyage to America. Some of their teachings seemed foolish to him, for, as Wesley confessed sarcastically, he was too learned and too wise to become engulfed in their emphasis on faith and piety. He further recalled a recent conversation with Peter Bohler, a Moravian who visited London on his way to America. Bohler declared that Wesley's efforts for holiness were shallow because he lacked genuine faith in Jesus Christ. "Preach faith until you have it," Bohler advised "and then because you have it, you will preach faith."[2]

Shortly after his experience with Bohler, Wesley's life was dramatically changed as he experienced an "evangelical conversion." Recalling this event, he explained:

> In the evening I went very unwillingly to a society in Aldersgate Street, where one was reading Luther's preface to the Epistle to the Romans. About a quarter before nine, while he was describing the change which God works in the heart through faith in Christ, I felt my heart strangely warmed. I felt I did trust in Christ, Christ alone, for salvation; and an assurance was given me, that he had taken away my sins, even mine, and saved me from the law of sin and death.[3]

Wesley's spiritual experience awakened him to the realization that many in England lacked faith and holiness. Consequently, this energetic preacher launched a crusade, encouraging others to seek faith in Christ and perfection as a child of God. Commencing a life of itinerant preaching, Wesley often

JOHN WESLEY

traveled nearly four thousand miles a year and averaged three sermons a day. Arising at four in the morning and traveling primarily on horseback, he preached throughout England, Scotland, Wales, and Ireland. Many Anglican clergymen objected to his revivalist techniques, did not approve of his preaching in their parishes without authorization, and closed their pulpits to him and his followers. Wesley, however, was not deterred by such opposition for he boldly proclaimed:

> I look upon all the world as my parish; thus far I mean, that, in whatever part of it I am, I judge it meet, right, and my bounded duty, to declare unto all that are willing to hear the glad tidings of salvation.[4]

As Wesley rode throughout the British Isles, he invited others to gather frequently, to pray, sing hymns, and study the word of God. Membership in these groups was open to all who desired spiritual edification. He also expected individuals who were influenced by his preaching to attend services of the Church of England on Sunday and to participate regularly in Holy Communion.

During his initial preaching excursions, Wesley did not attack any doctrines held by the church to which he belonged, but criticized the apathy, the worldliness, and the lack of faith and piety prevalent among many members of that religious community. Rather than establish a new denomination, Wesley struggled to initiate a reformation among members of the Anglican communion. Such action, however, eventually led to a disruption of England's established church.

The transition from societies in which people gathered to study and pray to a new religious community was a gradual process which began in 1739 and continued until 1791. One of the first steps in this transition was Wesley's formation of "United Societies" in London and other communities and the preparation of rules for these groups. According to these guidelines, members gathered to seek the power of godliness, to pray together, and to be strengthened by listening to the word of God. Members were encouraged to serve mankind and to help others work out their salvation. They were not to purchase, sell, or consume alcoholic beverages except in extreme necessity. They were to observe the Sabbath day and avoid every kind of evil. Each society was divided into classes of about twelve with a leader who had the responsibility of contacting every member of his class at least once a week.[5]

The movement from United Societies (which became known as Methodist societies) toward the creation of a new church continued during the 1740s. During that decade various elements of a missionary movement were initiated, including a "circuit system," "itinerant ministry," "class leaders," and "annual conferences"; Wesley appointed many lay leaders to direct the religious activities of congregations. These individuals did not claim authority to administer the sacraments, but they taught and counseled those who assembled together. When some of Wesley's followers were denied Holy Communion in the Church of England, he approved the administration of the Lord's Supper in the societies by Anglican priests who supported this religious movement. In 1746, Wesley read Peter King's *Account of the Primitive Church* (1691) which convinced him that bishops and presbyters were of the same order and that both these officers had the right to ordain. He further concluded that the scriptures did not advocate any specific form of church government.[6]

In the 1780s Methodist societies took other major steps toward separation from the Church of England. On 1 September 1784 Wesley ordained two men as deacons and the following day ordained them presbyters and set apart Reverend Thomas Coke (who had been episcopally ordained) as superintendent of Methodist churches in America. Shortly thereafter these three men sailed across the Atlantic and, acting under the direction of Wesley (who remained in the British Isles), helped establish a Methodist church in the young republic. Toward the end of that decade Wesley ordained others as presbyters, thereby rejecting explicitly the Anglican position concerning authority—that bishops alone have the right of ordination. Then in 1787 Wesley advised his followers to license all chapels and preachers, thereby admitting that they were dissenters in order to receive the privileges guaranteed Trinitarian Protestants by the Act of Toleration. Although Wesley had in reality severed his connections with the established church, throughout his life he insisted that he was a loyal member of the Church of England and refused to allow Methodists in England to officially announce their independent status. The actions of this resolute reformer, however, had precipitated a schism; shortly after Wesley's death in 1791 his followers in England acknowledged that the separation had been consummated.[7]

While Methodism was emerging as a distinct faith in England, it was transplanted to the English mainland colonies. About 1760 a lay preacher, Robert Strawbridge, migrated from Ireland to Maryland and near Sam's Creek in Frederick County organized a society according to the rules outlined by John Wesley. His itinerant preaching extended into the neighboring colonies of Virginia, Delaware, and Pennsylvania, where additional classes were constituted. Meanwhile, Philip Embury organized a Methodist class in his home in New York about 1765 and from there the movement spread into other communities.

After a significant growth of Methodism occurred during the American Revolution, especially in Virginia under the leadership of Devereux Jarratt, many members of this organization desired to sever their identity with the Church of England, a society which had lost prestige and clergy during the war. At that time most Methodist leaders in the new nation were lay preachers who claimed no special authority to baptize or administer the

FRANCIS ASBURY

Lord's Supper, and therefore members of this movement relied on Anglican priests to administer the sacraments. After several groups had initiated a schism, Methodists assembled in Baltimore; in the year 1784, the same year that Wesley had appointed Thomas Coke and Francis Asbury to be superintendents of Methodist bodies, delegates approved Wesley's plan of organization and formed the Methodist Episcopal Church. By refusing to accept Wesley's supervision of the church, approving Coke and Asbury as their leaders, and changing their titles to bishop, the Americans created a new church independent of the Methodist communities in England.[8]

The Methodist Church was organized in American during an era when there were fewer churches and ministers per total number of people than in any other age since the European colonization of this land.[9] Recognizing the skepticism and indifference toward organized religion which prevailed in the new nation, and knowing that large numbers were unable to attend church because there was no organized religious society in the community where they lived, vigorous Methodist leaders launched an effective missionary program designed to plant Christianity in the homes of the unconverted, and those who did not belong to a church. These Protestants solved, in part, the problem of the shortage of ministers by not requiring their preachers to be college graduates, and many dedicated Americans sacrificed the comforts of life to serve as itinerant preachers. Before their appointments Methodists were generally asked to answer four questions in the affirmative: (1) Are you converted? (2) Do you know and are you willing to abide by the rules of the society? (3) Can you preach adequately? (4) Have you a horse?

In addition to calling large numbers of preachers to travel throughout America, Methodists inaugurated an ingenious system enabling vast numbers living in rural communities to receive regular spiritual edification. These Protestants divided the country into conferences and districts and then subdivided the districts into stations and circuits. Preaching locations were determined within the circuits, and itinerant ministers were assigned to preach regularly in the designated places of worship. The circuits were called two-week, three-week, or four-week circuits depending on the period required to preach in each location. Traveling preachers, who almost lived on the back of a horse and generally slept in the homes of settlers living along established trails, were usually assigned to a circuit for only one or at the most two years and were given a small substance for their services. In areas where there was a Methodist meetinghouse, stationed preachers were appointed who in most instances derived much of their support from their own industry. But most communities prior to the Civil War were served by traveling ministers who had no secular employment.

One of the most famous circuit riders of the early republic was Peter Cartwright. At the age of sixty-eight, this itinerant had a circuit almost 500 miles by 100 miles. In order to carry his gospel message to the pioneers of

THE CIRCUIT PREACHER

frontier America, he rode through blinding snow storms and treacherous floods, and followed dusty trails in the burning summer heat. He traveled from forts to camps and from tents to log cabins. He preached in towns, villages, and farm communities, in homes, schools, and courthouses, and declared a message of salvation to innumerable farmers who gathered in the fields and groves of the old Northwest.[10]

Although Methodists were energetic supporters of a variety of interdenominational missionary programs, such as camp meetings, Sunday Schools, and Bible and tract societies, in most communities camp meetings were regularly conducted by Methodists themselves without the cooperation of other Protestants. In fact, Methodists sponsored more camp meetings than did members of any other denomination. Frequently camp meetings erupted into exciting spectacles in which enthusiasts demonstrated their emotional aspirations with a variety of physical demonstrations. During the exuberant meetings of the Second Great Awakening, people sometimes went into trances, jerked, rolled and crawled on the ground, barked like dogs, and fell to the ground as though they had been hit by a piercing cannon ball. Peter Cartwright declared that he had seen "more than a hundred sinners fall like dead men under one powerful sermon," and that he witnessed more than 500 people shouting in unison their praises to God.[11]

While some Americans defended the physical demonstrations as evidence of the power of the Almighty, others condemned the emotionalism as unhealthy hysteria, noting that while one group was supposedly being saved others were being intoxicated by the spirits, meaning the effects of alcohol or possibly evil spirits. No one, however, doubted that the camp meetings had a profound impact on many participants. After returning to their homes from an exciting religious experience, many settlers of the early republic decided to join one of the Protestant churches, and more united with the Methodists than any other denomination.

The tremendous success of the Methodists during the early nineteenth century is partly reflected in an examination of the annual reports of church membership. In 1786 the Methodists claimed a membership of 20,600. Twenty years later, in 1806, the membership had increased to about 130,600. Following the War of 1812, the increase was even more remarkable than the earlier growth, for in 1816, there were 215,000 Methodists, and by 1836 approximately 650,000. In one year, 1833, there was an increase in membership of 51,143; and in one ten-year period, 1826 to 1836, the growth was nearly 300,000. By 1850, approximately one-third of American Protestants were Methodists and for one century, from about 1820 to 1920, the Methodist Church was the largest Protestant community in the United States. Currently, this denomination stands second among Protestant groups in this country.[12]

During the era of spectacular Methodist growth there were a number of divisions in the movement. While some of these schisms have been healed, many have remained permanent. Currently there are more than twenty different bodies in America whose historical roots stem back to John Wesley.

A number of the divisions in Methodism occurred as a consequence of racial discrimination or the desire of blacks to unite in their own church. In 1787 a group of blacks in Philadelphia withdrew from the Methodist Church and in 1816 formed what is currently the second largest body of Methodists in the United States, the African Methodist Episcopal Church whose membership is more than one million. Another group, currently reporting more than a million members, separated from the mother church in 1796 in New York City and in 1848 adopted the name African Methodist Episcopal Zion Church. Shortly after the Civil War a number of free Negroes living in the South desired to form their own religious society and, with the approval of the parent group, organized in 1870 the Christian Methodist Episcopal Church, currently the fourth largest body of Methodists, with a membership of about half a million. Two other Methodist bodies consisting of black members are the Union American Methodist Episcopal Church and the African Union First Colored Methodist Protestant Church, Inc.

The most serious rupture in this religious movement occurred as a consequence of the slavery issue. In 1844 the main body was split into a northern and a southern church: the Methodist Episcopal Church was the northern branch and the southerners adopted the name Methodist Episcopal Church, South. It was not until 1939 that the two societies reunited, forming the Methodist Protestant Church. In 1968 this religious community merged with the United Brethren Church, creating the United Methodist Church. This is the largest numerical group in this family of churches with approximately eighty percent of all Methodists belonging to this communion.

The issues of discrimination and slavery were not the only divisive forces of this faith. Many schisms have resulted from groups rebelling against what they consider doctrinal innovations in the mother church. Other groups criticized the Methodist pattern of government, with some rejecting what they considered to be an autocratic polity in favor of a Congregational system providing for the autonomy of each congregation. The largest of these predominantly white churches, currently known for its theological conservatism, is the Free Methodist Church of North America. While many have classified the predominant Methodist system of government as episcopal because of the power extended to bishops, Methodists seek for equal representation of clergy and lay members in policymaking procedures, extending much authority to the Quarterly, Annual, and General Conferences. In the United Methodist Church the Quarterly Conference is the governing body of the local churches and consists of all the officials of a congregation. This assembly discusses future plans and programs, determines budgets, elects church officers, and sends delegates to the Annual Conference. At the Annual Conference all of the ministers and at least one lay member from each congregation meet

CAMP MEETING

to determine individuals who should be ordained to the ministry, vote on constitutional questions and elect lay and ministerial delegates to the General Conference. The highest policymaking body is the General Conference, which meets every four years. While a bishop presides, most business is conducted by committees. Reports of these groups become binding when adopted by the General Conference. Although there appears to be less freedom in this pattern of government than the local autonomy which exists in many other Protestant churches, Methodists believe that a genuine democratic spirit permeates their decision-making process.

One of the distinguishing characteristics of Methodism in modern America is that in most congregations a wide latitude of belief exists. Much freedom is apparent in the interpretation of basic Methodist beliefs; and in most congregations, liberal and orthodox members work harmoniously on a variety of church programs. In many congregations ministers do not require subscription to a specified creed by individuals requesting membership. But while there are practically no membership requirements in some local societies, many ministers specify that individuals desiring to unite with Methodists should indicate that they have committed their life to Christ. Since most Methodists reject many beliefs popularized by John Wesley and are known for their efforts to reinterpret the classical faith, there is currently no precise answer to the question, "What do Methodists believe?" Many ministers and laity would respond to this question by saying that they believe in Christ. Many would add that they believe Christians should express their faith by supporting a variety of social welfare programs and working conscientiously to solve the problems confronting men and women of the twentieth century. [13]

The inclusive nature of this religious community is aptly summarized in a series of statements which appear on printed programs circulated by members of the largest body of Methodists:

> If the United Methodist Church had no white members, it would be the seventh largest Negro denomination in the country. . . .
> If the United Methodist Church had no white members and no black members it would be the largest red denomination in the country. More American Indians belong to our church than to any other.
> If the United Methodist church had no white, black, or red members, it would be the largest yellow denomination in the country. One-half of all Japanese Americans who are Christians belong to our church.
> If the United Methodist Church had no English-speaking members, it would be the third largest Spanish-speaking denomination in the country.
> Our great church not only *sings* but demonstrates, "In Christ there is no east or west, in Him no south or north."

Distinguishing Beliefs

Traditionally, Methodists have emphasized the five points of Arminianism, especially that man plays a vital role in the salvation experience. He has the capacity, John Wesley taught, to accept or reject the gift of salvation when God offers this gift to mankind. God desires to save all mankind, Wesley added, but only those who accept Christ and do not fall will benefit from the atonement.

Sanctification is another doctrine that represents the historical tradition of this faith. Protestant reformers, including Luther and Calvin, did not make a sharp distinction between justification and sanctification. They considered justification not only as God's forgiveness of man and establishment of a new relationship with him, but also as the involvement of the Holy Spirit operating within man to produce a new holiness. According to most reformers, justification occurred when man obtained forgiveness of sins, and righteousness. John Wesley, however, emphasized justification and sanctification in separate classifications and taught that there is a possibility of complete sanctification or final perfection in this life. It is possible, Wesley added, for man to live a sinless life and be made perfect in love in this life. Wesley also emphasized that the Holy Ghost gives to individuals an assurance that they are children of God.

While describing their position concerning baptism, Methodists explain that baptism marks the beginning of growth in the Christian faith, and is the gateway into the Christian Church. Through infant baptism, they add, parents dedicate their children to God. Ministers instruct parents that the baptized infant is consecrated to God and that the parents or sponsors have a responsibility to bring up the child in the Christian faith.

There are a few differences in the beliefs of Methodists and doctrines generally held by Episcopalians. Unlike Episcopalians, Methodists do not generally endorse sponsors who act as spiritual parents and who are not physically related to the infants at baptism. Another difference in the faith of these religious communities is that Methodists do not endorse confirmation as practiced by Episcopalians. Instead of a service consisting of the laying on of hands of a bishop, in the Methodist Church there is a service of reception in which candidates renew vows made in their name at baptism. A third difference is that Methodists hold that the Lord's Supper is a memorial in which Christians remember the sacrifice of Jesus and promise to serve him. The bread and grape juice (Episcopalians use wine) signify the body and blood of Christ. The Lord's Supper is also considered by Methodists as a living experience, for this sacrament becomes a blessing and comfort to all worthy communicants.

Another basic difference in the beliefs of Methodists and Episcopalians is that while Episcopalians believe in apostolic succession, Methodists affirm that every man is his own priest. In harmony with most Protestants, Methodists teach that all believers constitute a priesthood whose influence and leadership help each to live closer to God. Methodists further assert that individuals should not administer the sacraments unless they have been ordained or appointed to serve as pastor to a church or circuit. A call from God is also deemed essential prior to ordination, and each preacher, it is believed, should declare publicly his faith in God before teaching others. According to Methodists, there are two orders: the office of deacon and the office of elder. Unlike Episcopalians, Methodists teach that the bishop is not a third order but is an elder set apart for a peculiar administrative task. In the Methodist church the bishop is not ordained but is consecrated.

Methodist church government is more like the Presbyterian system than the Congregational. Local congregations do not select ministers, and ministers are bound to serve where directed by bishops. Generally, the bishop, the congregation, and the minister approve an appointment before the minister becomes the spiritual leader of a congregation. The governing bodies of this church consist of lay and clerical representatives.

Miscellaneous Beliefs and Characteristics

Methodists are known for their emphasis on a triune God, evangelism, education, separation of church and state, freedom for all men, a concern and responsibility for the spiritual and temporal affairs of others, and for their opposition to the sale, distribution and consumption of alcoholic beverages. Methodist ministers are currently taking a more flexible attitude toward alcohol, there being a steady movement away from total abstinence. Some of the younger clergy are now accepting an occasional social drink.

Methodists are also known for their reinterpretation of classical Protestant theology. Most have rejected many elements of the traditional faith, including the traditional belief concerning the virgin birth of Christ, the fall, the atonement, and life beyond the grave.

10

The Baptists

America's largest Protestant community, the Baptists, is characterized by a multitude of distinguishing features. There are more than twenty-seven million adult baptized members of this denomination in the United States in comparison to about five million elsewhere.[1] Thirty-four percent of all American Protestants are affiliated with one of the twenty-one bodies comprising this family of churches, and over fifty percent of all church members enumerated by the National Council of the Churches of Christ in the U.S. are either Roman Catholics or Baptists. Moreover, the Baptist society was America's first convert faith, becoming the fastest growing religion in America at the end of the colonial period and remaining the largest Protestant denomination in the United States since the 1920s. Although this family of churches is known for its theological orthodoxy, it is also characterized by pluralism regarding historical roots and a number of basic doctrines.

Some Baptist historians contend that the historical roots of their faith stem directly back to the New Testament Church. They note that during the Middle Ages various Christian sects, such as Petrobrusians, the Paulicians, the Bogomils, and the Waldensians, taught principles that parallel modern Baptist beliefs, including the doctrine of believer's baptism.[2] Successionist historians have also advanced many theories regarding the manner in which Christ's church continued through the ages. Some have suggested that there was a chain of ordination preserving the authority which Christ conveyed to his apostles. Others have contended that the church was preserved by local groups who retained the essential principles or characteristics of New Testament Christianity.[3]

Most twentieth-century Baptist historians reject the successionist theories regarding a continuous history of the Baptist society from the first century to the present age. They assert that the successionists neglect or ignore basic differences in the beliefs of select medieval societies and of the modern Baptists; these significant differences, they aver, negate the possibility of a succession of the church. Moreover, many contemporary historians emphasize that there is no apparent connecting link between the so-called medieval Baptist societies which existed during different eras nor is there a visible connection between these medieval groups and the Baptists of the modern world. [4]

Although most twentieth-century Baptist historians insist that there was a disruption of the early Christian church, they claim that Christ's church was renewed when men gathered and worshipped according to the New Testament pattern. Some historians speculate that the recovery occurred in the early sixteenth century with the emergence of the Anabaptists of Switzerland. After Conrad Grebel (c. 1490-1526) of Zurich failed to convince Zwingli that the church and state should be separated and that the church should consist solely of regenerated Christians baptized after their conversion, a schism resulted and a new society was constituted, which spread into Germany, the Netherlands, and other parts of western Europe.

Other Baptist historians believe that the recovery emerged from the English Separatist movement. Modern Baptist history, some suggest, begins with John Smyth. Believing that the Church of England needed purification, Smyth became a Separatist and in the midst of increasing religious oppression joined others in a flight for freedom. This quest led many Separatists, including the Pilgrim fathers, to the Netherlands, where they secured temporary asylum in the first decade of the sixteenth century. While living in this new land, Smyth learned the tenets of the Mennonites or the Anabaptists (meaning to rebaptize) and was converted to the principle of believer's baptism. Subsequently, Smyth prepared an articles of faith and promoted the transfer of English Separatists to an Anabaptist society. Because of his activities in the Netherlands, John Smyth has gained the reputation among some historians as the "founder of the modern Baptist churches."

Another English Separatist who was influenced by the Mennonites was Thomas Helwys. Refusing to embrace Smyth's program of reform and deciding not to remain in exile, Helwys returned to England and with the support of about ten ardent followers organized the first Baptist church in England just outside the walls of London in 1611 or 1612.

Although Smyth is credited with initiating the rise of the first English Baptist society in the Netherlands and Helwys is recognized as the founder of the first Baptist church in England, there is no historical evidence indicating that either of these leaders proclaimed that immersion was the only proper mode of baptism. Since they probably retained the Anabaptist principle of baptism by affusion or pouring, some modern historians claim that the recovery movement did not occur until about 1640 when Baptists of England adopted the principles of baptism by immersion. According to one group of Baptist historians, after the proper mode of baptism was coupled with other Baptist distinctions, the renewal of New Testament Christianity became a reality.

Another popular explanation of the origin of the Baptists is that their modern historical roots stem back to the Free Church movement, which includes the Anabaptist and Mennonite tradition on the Continent and the Separatist tradition of England. This Free Church movement was characterized by liberty of conscience in the sense that each congregation was to be independently governed by God's influence and was to be free from all outside political and cultural influences. Therefore, some historians suggest that the recovery occurred when the principle that a church should be disciplined solely from within was coupled with other distinguishing features of the Baptists. Since about 1640, these historians note, the distinctive Baptist beliefs have remained essentially the same. [5]

Baptist opinions concerning the American origin of this denomination also conflict. The most popular view is that America's first Baptist church was organized under the leadership of Roger Williams in Providence, Rhode Island, in 1639. Since these early Baptists refused to acknowledge the authority claimed by ministers of other faiths, they initiated baptism among themselves, authorizing certain of their number to administer this ordinance. According to one account, Ezekiel Holliman, a layman, first baptized Roger Williams, who in turn baptized Holliman and about ten others. [6]

Williams remained a Baptist for only a few months. Shortly after helping others organize a Baptist society, Williams left the movement. He doubted the validity of his own baptism because of an absence of a visible succession of authorized administrators. In a letter to John Winthrop in 1649, Williams argued that he believed the practice of believer's baptism by "dipping . . . comes nearer the first practice of our great Founder Christ Jesus, than any other practices of religion . . . and yet," he continued, "I have not satisfaction neither in the authority by which it is done, nor in the manner." [7] On another occasion Williams acknowledged that he was dissatisfied with the prevailing creeds and with the various Christian institutions of his age. He insisted that an apostasy had occurred and that there was a need for a restoration of the purity of the "Primitive Church." [8] Failing to locate a church which, in his opinion, had received the necessary "special commission" to restore New Testament Christianity, Williams became a Seeker and died before his vision of a restoration had been realized. [9]

A few historians contend that the first Baptist church was constituted in Newport in 1638 under the direction of Dr. John Clarke, but since the records which indicate its being a Baptist society only date back to about 1648, most members of this faith agree that the earliest Baptist society was constituted in Providence. [10]

Although the Baptist persuasion was one of the earliest Protestant traditions to be transplanted in the New World, for over one hundred years Baptist growth in this land was exceedingly slow. In 1660 there were only four Baptist congregations in the English colonies of North America; all were in Rhode Island, two in Providence and two in Newport. The number of societies increased gradually to about twenty-two in 1700 and 132 in 1750. Membership in this denomination, however, rose sharply after 1760 and by 1776 there were about 430 Baptist meetinghouses in the new nation with an estimated membership of about 22,000. By 1795 membership had soared to more than 76,600 with 1,089 churches and 915 ministers. By 1800 the Baptist faith had become the largest religious community in the United States and retained that position until the early 1820s. At that time, the Methodists replaced the Baptists as the number one religion, numerically speaking, in the early republic. The Baptists regained numerical leadership among the Protestant churches in the mid-1920s and since that decade have remained America's largest body of Protestants, ranking second, next to the Roman Catholics, among all the American denominations.[11]

The remarkable growth of the Baptist Church in the late eighteenth and early nineteenth centuries was primarily the result of the inauguration of America's first effective missionary program. Recognizing the problems created by the frontier environment, the Baptists determined to carry religion to the rural farmers of the continent. The deficiency in the number of ministers was partly resolved by the ordination of many lay members who claimed an internal call from God but who had not secured a college education. For most of these early Baptist elders, preaching was an avocation rather than a profession. These dedicated preachers did not rely on parish contributions for their support but earned their livelihood from farming. The log cabin and frame homes of these farm preachers served as temporary meetinghouses and also as bases of operation. Frequently these dedicated pioneers left their homes and preached enthusiastically in surrounding communities. One leader who received a meager compensation for his ecclesiastical labors served hundreds of rural farmers. As a result primarily of conversions, the Baptists grew rapidly in numbers, becoming America's first convert religion.

Although Baptists emphasize the autonomy of each congregation, most local societies have united for the purpose of fellowship, for the promotion of educational and missionary work, and for the advancement of other church-sponsored programs. These loosely related groups of independent churches are usually called associations or conventions and are organized on local, state, and national levels. Membership consists of clergy and lay representatives of the affiliated congregations. On the national level, professional secretaries and administrators are hired to transform policies accepted by the representatives into effective programs. Although these bodies prepare recommendations, they claim no authority to enforce their decisions. The only serious recourse toward a recalcitrant congregation is to dismiss them from the alliance.

Even though these associations have historically remained advisory bodies, some congregations refuse to join one of the Baptist alliances. A few members of this faith insist that such unions are unscriptural and infringe on the independence of the local congregations. Since these strictly independent churches are not affiliated with a national group, they generally do not issue reports of membership and are therefore not enumerated on most statistics of church membership in modern America.

In addition to directing a variety of humanitarian programs, many Baptist alliances in the United States promote doctrinal uniformity among their adherents. Some alliances have prepared articles of faith which serve as guides for framing beliefs of a local congregation. Since associations generally strive to preserve the historic faith, some bodies will not admit into their organization congregations that endorse patterns of belief that conflict with the association's declaration of faith. Moreover, in order to become a member of most Baptist societies, individuals must subscribe to a local covenant. Consequently, in contrast to most Protestant faiths with memberships of more than a few million, there is a striking harmony of belief concerning essential Christian doctrines among members of most Baptist conventions. There are, however, differences of belief among many members of different associations, and a few alliances consist of many members known for their reinterpretation of the classical religion. Many members of the more liberal associations who do not adhere strictly to the traditional pattern of belief are not required to subscribe strictly to a local creed and share convictions popularized by various contemporary theologians.

The world's largest alliance of Baptists is the Southern Baptist Convention. Approximately forty percent of all Baptists in the United States are affiliated with this national body; among whites they are the overwhelming body. Some members of this alliance, which is known for its theological orthodoxy, believe that theirs is the only true church and will not accept baptisms unless administered by ministers of this convention. Others do not take such a strict stand, but members of all congregations comprising this union of churches endorse a local "church covenant" that harmonizes with the national declaration of faith. Although most Baptists living in early nineteenth-century America endorsed the five points of Calvinism, currently most members, in and out of this alliance, endorse Arminianism, including man's free will to accept or reject faith in the Lord Jesus Christ.

The Southern Baptist Convention was organized in 1845 after a series of controversies concerning slavery had precipitated a schism among American Baptists. After this alliance had been formed, the Southerners established a centralized organization for controlling various phases of their cooperative programs, such as foreign and home missionary societies. Previously, these programs were separate and independent organizations supported by different congregations. Prior to 1814, for example, at least sixty-five societies north of Philadelphia were raising money for domestic and foreign missions. The southerners decided that a national organization could more effectively direct missionary and other similar programs. Currently this convention is supporting home and foreign missions, hospitals, Sunday Schools, and many educational institutions. [12]

Throughout most of the nineteenth and twentieth centuries, a large percentage of the blacks in the United States have been affiliated with the Methodist and Baptist societies. Currently almost half of all Negroes are members of a Christian church and four out of every five who are church members are Baptists. More than ten-and-a-half million belong to one of three Baptist alliances: the National Baptist Convention, USA, Inc. (the largest Baptist black denomination), the National Baptist Convention of America, and the National Primitive Baptist Convention, Inc. [13]

One other Baptist alliance, the American Baptist Churches in the USA, has a membership of more than one million. This denomination, predominantly located in the north, is known for its more liberal theological position, its endorsement of open communion, its more tolerant position concerning integration, and its emphasis on Christian unity. Its ecumenical activities include membership in the National Council of Churches. It has also framed various recommendations suggesting that Baptist groups and other denominations, such as the Disciples of Christ and the Church of the Brethren, unite under a common bond of fellowship.

Although theological differences serve as a major factor in separating this religious community into many factions and even though some Baptists have become liberal, one of the distinguishing characteristics of the modern Baptist movement is that a high percentage of its members is earnestly striving to preserve the historic faith. In fact, of the American religious bodies (or groupings under general headings, such as Baptists, Methodists, and Lutherans) with memberships of more than four million, the Baptists would definitely be ranked as the most conservative body of American Christians.

One of the most significant contributions of the Baptists to the American heritage has been their emphasis on religious liberty and the separation of church and state; in the early nineteenth century members of this society witnessed a remarkable change in the religious climate of the new nation. By proclaiming the God-given, natural, and inalienable right of freedom of conscience, Baptists have played a significant role in advancing in this land the principle of religious liberty.

Distinguishing Beliefs
The following six beliefs are often cited by Baptists as their most distinguishing doctrines or practices:

First, *believer's baptism by immersion* is the correct Christian baptism—the immersion of a believer in water in the name of the Father, the Son, and the Holy Spirit. It is considered an act of obedience, symbolizing a believer's faith in Christ. Most orthodox Baptists will accept baptisms performed by other Baptist ministers. Some pastors of the Southern Baptist Convention, however, will only accept baptisms performed by ministers who belong to this alliance of churches. While most Baptists do not believe that baptism is necessary for salvation, they teach that faith in the Lord Jesus Christ is essential.

Second, *a regenerated church* is the doctrine that only converted souls who have been baptized by immersion are proper members of the church.

Third, *the Lord's Supper is a memorial* for Baptists, a symbolic act in which communicants testify that they remember the death of Jesus Christ. A Southern Baptist would add to this statement, "until he comes again."

Fourth, the Baptists hold for the *independence of each congregation.* The local congregation is an autonomous body and should operate through democratic processes under the direction of the Holy Spirit and the teachings of Jesus Christ. The church, they say, should not subordinate to the rule of any other religious body and is subject only to Christ, who stands at the head of each congregation.

Fifth, *separation of church and state* is insisted upon by Baptists.

Sixth, *religious liberty* is important to Baptists who assert that man is free under God in all matters of conscience and has the right to embrace or reject religion, to choose or change his faith, and to preach, teach, and worship publicly and privately, with due respect to the rights of others.

Miscellaneous Beliefs

In harmony with the beliefs of most Protestants, Baptists also teach that the New Testament is the supreme authority for determining religious truth and is the inspired word of God. Moreover, they generally believe in the Trinity; the incarnation; that men are saved by the grace of God, manifest through faith; and in a priesthood of all believers. Orthodox and liberal members of this faith are divided, however, concerning doctrines relating to the virgin birth, the fall, the atonement, and life beyond the grave, but since most Baptists are conservative, members of this denomination generally endorse the classical Protestant view.

en Stone by A.Newsam.

GEORGE FOX

The Society of Friends

11

One of the most unusual religious systems to emerge in the modern
European world was the Society of Friends. This faith, constituted during the
political turmoil of seventeenth-century England, was another powerful
movement that sprang from a profound personal experience of a conscientious leader. One of the most distinguished modern figures in this
movement, Rufus Jones (1863-1948), aptly described the founder of this
religious society, George Fox (1624-91):

> Fox ... was ... a man of unusual native capacity, of extraordinary
> depth of life, swift of insight, a born leader, a spiritual genius, a fine
> union of mystic, prophet and practical reformer, a rugged, fearless
> champion of a fresh and novel type of Christianity.[1]

Born in Fenny Drayton, Leicestershire, England, George Fox was the son
of a weaver and of a mother whom he respected as an "upright woman."
Although his parents considered directing him into the Anglican ministry,
they changed their plans and apprenticed their son to a shoemaker. As a
consequence of this decision, Fox learned a practical trade and received a
meager formal education. As a youth he was taught "to be faithful in all
things" and recalled that he "never wronged man or woman."[2] When he was
nineteen, the young man was invited by several nominal Christians to participate in a drinking bout. A custom had developed in which men continued to
drink until one refused to order another round and the individual who dared
suggest a cessation had to pay for all the liquor. Fox was grieved and highly
disturbed by the fact that members of a Christian church suggested that he
participate in such a "cankerous" vice. Abruptly leaving his associates, George
Fox completed his business and returned home. But he could not forget the

incident. Instead of sleeping that night, he remembered pacing back and forth, praying and crying to the Lord. In the midst of his anguish, Fox declared that the Lord comforted him, saying:

> Thou seest how young people go together into vanity, and old people into the earth; thou must forsake all, young and old, keep out of all, and be as a stranger unto all. [3]

On the morning following this religious experience, George Fox informed his parents that he was leaving home. When they inquired concerning his decision, he said that the Lord had instructed him to leave father and mother for His sake. Earning a livelihood as a shoemaker, Fox traveled from community to community, examining various beliefs expounded by professors of religion. This investigation led him to challenge many popular doctrines of that age. Consequently, in September 1643, George Fox not only "broke off all familiarity or fellowship" with young and old, but became a wandering seeker, initiating his quest for religious truth. [4]

During his wandering, George Fox learned the beliefs of Puritans, Separatists, and Baptists. He reclined in fields and orchards, reading the Bible. In his attempt to draw closer to the Lord, he fasted frequently and prayed fervently. As the months passed, Fox became increasingly disturbed with the sin prevalent in society and with what he regarded as deficiencies in the religions of his age. After concluding that none of the preachers were teaching the pure gospel of Christ, he said he heard a voice which declared, "There is one, even Christ Jesus, that can speak to thy condition." As Fox listened, his heart leaped with joy. He testified that the Lord commenced revealing to him heavenly wisdom. He learned, he said, that the Lord does not dwell in churches, temples, or holy places, but in the hearts of men. Everyone is enlightened by the "divine light of Christ." Although it shines in all of us, Fox declared, most people, even Christians, deny this light, hate it, and refuse to communicate with God. [5]

Four years after leaving home, the wandering Seeker became a traveling preacher. This stormy ministry began after Fox decided that a formal education was not an essential prerequisite for teaching others the gospel of Christ. His convictions precipitated a denunciation of salaried, professional clergy and of all historic Christian creeds. Such criticism encountered violent, brutal opposition, but the oppression did not prevent him from proclaiming his innermost convictions.

As early as 1650 a nickname for the followers of Fox was popularized. While George Fox was being interrogated by Justice Gervase Bennett at the time of his incarceration in the Derby jail, Fox told the judge to tremble at the word of the Lord. Replying to this admonition, Bennett called the prisoner a "quaker." Possibly the judge employed this term of reproach because it had been used previously to describe members of this movement who sometimes trembled or quivered with religious emotions.[6]

Meanwhile, the earliest disciples of Fox called themselves "Children of the Light" or "Friends." After 1665 the official name of this religious community became the Society of Friends; eventually, as the name Quaker lost its derogatory connotation, Friends incorporated this nickname into their patterns of expression.[7]

As this religious movement gained converts in the British Isles and spread to the western hemisphere, persecution intensified. Fox and his disciples were imprisoned and whipped by angry spectators. According to Fox, more than 1,000 Friends were incarcerated in 1656; in the winter of 1661 about 4,000 were placed in dungeons. Modern historians have estimated that between 1661 and 1689 approximately 12,000 Quakers were imprisoned in England and of these more than 300 died during their confinement.[8]

During the last half of the seventeenth century, hostility against these Protestants was as evident in the English mainland colonies as in Great Britain. After Quaker missionaries converted a few Virginians in the 1650s, political leaders enacted laws forbidding these Christians from settling, preaching, and worshipping in that colony. Meanwhile, the first Quakers, two lady missionaries who landed in what is today New York City, were promptly imprisoned and shortly thereafter expelled.

At the same time the Quakers were encountering opposition in Virginia and New Netherlands, they introduced their faith in New England. The earliest followers of Fox in the Bay colony were not only fined, whipped, imprisoned, and banished, but their bodies were mutilated by branding and by the clipping of their ears and tongues. Two male itinerants and one female missionary were also executed for violating a Massachusetts statute. The crime committed by these Friends was that they had returned to that colony after being banished on pain of death.

Eventually, members of the Society of Friends found several havens in America where they could worship in peace. In 1681, after the earliest Quaker immigrants were granted the right to settle in Rhode Island, New Jersey, and several other English mainland colonies, William Penn, a convert to this faith, was given a territorial grant by the English monarch. Although the king justified his actions by claiming that this charter was issued in return for a debt owed to Penn's father, possibly a paramount reason for this action was the king's desire to remove from England individuals classified as undesirable dissenters. Shortly after receiving this charter, Penn launched a "Holy Experiment" in Pennsylvania which included the right of good people of all religious persuasions to worship in peace. Many industrious Quakers were attracted to this province, settling mainly in and near Philadelphia. There they prospered and invited others to join them in building a land of liberty.

Viewing the development of this faith, it almost seems as though the early

Quakers thrived on persecution, for their growth during the first turbulent decades of their history was remarkable. In 1660, out of a population of approximately five million there were possibly 30,000 to 40,000 Friends in England and Wales, and by the end of the seventeenth century, there were probably more than 50,000 Friends in Great Britain and approximately 40,000 in the Western Hemisphere.[9] In 1688, after toleration was extended to Protestants throughout England and her American colonies, the rapidity of growth declined. In 1800, after a century of toleration, there were not appreciably more Quakers living in the world than there had been during the first five decades of the movement's history. Today the world membership is not significantly larger than it was in 1700; in 1971 the total membership of seven different bodies of Quakers in this country was about 127,000 and the world population, including the American Friends, was slightly over 200,000.

These membership statistics prompt individuals to ask why there was such a spectacular growth in the number of Quaker converts during its formative years and why the membership has remained relatively constant for more than 270 years.

Many factors explain the immediate popularity of Quakerism. The Friends' emphasis on equality and plainness of speech and dress appealed to many, especially those who were not classified as aristocrats. Fox's rejection of religious ritual and formalism, his emphasis on individual spiritual experiences, his humanitarian concerns, and his extension of the right to lay members and women to preach and participate in religious services and other meetings were powerful attractive forces. Salaried preachers who delivered sermons were replaced in the worship services by a membership who spoke or prayed as the Spirit directed. After Quakers gathered in homes or unadorned meetinghouses, they meditated. There was no opening prayer or singing of hymns. Silence was interrupted when a man or woman stood and spoke. According to Quaker belief, the person would then relate a message which was revealed through the Spirit of the Lord. Such a pattern of worship was appealing to many who were not satisfied with the ritual or the emphasis on preaching that characterized other denominations.

After its initial success, however, Quakerism lost some of its original vitality. The missionary zeal of the third generation of Quakers was not as apparent as among the earliest converts; during the nineteenth century, most attempts to spread this movement by means of direct proselyting activities were discontinued. Meanwhile, many children of the original converts lacked spiritual enthusiasm; prior to the American Revolution congregations of Friends seemed to have languished in sections of Delaware and in other parts of the American wilderness. During the American Revolution, this movement was further weakened as a consequence of the Quaker opposition to war. Following the birth of the new nation, influences from other denominations, strict membership requirements, and frequent excommunications—sometimes for marrying outside the faith—also hindered the growth of this religious community.

The strength of the movement also seemed to have been sapped partly as a consequence of debilitating schisms. While Fox contended that all men can know God and derive knowledge from the Lord without any intermediary in the form of church, sacrament, priest, or sacred scripture, some members felt differently about the Inner Light. Leaders of the faith were unable to agree on precise principles or procedures that would enable members to differentiate between truth and error or human reasoning and messages conveyed by the Spirit of God.

During the early history of this religious community, theological harmony in many congregations was maintained by employing the writings of Robert Barclay (1648-90) as a guide of religious truth. Barclay was a disciple of Fox who crystallized and defended with scriptural references the basic views of the founder of this denomination. In 1673 he published a Quaker *Catechism* and three years later brought forth his influential *Apology for the True Christian Divinity* (1676). In his writings, which passed through many editions and were widely circulated in this country, Barclay mentioned his belief in a trinitarian God who can only be known by the Spirit. Denying that Adam's sin was directly imputed to man, he described with an Arminian flavor his convictions concerning the fall and atonement, emphasizing man's vital role in the salvation experience. Barclay described in his popular works the Quaker belief in the Inner Light, and referred to the Bible as an important secondary source of religious truth which contained revelations of God to ancient saints. Considering life beyond the grave, this influential Quaker apologist felt that all men, regardless of their religious affiliation, would be judged according to their understanding and response to law and to the Inner Light. Moreover, Barclay rejected all outward, physical sacraments, and identified true worship as waiting and watching for the Light of Christ and then proclaiming to others the word and will of God.

While selections from Barclay's *Apology* served as a norm of faith in some Quaker societies, three emphases were visible in the early republic that shattered Quaker unity. Religious liberalism strengthened the Quaker tendency to resist creedal statements but carried this characteristic "to the point where it was scarcely necessary to believe anything in order to be a Quaker."[10] Meanwhile, an evangelical movement insisted on the endorsement of prescribed beliefs; while the liberal faction within this community became more tolerant of variations of faith, the evangelic wing remained intolerant of deviations from the classical theology. A third emphasis apparent among Quakers of the early nineteenth century was quietism, a mystic spirit based upon following the Divine Light.

By the middle of the nineteenth century, theological diversity had separated the American Quakers into at least three major bodies called the Hicksite, Wilburite, and Gurneyite Friends. After one observer investigated the Hicksite-Orthodox split, he confessed in bewilderment, "I didn't know you had enough theology to split over."[11]

Another aspect of this ecclesiastical movement has been the genuine concern of Friends for the welfare of others. In harmony with the teachings of George Fox, eighteenth-century Quakers led an attack on slavery, the first denomination in this land to do so. Influenced by the actions of two Quaker humanitarians, John Woolman (1720-72) and Anthony Benezet (1713-84), the Philadelphia Yearly Meeting repudiated slavery in 1758 and then in 1776 expelled all members who kept slaves. Yearly meetings organized in the South, however, were not as forceful in their actions against slaveholders. In the early republic, other Quaker leaders, such as Benjamin Lundy (1789-1839), continued the abolitionist crusade, denouncing all who supported the institution of slavery and aiding blacks who were seeking freedom in the northern states and Canada.

Members of this society have been interested in other social reform programs as well. Elizabeth Fry (1780-1845) gained a reputation for promoting prison reform in Great Britain. Dorothea Dix (1802-87) is recognized for her efforts to secure improved treatment of the insane. Susan B. Anthony (1820-1906) was a pioneer social worker, temperance leader, and advocate of woman and Negro suffrage.

In harmony with the Quaker heritage of concern for the oppressed, the American Friends Service Committee was organized in 1917 to assist English Friends with relief work in devastated regions of France, and to give conscientious objectors and others a constructive alternative to military duty through various forms of service. After the war the organization continued. During its history, the "AFSC" has sponsored many programs to promote international peace, to provide food, clothing, medical and social services to others, and to establish equal rights for all men and women, regardless of their race, creed, or nationality.

The Quaker spirit of humanitarianism, of equality, and of cooperation is reflected not only in their pattern of faith and worship and their social action programs, but also in their church organization and their Monthly, Quarterly, and Yearly Meetings. Every member, for example, may participate in the Monthly Meeting. When they gather at these sessions, Friends consider local church issues, such as Sabbath meetings, church property, and service projects. All, including men and women, have the same rights. No votes are taken, and decisions are made only after a unity of thought is clearly expressed. If there is no consensus of opinion, decisions are postponed for later discussion.

A Quarterly Meeting is formed by the assembly of members from several

Monthly Meetings. Four times a year these representatives gather to worship and consider business pertaining to their common interest.

The Yearly Meeting is an annual gathering in which Friends discuss issues on a much larger scope than is possible in other assemblies. Committees present their proposals for peace, social justice, race relations, education, temperance, and the advancement of other humanitarian goals, and Friends, by consensus or by employing democratic procedures, render decisions.

One of the largest organizations of Quakers is the Friends' General Conference, a national body comprising eight Yearly Meetings. This group is a Quaker body designed to promote fellowship and unite the actions of Quakers living in different parts of the country.[12]

Although there are various Yearly Meetings in America (five distinct Yearly Meetings are organized in Ohio), all representing different wings of the Quaker movement, there was a tendency, following World War I, for American Quakers to form organizations designed to reunite their members, to forget their differences, and to work harmoniously toward common objectives. Consequently, while major divisions within the movement have continued, the boundaries separating members are in some instances being weakened by Friends who are striving to identify beliefs which best represent their historic tradition.

Throughout the history of this movement education has had a high priority. Quakers held that everyone, including tradesmen, should secure the best possible education. In many instances, where there were no schools, Friends established educational institutions. Currently many members of this faith have received exceptional training in Quaker or public schools.

Like other religious communions, Quakerism has experienced many changes during its history. The plain Quaker clothing in most instances has disappeared, and the traditional language has been replaced by modern terminology. No longer are men and women separated in most gatherings; men now sit on the women's side of the aisle and women occupy benches once restricted to men. Music and pastoral sermons have been introduced in many American Quaker services. In this pastoral system, unprogrammed meetings have been retained but in some instances these meetings are held apart from the more formal services, or are incorporated into a Sabbath service in which the focal point is a sermon delivered by a full-time professional minister. The beliefs of some contemporary Quakers are similar in many respects to those popularized by modern theologians who are reinterpreting classical Protestantism. According to some Friends residing in twentieth-century America, life's quality, not adherence to particular forms or creeds or methods of worship, is the essence of true religion.[13] Even though the enthusiasm of the early Quaker missionaries has subsided, the spirit of toleration, of equality, and of concern for others, as reflected in the teachings of George Fox, has continued to dominate the convictions of many members of the Society of Friends.

Distinguishing Beliefs

Since most Friends of the twentieth century no longer embrace many beliefs popularized by Robert Barclay and a wide latitude of belief exists among these Christians, it is difficult to identify many distinguishing characteristics of contemporary Quaker theology. "Many, or most theological questions are left for the individual to decide." According to many Friends, "The essence of Christian faith is a way of life. Theological matters, such as original sin and our subsequent redemption by the sacrificial death of Jesus, the literal acceptance of the Bible, the mysterious union of the divine and human in Jesus Christ, life after death, and others are to be interpreted according to individual insight and growth." Another explanation of the current theological position of many Friends is that "Quakerism presents the believer with . . . challenges rather than imposing a standardized creed or rule of faith. This condition enhances growth of vision and understanding." [14]

Although changes have taken place in Quaker theology, there are a few beliefs that represent their distinct historical heritage that have remained popular. In harmony with the views of their earliest leaders, Quakers of today teach that there are two sources for determining religious truth, the Inner Light and the Bible. Every man, they assert, has the Inner Light (called the Seed, the Truth, the Light of Christ, and That of God in Every Man), and when individuals unite with this spirit, they can learn truth as did the prophets of old. They also teach that the Bible represents an important phase of man's spiritual history, and although they believe that this work contains mistranslations and errors of addition and omission, it is viewed as a book which informs man of the will of God as revealed to the ancient saints.

Quakers have also retained their peculiar belief concerning baptism and the Lord's Supper. While they teach that man should be cleansed spiritually, they say that baptism should be considered as occurring in a spiritual sense, without employing water. They further hold that the communion should be considered as the nourishing spirit of God in a purely symbolic sense.

Friends also emphasize the principle of religious liberty, separation of church and state, and the equality of men and women. Traditionally, they have also been opposed to war; many Friends are conscientious objectors. Moreover, they are often active leaders of various humanitarian programs.

12

The Unitarian
Universalist Society

During the sixteenth century there lived in western Europe a bold Spanish theologian named Michael Servetus. Servetus dared challenge the popular beliefs regarding God, baptism, and life beyond the grave and as a result was burned in effigy by the Catholics and at the stake by the Protestants. This Spaniard lived in an age when many leaders were earnestly attempting to recover the purity of the primitive Christian church. Inspired by the quest of other reformers, this freelance theologian joined the band of inquiring crusaders by reevaluating the traditional belief regarding God.

Fourteen years after Luther posted his Ninety-five Theses in Wittenberg, Servetus published a work entitled *On the Errors of the Trinity* (1531) which circulated widely and created an immediate storm in many European communities.[1] In many lands, Servetus was branded as a heretic and was hunted like a dangerous criminal. The uncompromising inquirer failed to realize that most Christians of the sixteenth century persistently held that the dogma of the Trinity should be encased in a sacred sanctuary and that no one should question decisions hammered out during generations of ecumenical debates.

In August 1553 Servetus was discovered in Geneva, promptly arrested, and accused of challenging the writings of the celebrated French theologian, John Calvin. "I was merely passing through the town," Servetus declared. "I was only planning on staying overnight. I am on my way to Naples to practice medicine. And I have not," he insisted, "attacked Calvin. It is true we disagree on theological issues; but a local, secular court should not be concerned with conflicting religious beliefs existing between citizens of different lands." His preliminary defense was considered inadequate and for months Servetus was kept in chains in a cold, dreary cell. His damp clothes hung on his freezing body for weeks without change. "Fleas are devouring me," Servetus grumbled. "My shoes are torn to pieces; and I have nothing clean to wear."[2]

Part of his trial consisted of his written duel with John Calvin. After months of bitter arguing, the court determined that Servetus had lost his debate with Calvin and was guilty of obstinate, incurable heresy. Servetus, the verdict read, had denounced the Trinity and had referred to the baptism of infants as an invention of the devil. Although Calvin urged that the dissenter be beheaded, the court ruled that he should be burned as a heretic.

After the trial, the wretched body of Servetus was chained tightly to a stake and placed over a pile of wood. His controversial book was forced under one of the chains which bound his body. A crown of straw and leaves sprinkled with sulphur was scornfully placed on his head. Then the executioner ignited the fire. Within a half-hour Servetus's agonizing screams were replaced by groans and then silence. The hunted heretic was dead.[3]

Michael Servetus was not the only nor the last theologian of the Reformation era to be executed for espousing anti-Trinitarian convictions. Between the end of the fourth and the middle of the sixteenth century, most outspoken critics of the Trinity were savagely persecuted. Throughout these intolerant years, however, a few Christians thoughtfully questioned the Nicene concept of God. The questioning led to reevaluations. The reevaluations precipitated an anti-Trinitarian movement and from this liberal tradition the modern Unitarian society emerged.[4]

As early as the second half of the sixteenth century, an anti-Trinitarian movement appeared in Poland, Hungary, and Transylvania, the forested region lying east of the Great Plain of Hungary. After the writings of Servetus were circulated in these lands, many Christians rejected the popular view of God as being three persons of one essence. In 1558 an Italian physician, Giorgio Blandrata (c. 1515-88), sought refuge in Poland where he promoted the emerging anti-Trinitarian movement. About five years later, Blandrata was summoned to be court physician in Transylvania. While there he continued to promulgate his radical views and converted an eloquent and persuasive Calvinist preacher, Francis David. Aided by a liberal edict of toleration issued by King John Sigismund, Francis David began directing the formal establishment of Unitarian societies in Transylvania in 1569.[5]

Meanwhile, Faustus Socinus (1539-1604), an Italian lay theologian, fled into Poland where he promptly became the recognized leader of the revolt against the Nicene concept of God. Socinus taught that Jesus was a mortal who did not live prior to his mortal birth but was given a secondary rule in the universe. He further insisted that this mortal teacher saved man not through his atoning sacrifice but by setting a proper example. Encouraging others to employ reason as a source of determining religious truth, Socinus insisted that many popular beliefs of that age, such as the Trinity, infant baptism, man's depravity, and unending hell were irrational, incorrect doctrines.[6]

The gradual, quiet penetration of Socinian and Arian views among English critics set the stage for a movement that began to focus on John Biddle, the recognized father of English Unitarianism. In the middle of the seventeenth century, Biddle commenced publishing boldly and clearly his Unitarian convictions by refuting the traditional belief of God as described by the Nicene Creed. Imprisoned for heresy, Biddle fell victim to the horrible conditions existing in the jails of that age and died in 1662 two days after being released from his diseased cell.[7]

Another Englishman of the seventeenth century who rejected the Nicene concept of God was the gifted poet John Milton. The innermost convictions of this illustrious writer were concealed in a work entitled *Christian Doctrine,* written for publication after his death. There is no scripture, Milton charged, informing us that Christ generated eternally from the Father; and there is no biblical passage specifying that God is three persons of one essence. The oneness of the Father and Son refers to a unity of love, charity, glory, and witness, Milton testified, but not of substance. Christ, he concluded, existed before the world was created, received from the Father a divine nature, is subject to the supreme Father, and is the mediator between God and man.[8]

After the passage of the English Toleration Act of 1689, the number of English critics of the Trinity increased saliently and some of the influential leaders of the Church of England openly avowed Arianism. One of the leaders of this movement was Samuel Clarke, who published in 1712 *The Scripture-Doctrine of the Trinity* in which he cited more than twelve hundred passages from the New Testament pertaining to the Godhead. After preparing this collection of biblical texts, Clarke concluded that the Father alone is the supreme God. Christ, he declared, is a subordinate being who existed before the creation of this world and should be worshipped as the mediator.[9]

After years of questioning and debating, one group of liberal dissenters agreed to unite and in 1774 Unitarianism was permanently organized in England. Attending the first service of this new society was an American, Benjamin Franklin, who at that time shared with many others serious doubts regarding the traditional interpretation of God.[10]

Shortly after the formal emergence of Unitarianism in England, a church of this religious persuasion was constituted in the United States at Boston, Massachusetts. In 1785 James Freeman persuaded his Anglican congregation to amend the Book of Common Prayer by revising all Trinitarian formulas and omitting from this liturgical manual the Nicene Creed and the Thirty-nine Articles. At that time the Church of England was in the process of reorganizing into the Protestant Episcopal Church; but Freeman, refusing to support this movement, steered his congregation along a new theological course.

Most early American societies that became Unitarian were formerly Congregational institutions. When members of these independent autonomous congregations hired a Unitarian preacher they suddenly transferred their

WILLIAM ELLERY CHANNING

ecclesiastical allegiance. By 1810 a majority of the pre-Revolutionary War Congregational churches of Boston had become Unitarian, and from this headquarters Unitarianism spread into other parts of New England and New York. Meanwhile, after Henry Ware became Hollis Professor of Divinity at Harvard, America's oldest college emerged as a reputable training ground for Unitarian preachers.[11]

While Unitarianism was growing in New England, Joseph Priestley, the noted English chemist, transplanted from England another form of this movement. At the end of the eighteenth century, Priestley began popularizing Socinianism in Pennsylvania, which at that time was probably the most popular form of this faith in England, but which never became one of the main historic streams of American Unitarianism. Although James Freeman had been a Socinian, most of the early Unitarian converts of New England in the late eighteenth and early nineteenth centuries adopted an Arian belief. Priestley's Socinian form of Unitarianism differed sharply from the New England Arian Unitarianism in that Priestley rejected Christ's premortal existence and denied His divinity.[12]

Theologically speaking, Unitarianism in early America was not only an anti-Trinitarian movement but it was also a reaction against many other forms of traditional Catholicism and Protestantism. Unitarians residing in the new nation rebelled against the belief that Adam's sin was imputed to mankind, that the Bible was infallible and should be regarded as the sole norm of faith. They further denied that the fall of Adam was a historical event and failed to recognize any necessity for an atonement, concluding that men were reconciled to God by following the exemplary teachings of the Savior. Early Unitarians were also assiduous critics of the doctrine of predestination and agreed that all creeds and confessions were but the commandments of men.[13]

Early American Unitarianism was also in most instances a reaction against Deism, the religion of the Enlightenment. This religion was a philosophy in which most adherents rejected all biblical miracles and denied the divinity of Christ. In the opinion of most Deists, God was a distant creator who allowed natural laws to operate the universe without any interference or sustaining help.

During the years preceding the Civil War, Unitarianism, especially in New England and New York, was not nearly as extreme as Deism. The Unitarian God was not impersonal or remote. Moreover, most Unitarians of the early republic accepted many of the biblical miracles and regarded the Bible as a valuable source for determining religious truth. In addition to believing that the Bible contained the word of God, they generally agreed that the purity of the scriptures had been altered by errors of addition, omission, and mistranslation; most insisted that reason should be adopted as another indispensable guide for determining religious truth. While members of this faith generally proclaimed that there was only one supreme God, most agreed with the foremost early leader of this movement, William Ellery Channing, when he declared that Christ was an inferior God and that the Holy Spirit was an influence emanating from the Father. [14]

Since a significant alteration in the beliefs of Unitarians has taken place during the past hundred years, the opinions of most modern Unitarians are more in harmony with the views of the Deists, Socinians, and transcendentalists of former ages than with the convictions of most Unitarians living in early America. The theology popularized by William E. Channing has been replaced by more liberal concepts, and moderns sometimes refer to the father of American Unitarianism as an Arian rather than a Unitarian. Unitarians, therefore, claim as members of their religious movement innumerable liberal thinkers who questioned the orthodox Christianity of their ages. Included in this list of former Unitarians are a number of the early presidents of the United States, such as John Adams, Thomas Jefferson, James Madison, and John Quincy Adams. Unitarians also include in their list of illustrious proponents Daniel Webster, John Marshall, Florence Nightingale, Clara Barton, Susan B. Anthony, Dorothea Dix, Charles Darwin, Horace Mann, and Albert Schweitzer. They also claim as official or unofficial members a prolific number of famous authors, among whom are Charles Dickens, Ralph Waldo Emerson, Henry David Thoreau, Walt Whitman, Henry Wadsworth Longfellow, Oliver Wendell Holmes, William Cullen Bryant, James Russell Lowell, Louisa May Alcott, Mark Twain, Bret Harte, and Thomas Wolfe. [15]

While Unitarianism emerged as a reaction against the popular medieval concept of God, Universalism arose in part because many Christians refused to endorse the medieval view of an unending hell. Universalists replaced the concept of an everlasting punishment for unregenerates with the belief in the final, universal salvation of all moral beings from sin and death. Throughout the Middle Ages and during the era of the Reformation critics expressed a belief in the salvation of all mankind, but it was not until after the Reformation that the modern Universalist society was constituted.

In the middle of the eighteenth century, after many seeds of theological revisions had been planted, James Relly organized a group of believers into the first English Universalist Church. One of the followers of Relly, John Murray, subsequently inaugurated the formal organization of Universalism in the United States in 1779. This movement, like Unitarianism, spread from Massachusetts into other parts of New England and New York, but did not attract many converts in the South.

The strength of Universalism in the new nation was dissipated by theological disputes and schisms that divided many congregations. Although Universalists were bound together by the belief in universal salvation, members disagreed vehemently as to whether or not there would be any punishment hereafter for the less valiant children of God. Some contended that immediately after death, the righteous would enter a place of peace and happiness

JOHN MURRAY

while the wicked would enter a state of remorse called the spirit prison. After Christ's crucifixion, some explained, the Savior preached to the spirits in prison and all, through the persuasive power of God, will eventually be converted and welcomed into heaven. Other Universalists of the early republic held that after death all mankind would immediately enter heaven. Members also disagreed regarding baptism (candidates for and mode of baptism), the concept of God (some endorsed the Arian view and others the Trinitarian), and the Lord's Supper (some did not perceive the need for any sacraments).[16]

Although opponents of this movement censured Universalists for encouraging licentious behavior, Universalists replied to such charges by insisting that in order to obtain genuine happiness in this life men must learn to live in harmony with the exemplary teachings of Christ.[17] When we deviate from such a guide we suffer hell on earth.

As the nineteenth century drew to a close, liberal concepts increased among members of this faith and the theological affinity of the Universalists and Unitarians increased. Recognizing parallels of belief, leaders of these societies sought unification and in 1961 the two societies merged, creating a voluntary association of independent churches in the United States and Canada.

Although the Unitarian Universalist Association currently reports a membership of less than 200,000, their leaders insist that most people who endorse Unitarian convictions have not officially united with the society. They also specify that this movement is a thinking man's religion in which seventy-seven percent of the members have college degrees. It is a faith that appeals especially to educated professional men and scientifically oriented individuals residing in urban America.[18]

Today there is a tremendous latitude of belief among members of this association. Although the society endorses no specific creed, every member is encouraged to prepare his own articles of faith and to continually revise his beliefs as his understanding increases. This society is also one of the few religious movements in America in which atheists, agnostics, and theists worship comfortably together and freely express their convictions. They agree that there is possibly no more than one God and sometimes jokingly admit that members of this church pray "to whom it may concern." [19]

Another characteristic of this movement is that Unitarian Universalists regard their institution as a social and educational agency inspiring man to advance freedom of conscience, promote truth, guard the democratic processes in human relations, and foster the establishment of a universal brotherhood in the world.[20] One of the major thrusts of this movement in contemporary America is the conscientious support which members give to many social action programs, including the Red Cross, agencies of the United Nations, women's rights, and the modern movement of Planned Parenthood.

The beliefs of one member of this society were clearly summarized a few years ago in an advertisement appearing in a community newspaper:

Do Unitarians
Believe in
Anything?

We believe in brotherhood; . . . in Civil rights; in the United Nations; in upgrading our educational system; in an attack on the problems of poverty; in the nuclear test ban treaty. . . . Many of us even believe in God. [21]

Distinguishing Beliefs

There are a multitude of beliefs held by members of the Unitarian Universalist Association that differ from the convictions of most other Christians. The following beliefs represent the unusual flavor of their pattern of thinking.

According to Unitarian Universalists, there is no scriptural warranty for the dogma of the Trinity. The belief is generally considered a doctrine of no religious value. Some members are theists, others are agnostics, and some are atheists.

Most members of this association believe that the Bible does not teach that Jesus was God, but conveys the idea that Jesus was a religious leader (a Messiah), a man, not an all-powerful, infallible divine being. Jesus of Nazareth is cherished along with Moses, Buddah, and many other great teachers as a naturally inspired leader.

The Unitarian Universalist Association endorses no creed. Every individual is not only free to form his own religious beliefs, but is encouraged to do so. Although the Bible is considered a valuable account of man's experiences, it is not viewed as an infallible guide to ecclesiastical truth. They say that since Biblical writers were subject to error and taught incorrect religious concepts, doctrines should not be endorsed solely because they are taught in this history.

Members of this faith also generally teach that beliefs should not be viewed as a body of unchanging doctrines but should be considered in the light of continual growth. The ultimate source of truth is man, they contend; and reason and emotional response are generally substituted in this movement for divine inspiration and revelation.

The increasingly dominant belief of this faith is concern with the present life; emphasis on freedom and peace; promotion of an idealistic gospel of social programs built upon the philosophies of men; and humanism, the exaltation of man at the exclusion of divine elements. [22]

Members of this religious community also teach that man, who is a product of evolution and stands high on the evolutionary stages of life, is essentially good and is invested with inestimable potential. This optimistic view of man's nature does not suggest, however, that man does not sin; although man is subject to error, he is considered capable of creating a harmonious society based on justice and cooperation.

Biblical accounts of events such as the fall and atonement are sometimes classified by Unitarian Universalists with Aesop's fables or other such narratives, although some would say that Aesop's fables contain more ethical concepts than most orthodox Christian views of the fall and atonement. Mythology is generally regarded as a means of communicating elements of truth in a particular and important form. [23]

The need for sacraments has been eliminated by members of this association. Baptism of infants and, less frequently, of adults, by sprinkling is sometimes performed, but this rite is regarded solely as a symbolic act of dedication. In the case of infant baptism, parents make covenants for their children. The Lord's Supper is also administered in many of their societies, and this rite, like baptism, is viewed in symbolic terms. Since sacraments are not emphasized nor considered necessary, Unitarian Universalists regard the concept of authority as an irrelevant belief. [24]

Unitarian Universalists generally emphasize the present life rather than a life beyond the grave. Rejecting the traditional Catholic and Protestant view of a heaven and hell, most members of this faith "respect deeply the ruling passion for a continuous life." The nature of this future existence, however, is considered beyond man's definite knowledge. [25]

Part Three
Native American Religions

The Christian (Disciples of Christ) Society and Church of Christ

13

While a majority of the major religions in this land are transplanted faiths, some of the largest denominations in the United States are indigenous to the American soil and after their inception were transplanted to nations throughout the world. The majority of these well-known native American faiths were constituted during the nineteenth century, especially between 1830 and 1890, and most of these societies are currently distinguished by their theological orthodoxy and their missionary zeal.

The first religious development in America that precipitated the creation of a number of enduring religious societies was the restorationist movement. Following the American Revolution, a number of theologians vehemently condemned all the popular creeds of Christendom. Urging all disciples of Christ to return to the purity of New Testament Christianity, these preachers taught that the Bible should be regarded as the only standard of faith, that every congregation should be autonomous, and that all men are endowed with the capacity to accept or reject God's gift of salvation. Although these resolute leaders were divided concerning the doctrine of the Godhead, they rejected the use of the term "Trinity," claiming that such a word was unscriptural. Some of these modern reformers were Arians, holding that the Father and Son were separate and distinct beings or spirits, while others believed that the Father and Son were of the same divine essence.

One of the remarkable characteristics of the early American restorationist movement was that it sprang forth almost simultaneously in many different parts of the new nation and was initiated by leaders who were formerly affiliated with a variety of Protestant faiths. About 1793 James O'Kelly, a North Carolinian who had been one of the outstanding Methodist preachers in the South, launched this reorientation of Christian thinking. Rejecting what were considered authoritarian characteristics of Methodism, O'Kelly helped organize independent congregations in Virginia and North Carolina which eventually adopted the name "Christian Church." During the initial months of its inception, about one thousand joined this religious community. By 1809 this faith reported about 20,000 members, most living in Virginia and North Carolina and western regions settled by emigrants from these two coastal states. [1]

Shortly after southern farmers united in their pursuit of New Testament Christianity, Abner Jones and Elias Smith initiated a similar movement in Vermont. Withdrawing from Calvinist Baptist societies, these two men organized autonomous congregations in Vermont and other New England states. From New England the restorationist movement spread into New York, Pennsylvania, and Ohio and by 1830 reported 50,000 followers, including settlers living in Alabama and Missouri and states situated north and east of these outlying regions.[2] Rejecting the historic creeds and all the churches then constituted in America, the followers of Jones and Smith endorsed the name "Christian denomination," but they also called themselves Eastern Christians or members of the Christian Connexion.

Early in the nineteenth century, the Eastern Christian faith expanded into many sections of the new nation and formed a loose alliance with the followers of O'Kelly. After Christians living in the South recognized their affinity with the Eastern Christians, a national advisory body was organized in 1808. Although this general conference was divided in 1854 as a consequence of the slavery issue, it was reunited in 1894. Then in 1931 many of these independent societies, especially those located in New England and other northern states, combined with the Congregational Church and thirty years later helped form the United Church of Christ. [3]

Another wing of the restorationist movement emerged in Kentucky under the leadership of Barton Stone. Prior to his ordination as a Presbyterian minister, Stone confessed that he had rejected predestination and the popular view of the Trinity in favor of the Arminian view of free will and the Arian belief that the Father and Son are two distinct beings. When Stone was asked during his preordination interview, "Do you receive and adopt the [Westminister] Confession of Faith?," he recalled saying, "I do, as far as I see it consistent with the Word of God." Doctrinal differences, however, led him to withdraw from the jurisdiction of the Presbyterian Synod at Lexington, Kentucky, and in 1803 Stone and four associates formed the Springfield Presbytery. One year later they dissolved the presbytery, organized independent congregations, and initiated a program designed to restore the Apostolic Church. Denouncing what they called "man-made creeds," these leaders urged others to acknowledge the Bible as their only rule of faith and practice, to endorse the exclusive use of the name of Christian, and to unite under the banner of universal charity. [4]

While many Americans were contemplating a religious restitution, Alexander Campbell, one of the most celebrated and influential restoration theologians, began his quest to reestablish the ancient Christian order. Campbell's faith in the popular creeds of Christendom had been shaken while studying theology in Scotland. When he arrived in America in 1809 he united with his father, Thomas Campbell, in rejecting all denominations and endorsing the New Testament as the only guide for religious truth. In that same year, Thomas Campbell had withdrawn from the Presbyterian Church and had organized the Christian Association of Washington County, Pennsylvania, an event that is sometimes heralded as the beginning of a new religious society. In his *Declaration and Address* (1809) this former Presbyterian preacher, who had preceded his son to America, outlined a program designed to cure the problems of fragmented Protestantism by returning to the pure teachings of the apostles of Christ.

A few years after Alexander Campbell pledged his allegiance to the principles outlined in his father's *Declaration and Address,* he was immersed by a Baptist elder and led the independent congregation of about thirty who supported him into the Baptist fold. One year later, in 1813, he united this society (called Brush Run) with the Redstone Baptist Association. After joining that alliance, Campbell denounced all popular confessions of faith and rationalized that instead of submitting to these Baptist representatives a traditional creed, he had presented a declaration of belief that was not binding as a term of communion. As this nominal Baptist continued to expound unorthodox views, he encountered increased opposition. Consequently, in 1823, he became pastor of a Baptist society in Wellsburg, West Virginia (then Virginia), composed mainly of members dismissed from his former congregation. Although most Baptists insisted that Campbell was not loyal to the historic faith, the controversial leader was welcomed in 1824 into the Mahoning Association. Shortly after this Baptist alliance had been formed (primarily by individuals living in eastern Ohio), many of its members weighed sympathetically the restorative ideas popularized by Alexander Campbell. [5]

The basic beliefs of Campbell were fanned into many parts of the early republic through his publication, *The Christian Baptist.* In 1824, one year after the inception of this periodical, Campbell began a series of thirty-two articles entitled "A Restoration of the Ancient Order of Things." "All the famous reformations in history," he said, were alterations "of creeds and of clergy" rather than of religions; all these reorientations of Christian thinking had "left religion where it was." "Human creeds," he added, have been "reformed and re-reformed" but have remained "erroneous." [6]

While Alexander Campbell was contending that in many respects the teachings of contemporary churches failed to harmonize with New Testament standards, Walter Scott presented in eastern Ohio a doctrine which became one of the distinguishing beliefs of the Disciples of Christ. In September

1827, shortly after Scott was called by the Mahoning Association to preach in Ohio unbound to any creed or congregation, he enumerated six basic principles of the gospel: faith, repentance, believer's baptism, remission of sins, reception of the Holy Ghost, and eternal life. One contemporary reported that after Scott proclaimed these views of salvation in Braceville, Ohio, "great excitement" erupted. "It was common practice," this same observer claimed,

> for him [Walter Scott] to illustrate the five items [leading to eternal life] ... by holding up his left hand and using his thumb for Faith, and so on; then contrast it with the five points of Calvinism; and thus he made the Scripture order of the gospel so plain, that little boys could carry it home.[7]

Although a few Baptist congregations withdrew from alliances of Baptist societies or were expelled from associations in the late 1820s because of their endorsement of Campbell's views, many historians date the rise of a new denomination, the Disciples of Christ, with the dissolving of the Mahoning Association in August 1830. When delegates assembled in Austintown for their annual meeting, they severed all connections with the Baptist faith by agreeing to discontinue their annual gatherings and return to the primitive purity of New Testament Christianity.[8]

Shortly before the Mahoning Association was dissolved, Campbell commenced publishing another periodical, *The Millennial Harbinger* (which soon replaced *The Christian Baptist*), in which he announced that groups were already restoring the ancient gospel and predicted that his blissful revolution would produce a state in society far surpassing the righteousness, peace, and joy that had resulted from any previous revolt since the great apostasy from Christian institutions.

Although Campbell believed that the "Reforming Baptists" who contended for the "ancient gospel" could "legitimately assume the name 'Christian,' " he preferred not to use that title for he did not want to be identified with the Eastern Christian movement led by Abner Jones and Elias Smith. While Campbell recognized many parallels between his convictions and those espoused by Jones and Smith, he concluded that Eastern Christians had failed to restore the gospel as taught by those who were called "Christians first at Antioch." They did not immerse for the remission of sins, Campbell said, and they incorrectly believed that the Father and Son were separate and distinct beings. Consequently, to avoid being confused with the Eastern Christians, Campbell suggested that individuals who endorsed his interpretations of the New Testament continue calling their local congregations "churches of Christ" and refer to the people and the general movement as the "Disciples of Christ." Meanwhile, this reformer vehemently opposed the popular designation of "Campbellites," for he insisted that Christians should not be identified by the names of human leaders.[10]

Even though Alexander Campbell did not unite his followers with Eastern Christians, he agreed with Barton Stone in 1832 to encourage unity among those who endorsed their basic convictions. Since these leaders did not claim authority to establish a national organization, they advised their followers to cooperate rather than compete. While many Christians and Disciples adopted fellowshipping programs, some groups refused to enter an alliance or other cooperative adventure. So, throughout its history, this denomination has remained essentially a fellowship of autonomous congregations.

The merging of the forces launched by Campbell and Stone is most remarkable when one examines the conflicting beliefs of these two influential leaders and realizes that Campbell failed to unite with Eastern Christians because of theological diversities. Campbell and Stone, for example, disagreed on the frequency of administering the Lord's Supper; Campbell insisted that the ordinance should be administered weekly while Stone concluded that a less frequent administration was more desirable. Eventually Campbell's suggestion became one of the identifying characteristics of the Sabbath services of the Disciples of Christ. Another issue precipitating conflict centered on the subject of baptism. Was baptism by immersion essential for salvation and entrance into the church? Stone replied, "No." Campbell, however, contended that this ordinance was necessary for entrance into the church and was God's method of "formally" remitting sins. Moreover, the two men disagreed on the concept of the Godhead, Stone being an Arian and Campbell asserting that the Father and Son are of the same divine essence. The proper name for this denomination also served as a factor creating discord. Stone and most of his followers recommended that they retain the title of "Christians," while Campbell preferred the name, "Disciples." [11] This latter issue has not yet been fully resolved, for various congregations have retained their favorite identification. In 1957, however, a main branch of this movement adopted the name "International Convention of Christian Churches (Disciples of Christ)."

During its formative years, the Disciples rode the wave of the frontier as its crest swept across the prairies of western America. After Stone's thousands combined in 1832 with the twenty or thirty thousand Disciples, the community witnessed constant conversions. By mid-century there were more than 100,000 adherents; during the decade preceding the Civil War, almost a twofold increase occurred. Not suffering from the debilitating effects of the slavery issue which plagued many American churches, the Disciples continued to grow during and after the temporary disruption of American democracy. In 1870 there were approximately 350,000 members and in 1890 the number had reached more than one-half million. [12]

The most devastating schism in this denomination occurred in the twentieth century at a time when its membership was more than one million. [13] In 1906 the conservative wing of the movement rebelled against the endorsement of missionary societies and the use of organs in their Sabbath services. While these latter two innovations (which were considered out of harmony with teachings of the New Testament) precipitated the rupture, the appearance of liberal tendencies among Disciples served as the primary underlying force that led to the rise of the Church of Christ.

During the first half of the twentieth century, the Church of Christ was one of the fastest growing religious societies in America, and its growth has continued during the past few years when some communions are concerned about the lack of increase or the loss of membership. While a growing minority of Disciples in contemporary America are reinterpreting classical Protestantism, members of the Church of Christ continue to be identified by their orthodoxy, with some members advancing many beliefs popularized by fundamentalists.

Although Christians, Disciples, and members of the Church of Christ have not adopted any articles of faith, they have endorsed a slogan which aptly characterizes their theological heritage:

> No book but the Bible.
> No name but the divine.
> No plea but the gospel.
> No aim but to save.
> In Christ—unity.
> In opinions—liberty.
> In all things—charity.

Distinguishing Beliefs

There are many parallels in the teachings of Christians (Disciples of Christ) and Baptists. For example, Disciples generally endorse most of the distinguishing beliefs that characterize the Baptist faith: (1) believer's baptism by immersion, (2) regenerated church, (3) Lord's Supper as a memorial, (4) autonomy of each congregation, (5) religious liberty, and (6) separation of church and state.

There are, however, a few differences in the historic Baptist faith and beliefs generally held by Disciples. Although Baptists insist that creeds have no authority over conscience, they generally endorse creeds as guides to interpreting the Bible. Disciples, however, reject all creeds as tests of church membership, belief, worship, and practice.

Although Disciples believe that God is three persons of one divine essence, unlike most Protestants they do not believe in using the word Trinity for they say such a term is unscriptural.

Other differences in the historical beliefs of Baptists and Disciples pertain to the doctrines of remission of sins and reception of the Holy Ghost, and the practice of the Lord's Supper. Disciples generally teach that remission of sins and reception of the Holy Spirit follow baptism. Moreover, Disciples

ALEXANDER CAMPBELL

generally observe communion weekly, while this ordinance is usually less frequently observed by Baptists.

After the division occurred in the Disciples movement in 1906 and the Church of Christ was organized, members of the Church of Christ retained or endorsed a number of beliefs that are currently rejected by most Disciples. These teachings coupled with the distinct beliefs held by Disciples as cited above provide a summary of the most distinguishing characteristics of the doctrines and practices of the Church of Christ.

Two beliefs that helped facilitate the schism of 1906 have remained points of theological debate. Members of the Church of Christ continue to insist that missionary societies should not be established and that God has not given men license to add to acts of worship with mechanical music. They explain that because there is no command in the New Testament to have music in the services except singing, there should be no instrumental music in Christian worship.

There are other differences in the faiths of these two bodies that have cemented the schism. While Disciples are divided concerning the subjects of the inspiration of the Bible and Biblical miracles, many members of the Church of Christ believe in the verbal and plenary inspiration of the Bible and generally hold that miracles occurred precisely as described in the Old and New Testaments.

Members of the Church of Christ further hold that unleavened bread and fruit of the vine should be used in the Lord's Supper and insist that there is but one basis for divorce and remarriage: adultery on the part of one of the parties.

Individuals who belong to this religious community also do not believe that their society is a denomination, for they say that this term implies division or denotes many parts. They explain that they are not part of Christendom but are members of the only true church, the body of Christ.

Members of the Church of Christ, moreover, do not join in unification efforts with other churches. Although some Disciples do not support current ecumenical programs, others are taking an active part in the movement to create Christian unity. Disciples are affiliated with the World Council of Churches and with the National Council of the Church of Christ in the United States.

Miscellaneous Beliefs

In most instances, other than those cited as distinguishing beliefs, orthodox Disciples and most members of the Church of Christ subscribe to the historical Protestant faith. Liberal Disciples, however, have adopted many new interpretations of Protestant theology and share many convictions popularized by contemporary theologians.

The Church of Jesus Christ of Latter-day Saints

14

During an era in American history when restorationist theologians were seeking a recovery of New Testament Christianity, when utopian societies and various humanitarian movements were forming, when great awakenings were responsible for mass conversions, and churches were engaged in a bitter war of words, a teenage farm boy named Joseph Smith (1805-44), who lived near Palmyra, New York, initiated his religious quest. For about three years this lad investigated the different faiths of America. Before his family migrated from Vermont to western New York his father had participated in the organization of a Universalist society; after arriving at the Finger Lake country some members of his family joined the Presbyterian Church while others leaned towards Methodism.[1] Joseph Smith, however, became confused in the midst of what he called a "tumult of opinions." "Considering that all [denominations] could not be right, and that God could not be the author of so much confusion," he said, "I determined to investigate the subject more fully." After reading the counsel of James, "If any of you lack wisdom, let him ask of God, that giveth to all men liberally" (James 1:5), he decided to follow the admonition.[2]

Joseph Smith testified that in the spring of 1820 he knelt in prayer in a peaceful grove, asking the Lord which church he should join. As a consequence of this petition, he claimed to have received a glorious vision. The Father and Son appeared to him, he soberly declared, and Jesus Christ instructed him that he should join none of the religious societies. He was told, he added, that the apostasy was a reality and "that all religious denominations were believing in incorrect doctrines." Furthermore, he received on that occasion "a promise that the fulness of the gospel should at some future time be made known unto me."[3]

Joseph Smith's "first vision" initiated what he claimed was a series of remarkable communications with God and angelic messengers. One cannot fully understand the life of this religious leader nor the beliefs of his followers without considering his assertion of a divine calling. Joseph Smith professed that his understanding of the Godhead and of the basic doctrines of the church which he organized were not based on human reason or his interpretation of the Bible but on personal communications with deity and angelic messengers in the form of visions and direct revelations.

During the 1820s, for example, this young man claimed that he was frequently enwrapped in heavenly visions during which an angel, by the name of Moroni (the son of Mormon, an ancient American prophet, writer, and general mentioned in the Book of Mormon), appeared to him. During these visitations, Joseph Smith said that the angel informed him that there was "a book deposited, written upon gold plates, giving an account of the former inhabitants of this continent, and the source from whence they sprang. He also said that the fulness of the everlasting gospel was contained in it, as delivered by the Savior to the ancient inhabitants."

According to Joseph Smith, on 22 September 1827 he traveled to the Hill Cumorah, located near his farmhouse, and secured the ancient record, after which he translated the work through the gift and power of God by means of Holy Interpreters called the Urim and Thummim. Most of the translation, he wrote, occurred between April and June 1829, with Oliver Cowdery, a former schoolteacher of the Genesee country, acting as scribe. In the summer of 1829 Joseph Smith located a publisher in Palmyra; in March 1830 the work, entitled the Book of Mormon, was available for sale.[4]

Individuals who believe that Joseph Smith was a prophet of God accept the Book of Mormon as the word of God. This body of scripture, they explain, does not replace the Bible but is a supplement to that sacred work. Since one section of this record describes the visitation of the resurrected Christ to his "other sheep" living in America and his teachings to these people, this portion is sometimes referred to as a fifth gospel.

Members of the church established by Joseph Smith, known as The Church of Jesus Christ of Latter-day Saints, maintain that the Book of Mormon is a valuable guide for determining religious truth, unlocking many mysteries in the Bible. Latter-day Saints read within its covers answers to questions that have precipitated theological confrontations among Christians, such as prerequisites for and mode and purpose of baptism, and the significance of the Lord's Supper. Information concerning life beyond the grave, especially the spirit world and the resurrection, is also presented in the writings of men regarded as ancient prophets. Moreover, this work unfolds tenets that were not taught by Americans prior to 1830. Heralded by Latter-day Saints as a new witness for Christ, the book discusses a distinct concept of the

JOSEPH SMITH

THE EIGHT WITNESSES

fall of Adam and a unique view of the limited and universal natures of the atonement.

Included in the original and subsequent publications of the Book of Mormon is a statement signed by three men, Oliver Cowdery, David Whitmer, and Martin Harris, testifying that the plates were shown to them by a messenger from God and that they heard a voice from heaven verifying the translation of the record as correct. The book also contains eight other men's testimonies that they beheld the plates and saw the engravings which had the appearance of an ancient record and were of curious workmanship. "As many of the leaves as the said Smith has translated," they declared, "we did handle with our hands." Since "we have seen and hefted, [we] know of a surety that the said Smith has got the plates of which we have spoken."[5]

Another distinct aspect in the history of this movement is that an array of witnesses verified the reality of many of the visions claimed by Joseph Smith. On about eight different occasions, friends of the "Mormon prophet" reported having been with him when visions occurred and seeing the messengers from God.[6] Oliver Cowdery declared that he was present with Joseph Smith when John the Baptist laid his hands on his own and Joseph Smith's heads, restoring to the earth the Aaronic Priesthood and giving them the authority to baptize. Oliver Cowdery also testified that he was with Joseph Smith when the higher or Melchizedek Priesthood was restored by messengers of God, conveying the right to organize Christ's church in the latter days and to confer on others, by the laying on of hands, the gift of the Holy Ghost.[7]

Shortly after the Book of Mormon was published, Joseph Smith gathered a number of his followers in Fayette, New York, where he organized The Church of Jesus Christ of Latter-day Saints on 6 April 1830. From western New York this religious movement spread throughout the United States and Canada, and before the church was ten years old Mormon missionaries were preaching in England. From Fayette, the headquarters of the church was moved to Kirtland, Ohio, in 1831, and during most of the next decade there were two major gathering places for Latter-day Saints, northeastern Ohio and western Missouri.

While Mormon missionaries were preaching that New Testament Christianity had been restored through a modern-day prophet, Latter-day Saints experienced greater persecution than that encountered by members of any other Christian faith in early America. Approximately 1,000 members of this religious community were driven from Jackson County, Missouri, in 1833. In 1838 most of the Ohio saints emigrated amidst threats from irate mobs; during the winter of 1838-39, after the governor of Missouri had ordered the extermination or expulsion of all Mormons, approximately 10,000 Latter-day Saints were forced from their homes by the Missouri militia. Seeking refuge in Iowa and Illinois, many exiles gathered in a place they named Nauvoo, adjacent to a great horseshoe bend in the Mississippi River. There they drained the swamps and erected a town which had within five years a population of slightly more than 11,000 people. Growth was spectacular and contemporaries reported in the early 1840s that Nauvoo was the largest town in Illinois; but peace did not continue. In 1844 Joseph Smith, the Mormon prophet, was shot and killed by a mob in Carthage, Illinois. Shortly thereafter, hostile groups forced most members of this faith to leave Illinois, and in 1846 a general exodus west commenced.

Under the direction of one of the greatest colonizers in history, Brigham Young, Latter-day Saints sought a new home in a desert oasis. Adjacent to the towering peaks of the Rocky Mountains and near the shores of the Great Salt Lake, most of the American followers of Joseph Smith gathered. From this "Zion" in the top of the mountains, these people established under the direction of Brigham Young more than 350 western settlements, and since 1847 Salt Lake City, Utah, has been the religious center for Latter-day Saints throughout the world.

Then a new wave of oppression struck the Latter-day Saints. The practice of plural marriage had been unfolded by Joseph Smith and publicly announced in Salt Lake City in 1852. During the 1880s, nearly 1,300 Mormons in Utah, Idaho, and Arizona were imprisoned for violating the anti-polygamy laws enacted by Congress. To accomplish the destruction of Mormon political and economic power in the West and to force Latter-day Saints to discontinue the practice of plural marriage, the national government ordered the disincorporation of this religious society and the escheatment of all its property not used exclusively for religious worship. This pressure from the national government ceased after political and economic changes were inaugurated by Mormon leaders and after the fourth president of the church, Wilford Woodruff, issued a manifesto in 1890 announcing that no more plural marriages would be sanctioned.[8] Gradually the number of Saints who had more than one wife declined, and this marital practice was discontinued. Meanwhile, it had been lived by only about 10 percent of Latter-day Saint families.

While more than 90 percent of all Christians who believe in the divine calling of Joseph Smith are members of The Church of Jesus Christ of Latter-day Saints, there have been a number of permanent divisions in this religious movement. Two issues which precipitated schisms among Latter-day Saints were succession in the presidency and plural marriage. Some of the followers of Joseph Smith did not accept the leadership of Brigham Young. Remaining in the East, one group formed the Reorganized Church of Jesus Christ of Latter Day Saints in Amboy, Illinois, on 6 April 1860. Members of the Reorganized Church, whose headquarters for more than 205,000 world adherents (1971) is Independence, Missouri, maintain that Joseph Smith's son, Joseph Smith III, was the rightful successor to the Mormon prophet; since the reorganization these saints have taught the principle of lineal succession in the presidency. Other issues, including the concept of God, temple

RESTORATION OF THE PRIESTHOOD

work, church scripture, and ecclesiastical polity have prevented a healing of this rupture.

After Latter-day Saints discontinued performing plural marriages, a few members of this movement refused to abandon the principle, and several offshoots have retained this practice. The largest of these sects has a membership of less than 4,000 and is generally referred to as the "Fundamentalists."

During the twentieth century, The Church of Jesus Christ of Latter-day Saints experienced rapid growth, being by percentage one of the fastest growing denominations in the United States. In 1900 world membership numbered 268,000 with 90 percent of all Latter-day Saints living in Utah, Idaho, and Arizona. By 1925 the membership had doubled; during the ensuing twenty-five years there was another two-fold increase, so that by 1950 membership had reached one million, with more than 90 percent of the adherents living in the United States. Two decades later the church reported a membership of nearly three million with more than two and one-fourth million residing in this land.

The significant increase in LDS membership in recent years has been accompanied by a major expansion in membership as well. In 1950 less than 100,000 members lived outside the United States but in 1970 more than one-half million Latter-day Saints were living in Canada, Latin America, Europe, the isles of the Pacific and eastern Asia. As a consequence of this extension beyond the borders of the fifty states, this religious society is currently emphasizing its international character. There is, for example, a rapid multiplication of books, magazines, and lesson manuals published in foreign languages. These works reflect a conscientious effort to relate the message of the restoration to people living throughout the world.

Latter-day Saints not only teach that there has been a restoration of the basic doctrines taught by Christ and his apostles, but they indicate that their basic pattern of church government harmonizes with New Testament Christianity. They say that Christ stands at the head of the church and directs a president regarded as a "prophet, seer, and revelator." Included among the highest officials, called general authorities, are twelve apostles, who are considered, like the apostles of old, to be special witnesses of Jesus Christ. Each year these men are also sustained by the membership of the church as living prophets.

Since instructions to local leaders and church members are constantly flowing from individuals regarded as divinely inspired apostles and prophets, the basic government of this church has often been referred to as a theocracy. There are, however, democratic elements in this religious society, for no officer serves without the sustaining vote of the people. Although the theocratic elements outweigh the democratic characteristics, much power in this church resides with local bishops. These leaders of Mormon wards (congregations of about five hundred members) serve without financial remuneration, earning their livelihood from various economic pursuits, and have the responsibility of interpreting and applying the directives of the general authorities. These men also preside over various church meetings in which the membership participates in teaching, preaching, and administering.

Throughout the history of this denomination there has been an emphasis on the role of the church in providing for educational, recreational, and other temporal needs of its members. Currently this religious society is sponsoring one of the most comprehensive welfare programs in America, one designed to help people help themselves. Latter-day Saint bishops are given the responsibility of seeing that no one in the ward is hungry, cold, or insufficiently clad. Counseling, job training, and medical care are also available for those in need. Latter-day Saint men functioning as home teachers and members of a women's Relief Society are assigned to visit each Latter-day Saint home at least once a month and these men and women have the responsibility of helping bishops discover and appraise the needs of others. In addition to gathering and storing food, clothing, and bedding for emergencies, members of this church are instructed to produce many of the necessities of life and to work for that which they need. Under the direction of local leaders, church members operate farms, cattle ranches, and dairies, and maintain canning, clothing, and soap factories. These farms and industries are manned primarily by church welfare recipients themselves and individuals who voluntarily donate their time. The products of their labors are shipped to storehouses where they are freely distributed to needy members and destitute families living in Mormon communities.

Throughout the history of the movement, Latter-day Saints have emphasized missionary programs. Every year thousands of young men and women voluntarily accept a call to labor for approximately two years in mission fields located in the United States and many other nations of the world. These missionaries, most of whom are in their early twenties, are self-supporting or are assisted financially by members of their families or friends. After returning to their homes, they provide experienced leadership in the local congregations where there are no salaried clergy.

In the midst of an era when many forces have combined to disrupt the American family, Latter-day Saints have inaugurated a program to strengthen their families. Monday night is generally set aside as "family home evening," a time when families organize activities, study and discuss the gospel, and participate in a variety of recreational events. Every family is provided a lesson manual for this occasion which provides various suggestions for learning and living principles exemplified by Jesus Christ.

Since Latter-day Saints take upon themselves the name of Jesus Christ and believe in following his exemplary life, they classify themselves as Christians but not Protestants. Joseph Smith was not a member of any religious society when he organized the church of Christ in preparation for the Savior's millennial reign.

Theologically speaking, throughout the history of this religious community, Latter-day Saints have been known for their orthodoxy, retaining the basic beliefs introduced by Joseph Smith. They further proclaim that while there is good in all churches, the "restored church" is the one and only true religion on the face of the earth, explaining that this is the only society teaching the fulness of the gospel of Christ and the only faith endowed with God's authority to perform ordinances. This belief in the one and only true church is not as exclusive as it sounds. Latter-day Saints teach that all people, either in this life or in the spirit world and prior to the final judgment, will be granted the privilege of accepting or rejecting the pure gospel of Christ.

During the twentieth century the image of this religious community has changed considerably. As a consequence of the accomplishments of Latter-day Saint businessmen, politicians, educators, and athletes, this faith is gaining the respect of many people. Broadcasts of the famous Salt Lake Tabernacle Choir, presentations of the Hill Cumorah Pageant, Mormon exhibits at information centers and fairs, and international activities of Brigham Young University students have contributed to the creation of a respected image among people in this country and in many other nations throughout the world.

Distinguishing Beliefs[9]

In many respects, the beliefs of Latter-day Saints are different from those held by most Catholics and Protestants. The following beliefs are examples of the doctrine and practices of Latter-day Saints that are not generally endorsed by other Christians.

Members of this religious community teach that the Bible, latter-day scriptures (including the Book of Mormon), and latter-day revelation are sources enabling Christians to determine religious truth. Latter-day Saints "believe all that God has revealed, all that he does now reveal, and . . . that he will yet reveal many great and important things pertaining to the Kingdom of God." And they hold that, since doctrine emanates from scripture and latter-day revelation, any change in the policies of the church will come from the prophet who directs the affairs of Christ's church on earth.

Latter-day Saints also teach that the Godhead is comprised of three separate and distinct personages: God the Father, God the Son, and God the Holy Ghost. They believe that these glorified personages are full of transcendent knowledge, power, mercy, love, and justice. They also teach that the Father and Son have tangible bodies of flesh and bones. Moreover, the Father and Son are considered as spiritual beings because spirit, not blood, flows through their bodies. (Spirit is defined as matter which is finer, or purer, and can be discerned only by purer eyes.) God literally created man in his own image, they explain, meaning not only with Godlike attributes but also with a physical resemblance.

Latter-day Saints also declare that God the Father is the literal parent or father of the spirits of all mortals. While the spirit element has always existed, individuals were clothed with spirit bodies before man's mortal creation, and Jesus was the firstborn in the spirit world. The premortal spirit body, they add, is similar in appearance to the earthly body.

According to Latter-day Saints, the war in heaven described in the Book of Revelation occurred before the physical creation and prior to the fall of Adam, who is also called Michael in the Bible. Satan, who was another spirit child of God, sought to destroy man's free agency while Christ championed his Father's plan designed to preserve man's free will. The Father's plan was accepted. Lucifer and one-third of the children of God rebelled, were cast from heaven, and were deprived of the opportunity of obtaining bodies and living as mortals.

Another distinct doctrine of this faith pertains to the Holy Ghost. They say that the third member of the Godhead, the Holy Ghost or Holy Spirit, is a personage of spirit, meaning an entity or individual who is a spirit. He is considered as the comforter, testator, sanctifier, spirit of truth, and messenger of the Father and Son.

While considering the creation, Latter-day Saints assert that God created the world by organizing chaotic matter. The word *create*, they claim, means to organize rather than to make out of nothing.

It is also the belief of Latter-day Saints that various types of beings serve the Lord as angels, such as premortal spirit children of God, translated beings, spirits of just men made perfect, and resurrected personages. They further state that, after rebelling against God, Satan and his followers became fallen angels and now labor to overthrow the kingdom of God, including seducing and leading people astray.

Another distinguishing Latter-day Saint doctrine is the view of the fall. If Adam had not transgressed, they explain, he would not have fallen, but he and Eve would have remained in the Garden of Eden in a state of their original creation, which was a state of innocence. In this condition they would have had no children. They also could not have sinned nor performed righteous acts; and if there be no righteousness, there can be no happiness. "Adam fell that men might be; and men are, that they might have joy." In some respects, therefore, they teach that man benefits from the fall; and men will be punished for their own sins and not for Adam's transgression.

Latter-day Saints further affirm that through the atonement of Christ all men will be resurrected, and that through this redemption "all mankind may be saved, by obedience to the laws and ordinances of the gospel." Because of the grace or goodness of God, Jesus took upon himself the sins of every man, woman, and child. Men are therefore saved by the love, mercy, and condescension of God towards his children; men should grow in grace until they are sanctified and justified by God. The way of salvation, they add, includes not only the grace of deity but also depends on individual merit and reception of the ordinances of the gospel. The church is viewed as an institution established by the Lord to aid in the salvation of men.

It is also the belief of these Christians that faith and repentance should precede baptism by immersion for the remission of sins. After baptism follows the laying on of hands for the gift of the Holy Ghost. In order to perform ordinances such as baptism, which is considered essential to enter the kingdom of God, Latter-day Saints teach that a man must be called of God by prophecy and by the laying on of hands by one having the authority. This power of God, or priesthood, they testify, was restored to the earth by John the Baptist and by Peter, James, and John.

Active members of this religious community partake of the emblems of the Lord's Supper (bread and water) weekly in remembrance of the body and blood of Christ. During this ordinance, members renew the covenants which they made at baptism and the faithful are promised that the Spirit of God will abide with them.

Another belief of this faith is that the Lord established through men raised up for that very purpose the Constitution of the United States to protect the rights of mankind and help men to exercise their moral agency more fully.

A Latter-day Saint health code, known as "the word of wisdom," affirms the use of meat, fruit, vegetables, and grain, but directs members to refrain from the use of wine and strong drink (meaning alcoholic beverages), tobacco, and hot drinks (interpreted as tea and coffee). Harmful drugs are also considered a violation of the spirit of the word of wisdom, and compliance with these prohibitions has become a measuring rod which in part determines personal worthiness of Latter-day Saints.

According to a statement issued by the Public Communications Department of The Church of Jesus Christ of Latter-day Saints on 9 September 1974, "Blacks are welcomed into church membership, and their numbers are growing. . . . Faithful church members of all races, including blacks, have the right to the saving ordinances of the gospel which qualify them for a place in the celestial kingdom after death." Although many adults of all races (including Caucasians) in the church do not hold the priesthood, "the very core of church doctrine is that all persons in the world are literally spirit sons and daughters of the same Heavenly Father, which makes all men brothers and . . . those who do not hold the priesthood are as precious in the sight of God as those who do."

Latter-day Saints also teach that there will be in the last days a literal gathering of Israel and a restoration of the Ten Tribes. A "Zion," they explain, will be built upon the American continent and the Jews will gather in Palestine. They further predict that Christ will personally return to the earth and usher in the Millennium, a thousand-year period during which Christ will reign on earth. During this era of peace, they state, there will be two capital cities, one in Jerusalem and the other in Independence, Jackson County, Missouri.

Latter-day Saints further believe that at death the spirits of all men enter the world of spirits. The righteous enter paradise, a state of rest, peace, and happiness. The wicked enter a spirit prison, where they suffer mental anguish. In the spirit world all will be granted an opportunity to embrace the gospel of Christ, and all who would have received the truth if they had been granted such an opportunity in this life will accept the gospel in the spirit world. After all men are resurrected with bodies of flesh and bones, all, except the sons of perdition (those who deny Christ and rebel against him after gaining a perfect knowledge of the gospel) will be assigned to one of three degrees of glory. Individuals who participate in the resurrection of the unjust but do not deny the Holy Spirit will enter the lowest of the three kingdoms, the telestial glory. Honorable children of God who fail to embrace the fulness of the gospel but do not deny Christ will enter the terrestrial world and receive of God's glory but not of his fulness. The most faithful children of God will enter the celestial glory, receive of God's fulness and glory, and dwell in the presence of God the Eternal Father and his son, Jesus Christ.

Latter-day temples are considered sacred sanctuaries where faithful members worship and participate in sacred ordinances that are performed in no other buildings. In these "Houses of the Lord," Latter-day Saints perform by proxy baptisms for the dead. This vicarious service for their ancestors and others who have died is the program ordained by the Lord by which all worthy children of God may return to his presence. Since they teach that a man must be born of water and the spirit before he may enter the kingdom of God, an individual, they explain, may learn the gospel in the spirit world and receive baptism (an earthly ordinance) through the work of a proxy.

Another temple ordinance of Latter-day Saints is the endowment, which prepares, in their view, members to receive the fulness of God's blessings, preparatory to man's entering the presence of God.

Latter-day Saints are also married in temples for time and all eternity. Couples who keep the terms and covenants which they make in these "holy places" are promised that they will be privileged to be husband and wife in the eternities, will receive the title of "gods," will have eternal increase, and will have their faithful mortal offspring with them after the resurrection.

Latter-day Saints not only believe that the same basic organization that existed in the Primitive Church (including apostles, prophets, pastors, teachers, evangelists, etc.) has been reestablished in the latter days, but maintain that members of The Church of Jesus Christ of Latter-day Saints are blessed with the same gifts manifest among early Christians, such as the gift of healing, prophecy, visions, revelation, tongues, and interpretation of tongues.

Miscellaneous Beliefs

Latter-day Saints also believe that members should pay a tithe (contribute one-tenth of their income to the church), plus be willing to make other contributions and support financially other worthy projects.

A summary of three other beliefs held by Latter-day Saints is found in their "Articles of Faith":

We claim the privilege of worshiping Almighty God according to the dictates of our own conscience, and allow all men the same privilege, let them worship how, where, or what they may.

We believe in being subject to kings, presidents, rulers, and magistrates, in obeying, honoring, and sustaining the law.

We believe in being honest, true, chaste, benevolent, virtuous, and in doing good to all men; indeed, we may say that we follow the admonition of Paul—We believe all things, we hope all things, we have endured many things, and hope to be able to endure all things. If there is anything virtuous, lovely, or of good report or praiseworthy, we seek after these things.

15

The Seventh-day Adventists

Late in the second decade of the nineteenth century, William Miller (1782-1849), a farmer from Low Hampton, New York, commenced a serious, methodical examination of biblical prophecies. Although a former deist, Miller became converted to the Christian belief that Jesus is the Christ, after which he concluded that the chronological portions of the Bible should be examined as conscientiously as other parts of that sacred work. As he studied and contemplated, Miller decided that Daniel 8:14 was a key unlocking the mystery of the Second Coming. This scripture read, "Unto two thousand and three hundred days; then shall the sanctuary be cleansed." Believing that a day in symbolic prophecy represents a year, Miller thought that after a period of 2300 years the sanctuary (which in his opinion meant the earth) would be purified by fire at the time of the Second Coming. His next problem was to determine the starting point for the 2300 years.

As Miller continued his investigation of biblical prophecy, he read Daniel 9:24, which said, "Seventy weeks are determined upon thy people and upon the holy city." According to Miller's analysis, "determined" in that passage meant "cut off" and the seventy weeks (or 490 years) to be cut off pertained to the only period of time mentioned in the preceding chapter, or the 2300 years. The next step in Miller's chain of interpretations was to conclude that the two periods mentioned in Daniel chapters 8 and 9 began simultaneously—in 457 B.C., the date referred to in Ezra as the year of the command to rebuild and restore Jerusalem. Consequently, according to Miller's calculations, Christ would return 2300 years after 457 B.C., or about 1843.[1]

For nine years after calculating an approximate date in which he believed Christ would return, Miller informed only a few relatives and intimate friends of his biblical discovery. During these years, he became a Baptist and, although he was not ordained, in 1833 he secured a license to preach.

Early in the 1830s, William Miller publicly announced that the ancient prophets had predicted Christ's Second Coming and that he had correlated their prophecy with the current calendar. With astonishing rapidity, the advent message gained momentum. Several hundred ministers of different faiths and more than 50,000 converts joined the Advent movement launched by Miller. Although it was not his original intention to organize a new religious society, some of Miller's supporters either withdrew voluntarily or were excommunicated from their congregations and formed independent religious societies.

For many years Miller hesitated to be more precise than to predict Christ would come about 1843. After it was reported in the New York *Herald,* however, that he had fixed April 3 for the advent, Miller wrote an article on 4 February 1844 for the *Signs of the Times,* in which he identified clearly his position concerning the date of the Second Coming. "Jesus Christ will come again to this earth, cleanse, purify, and take possession of the same, with all his saints," Miller announced, "some time between 21 March 1843 and 21 March 1844." He further insisted on that occasion that he had never designated a specific day, month, nor hour for the return of the Savior.[2]

Excitement and tension mounted as 21 March 1844, the last anticipated day for the Second Coming, approached. While converts to the movement increased, hostility itensified; and Miller was denounced in his own country as a "fanatic," a "liar," a "deluded old fool," and a "speculating knave." Amidst growing criticism, the third week of March 1844 passed without any startling ecclesiastical interruptions. Miller was disappointed and perplexed. While confessing that he had erred, the Advent leader asserted that "the day of the Lord was near, even at the door." [3] But a failure in his biblical interpretations was evident and, disillusioned, many abandoned the movement.

The most dramatic event in the history of the Millerites, however, had not yet transpired. After a reevaluation of the scriptures, one of Miller's followers noted that according to Habakkuk 2:3 and Leviticus 25:9 there was to be a "tarrying time" of seven months and ten days, after which the earth would be purified. In August 1844, during an Adventist camp meeting held in Exeter, New Hampshire, a new expectation date, 22 October 1844, was proclaimed. Although Miller had previously resisted setting an exact date for the coming of the Bridegroom, early in October of that year he was converted to the "seventh month movement" and on October 9 proclaimed that Christ would return on October 22. [4]

Preparations for the Second Coming were hastily renewed in many American communities. During the third week of October 1844 hundreds suspended their work to contemplate, to attend meetings, and to warn their neighbors. Some turned their possessions into cash and paid their debts. Others disposed of their substance and gave alms to the poor. But there was no general selling of farms by the Millerites, and reports describing the preparation and adorning of ascension robes were branded by Miller as "false and scandalous."[5]

On 22 October 1844 thousands gathered in homes, fields, and houses of worship, watching and waiting for the coming of Christ; but again the pronounced time passed, leaving many lonely, confused, and humiliated. As William Miller confessed, the adventists' expectation of the Second Coming proved premature. Whereas the era between 21 March 1843 and 21 March 1844 was a period ending in much disappointment, 22 October 1844 was the day of the "Great Disappointment." Although the Millerites disbanded and many returned to their former churches, a number of religious societies trace their historical roots back to phases of this movement, the largest of these Adventist churches being the Seventh-day Adventists.

Although Seventh-day Adventists teach that throughout the history of Christianity groups have maintained beliefs that parallel their interpretations of the gospel of Christ, they claim that the modern history of this faith occurred after the "Great Disappointment" of 1844 when three segments of the Millerite movement fused.

One of the zealous leaders who emerged in the spiritual vacuum created by the disintegration of the Millerites was Hiram Edson .(1806-82). Early in the morning of 23 October 1844, fearing the jeers and scorn of those who had refused to attend his Adventist cottage meetings, Edson strayed into a secluded cornfield in Port Gibson, New York. There, after a night of great anticipation followed by intense grief, Edson pleaded to the Lord, seeking an answer to the disappointment that gripped him and his religious associates. Suddenly, he testified, he received an overwhelming conviction that on 22 October 1844, Christ, instead of returning to this earth, entered for the first time a second apartment of the heavenly sanctuary. There he commenced a second phase of his ministry, a work in that holy place that was necessary before the Second Advent.[6] According to Seventh-day Adventists, on that date Christ began the "investigative judgment." The Savior commenced determining those eligible to enter God's presence and will continue this ministry until he leaves heaven and returns personally to this earth. While these Adventists admit that Miller unfolded many correct concepts, they contend that he erred in interpreting the sanctuary as this earth (instead of a second compartment of heaven) and in determining a precise date for the Second Coming.

While Edson's interpretation of the "cleansing of the sanctuary" grew in popularity, another group of former Millerites increased in strength under the leadership of Joseph Bates (1792-1872) of New Bedford, Massachusetts. In 1821 this unusual sea captain discontinued drinking "ardent spirits" and during a subsequent voyage resolved not to drink wine. Later he gave up smoking, chewing tobacco, and drinking tea and coffee and became a temperance leader in Massachusetts. At one time Bates captained a "temperance vessel" in which he ordered the crew not to consume alcoholic beverages, to discontinue swearing, and not to wash or mend clothes on Sunday. Early in the 1840s, he discarded meat from his diet and eventually became one of the enthusiastic contributors and supporters of the Seventh-day Adventist health code. This program includes abstinence from liquor, tobacco, tea, coffee, and meats classified in the Old Testament as unclean (such as pork, lobster, and crab).

After retiring with a modest fortune, Bates accepted Miller's views concerning the Second Coming and in 1839 became an itinerant Adventist preacher. After the "Great Disappointment," he was converted to the doctrine that the seventh day is the Sabbath of the Lord and in 1846 published a tract, *The Seventh Day Sabbath, a Perpetual Sign,* in which he defended Saturday as the true Sabbath on the basis that the Ten Commandments was a moral guide which should not be changed. Traveling westward from New England, the pioneer Adventist preacher gathered followers in Michigan, Indiana, Illinois, Wisconsin, and Iowa.[7]

The foundation of this native American religion was not completed until a third force—the "spirit of prophecy"—was added to the movements promoted by Hiram Edson and Joseph Bates. According to Seventh-day Adventists, this prophetic gift was the contribution of one of the cofounders of their society, Ellen Gould Harmon White (1827-1915).

Born on a farm near Gorham, Maine, Ellen Harmon was reared in Portland. When she was nine, Ellen was struck by a rock thrown by a classmate and suffered a broken nose and a possible concussion. For three weeks, she remained unconscious; after she recovered, her face was blemished by a broken nose. This disfigurement caused serious embarrassment and emotional distress which impaired her general health; for several years she was unable to breathe properly through her nose. When she attempted to return to school at the age of twelve her health again interrupted her education. Although she received little formal training after her ninth year, she learned by the help of her conscientious parents and later by reading and conversing with others.

While Ellen's parents were members of the Methodist society in Portland, she did not unite with the group until after she had heard Miller preach in Portland, had accepted his views on the Second Coming, and had claimed a converting experience. When she was baptized on 26 June 1842 she requested that the ordinance be performed by immersion, after which she was admitted into full fellowship in the Methodist Church.

Ellen Harmon remained a Methodist for only a few months. After William Miller returned to Portland in 1842, the young woman acknowledged her endorsement of his prediction, and she, her parents, and other members of her family were disfellowshipped from the Pine Street Methodist Church.[8]

As 22 October 1844 approached, Ellen Harmon sincerely tried to prepare herself for the return of the Savior. For weeks, the young convert to Protestantism had prayed earnestly and evaluated her innermost thoughts and emotions. When the anticipated date of the Second Coming passed without any miraculous manifestations, Ellen was gravely perplexed and disappointed. Believing that the signs of the times clearly indicated that the "end of all things was at hand," she decided to continue preparing for the eventful day of Christ's return.

In December 1844 Ellen Harmon united in prayer with four other women and while praying received her first vision. The seventeen-year-old woman said that the power of God rested upon her. "I seemed to be surrounded with light," she testified. "[I] saw a straight and narrow path, cast up high above the world." Under the direction of God, she continued, Advent people were traveling toward a heavenly city. Some fell by the wayside, but 144,000 marched over a sea of glass to the gate of the city. Upon their arrival, "Jesus raised his mighty, glorious arm, laid hold of the pearly gate, swung it back on its glittering hinges," and welcomed those who were worthy to enter. After being given "harps of gold," the 144,000 gathered near the tree of life and throne of God and, touching their golden harps, "sat down to look at the glory of the [heavenly city]." [9]

After informing a small group of Adventists in Portland that she had beheld a glorious vision, Ellen was comforted by their decision that it was light from God. Shortly thereafter, she said she received other visions. Throughout the remaining years of her life, Ellen Harmon acted as an instrument in God's hand, revealing light and knowledge to the inhabitants of the earth. Present-day custodians of her estate estimate that she received at least two thousand visions.

Ellen Harmon lived for eighty-seven years, although at the time of her initial report of a vision and for many years thereafter she complained that her health was so poor that she suffered constantly. In her reminiscences, this woman specified that she was "unusually sensitive," was plagued with emotional and physical problems and was subject to fainting spells. But notwithstanding her nervous disorders and serious illness, Ellen Harmon stated that on many occasions when her body seemed to be in an unconscious state, heavenly beings sent from God would instruct her. [10]

During one of her earliest visions, Ellen maintained that an angel informed her to publicize the information which she received from heavenly channels. In response to this command, Ellen said, she went forth reluctantly to bring others "the light and peace of Jesus." During her travels she met James White (1821-81), a twenty-three-year-old Adventist preacher. This acquaintance developed into a genuine love; and on 30 August 1846 the two religious leaders were married, after which they united in proclaiming their distinct message to mankind.

After learning the views of Joseph Bates in 1846 Ellen White received a

ELLEN GOULD HARMON WHITE

vision which seemed to substantiate his teachings concerning Saturday as the proper day for worshipping the Lord. James and Ellen White then joined Bates in unifying and strengthening the new Sabbath Adventist movement.

Eventually Mrs. White became acquainted with Hiram Edson's view concerning the religious event of 22 October 1844. Through "prophetic insight" this influential woman confirmed the belief that on that historic date, Christ entered the holy of holies and appeared in the presence of God "to make an atonement for all . . . entitled to its benefits."[11] Meanwhile, Bates, Edson, and many others concluded that Ellen G. White possessed the gift of prophecy. Subsequently, many segments of the former Millerite movement fused, and the work of gathering converts progressed more rapidly.

Ellen G. White was not only a pioneer Adventist preacher, but she was also a prolific writer. During her adult life, she wrote about sixty books, forty-four of which are currently in print. She also contributed about 4,600 articles to church periodicals. In the opinion of Seventh-day Adventists, her most significant literary accomplishment was a five-volume Bible commentary entitled, *Conflict of the Ages.* Another of her popular publications, *Steps to Christ,* has been translated into eighty-five languages. [12]

Seventh-day Adventists do not regard the writings of Ellen G. White as an addition to the Bible. Members of the denomination emphasize that Mrs. White possessed the gift of prophecy, one of the gifts promised by Christ to his Church to unify and strengthen Christians. Rather than considering these writings as scripture, though, Adventists employ them as a key disclosing what they consider to be proper interpretations of the Bible.

The publications of James White also became a significant element in advancing this religious community. In 1849 he began publishing *Present Truth;* a year later the name of this paper was changed to *The Advent Review and Sabbath Herald.* After a group of Adventists in Michigan offered to build a printing office for White, the *Review and Herald* was moved in 1855 from Rochester, New York, to Battle Creek, Michigan.

The early organization of this religious society was informal and lacked an official name. Converts were at first referred to as "Sabbath-keepers" or "believers in the Second Advent." However, more than a decade after the initial disciples commenced gathering, members met in Battle Creek and on 1 October 1860 adopted the name "Seventh-day Adventist," to reflect their distinctive beliefs. Three years later, when their membership was 3,500, another meeting was held in Battle Creek, during which the formal denominational organization was finalized. Since 1903 the world headquarters of this faith has been in Washington, D.C.[13]

The Seventh-day Adventist organization has a representative system of church government. Congregations govern themselves through officers, which include a minister and lay members. Local elders, deacons, deaconesses, and other leaders are nominated by the membership and voted upon by the congregation. Officers within a defined geographical area are elected to serve as representatives in conferences, and this body has direct responsibility for church and evangelistic work within its region. Work pertaining to larger geographical areas is supervised by other bodies, including a general conference which holds sessions every four years. All units of this church, except for the local congregation, have elected officers who devote full time to various church-related activities.

Ministers of this religious community are graduates of Seventh-day Adventist colleges and are ordained after two or more years of internship. As in many other faiths, ordained ministers are appointed pastors of congregations and only these men may baptize and conduct weddings. [14]

Following the formal organization of this denomination in May 1863, Adventist preachers carried their particular message of salvation from the northern states to many other parts of the nation and throughout the world. In the 1880s, after Adventist societies were constituted in the South, members were fined, imprisoned, and forced to serve in chain gangs for violating Sunday laws. Before 1890 the movement had not only spread across the United States, but had been carried into Canada, Europe, South Africa, and Russia. During the last decade of the nineteenth century, Seventh-day Adventist missionaries introduced their beliefs into India, South America, and Japan. At the turn of the century, this society reported a world membership of 75,767. [15]

During the twentieth century, the numerical growth of this denomination was greater outside the United States than within U.S. borders. In the mid-1960s, when church membership in the United States and Canada was 380,855, more than 300,000 members resided in three other geographical regions—Latin America, Africa, and the Far East—and more than 200,000 lived in Europe. Out of a membership of one and one-half million, 24 percent resided in North America. This ratio has remained constant during the past few years; in 1970 approximately one of every four Adventists lived in the United States.

There are other distinguishing characteristics of the Seventh-day Adventist faith in contemporary America. Members of this religious community have remained, theologically speaking, orthodox, retaining the basic beliefs unfolded by the cofounders of their society. They have also retained their zealous evangelistic spirit. Missionaries have labored in approximately two hundred countries, teaching others in nearly a thousand languages. Many people have been introduced to their religion by listening to the "Voice of Prophecy" radio program and by reading their popular monthly magazine, *Signs of the Times.* Early in the 1960s more than 50,000 members (three and one-half percent of their world membership) were employed by the church for evangelistic, educational, medical, publishing, and other ecclesiastical activities. Currently this denomination is recognized for its support of educational institutions. Next to the Roman Catholics and Lutherans, they maintain the largest parochial school system in the United States. Seventh-day Adventist hospitals, sanitariums, and clinics are also recognized for their efficiency in serving others. Members are distinguished by their conscientious study of the Bible, by their genuine support of welfare and civil defense programs (including mobile disaster-aid units and disaster-preparedness classes), and by their smoke clinics, temperance programs, and food factories, which produce high-protein foods especially designed for vegetarians. While these Protestants are willing to serve in the military, they believe in noncombatant service, and many Seventh-day Adventists have won recognition for courageous activities in the Medical Corps of the United States Army.

Distinguishing Beliefs [16]

Although many Americans recognize that one of the distinguishing beliefs of the Seventh-day Adventists is the observance of the Sabbath on Saturday, there are many other doctrines and practices held by members of this church that differ from beliefs generally held by Christians living in the contemporary world.

While explaining their position concerning the Sabbath, Seventh-day Adventists teach that this special day should be observed from sundown Friday to sundown Saturday. They also teach that this seventh day is sacred because it was designed to be a memorial to God's creative power and is a sign of his authority.

Another unusual belief of members of this religious community is that while the Bible is the sole rule of faith and practice and that all theological beliefs and practices should be judged according to the information contained in that work, the writings of Ellen G. White provide a lesser light leading individuals to this greater light. God, they claim, has relayed his desires and admonitions to mankind through this messenger, and the counsel and writings of Ellen G. White have served as a major factor in maintaining doctrinal unity in this church.

Seventh-day Adventists also hold a distinct view concerning Christ's participation in the judgment. According to members of this faith, Christ's intercession in man's behalf in the heavenly sanctuary is as essential to the plan of salvation as was his death on the cross. Christ's sacrifice on the cross, they explain, was an atonement for sin, was provided for all men, and was the beginning of the work of reconciliation. It will, they hold, be efficacious for all who repent, accept the grace of God, and surrender their lives to God. Christ's work of atonement in the heavenly sanctuary, Seventh-day Adventists continue, refers to the application of the benefits of salvation which were provided at Calvary to all believers according to their needs. It is also their conviction that since 1844, when Christ entered a heavenly sanctuary, the Savior in the "investigative judgment" has been determining the destinies of all men. There the "High Priest" intercedes as the lives of men are called into judgment.

Another peculiar doctrine of members of this religious community is that the soul of man is the entire man and that the spiritual body cannot exist independent of the physical body. All men, they say, rest in the tomb until the resurrection morning, and during this period of slumber, all men are in a state of total unconsciousness. Moreover, they declare that the wicked will not suffer everlasting punishment (in the traditional sense of the term of burning eternally in hell), but will be annihilated.

Seventh-day Adventists further testify to the world that the second coming of Christ is near. This coming, they affirm, will be literal, physical, and visible to all mankind. After Christ returns, members of this faith teach that the millennium will be inaugurated. During the thousand years, the righteous will make the new earth their celestial home; and at the end of the millennium, Satan will be loosed for a season, after which he will be destroyed with all the unrepentant inhabitants of the earth.

One of the requirements for membership in this faith is strict abstinence from liquor, tobacco, tea, coffee, and meats which they teach are classified in the Old Testament as unclean. Many members are also vegetarians.

"Attendance at motion picture theaters is frowned on by the church," women are advised not to resort "to the overuse of cosmetics," and wearing much jewelry is considered a "display of pride and vanity." Active members also refrain from card playing and dancing.

Several beliefs of the Seventh-day Adventists parallel some of the most popular distinguishing beliefs of the Baptists. For example, Seventh-day Adventists teach that baptism should be observed by all of sufficient maturity to understand its meaning and should be performed by single immersion. Like Baptists, they also state that the Lord's Supper should be regarded as a commemorative ordinance in which communicants celebrate the Savior's death. Approximately four times a year members of this faith observe the Lord's Supper by partaking bread and wine, elements which are viewed as symbols of the flesh and blood of Christ.

Unlike Baptists, however, Seventh-day Adventists believe that the ordinance of the Lord's Supper should be preceded by a preparatory ordinance of foot washing.

Miscellaneous Beliefs

Although Seventh-day Adventists employ the writings of Ellen G. White as a key to unlock the mysteries of the Bible, in harmony with the views of most Protestants they insist that the Bible is the sole rule of faith and practice. Most also hold that the Trinity consists of God the Father, God the Son, and God the Holy Ghost. A few members, however, depart from this historic belief concerning God by claiming that the Father and Son are distinct beings or spirits.

In harmony with a tenet held by many orthodox Protestants, Seventh-day Adventists also insist that the popular theory of evolution should not be considered as a correct explanation of the origin of man. It is the belief of members of this church that God created the earth and all life as explained by individuals who endorse a literal creationist view.

The belief of Seventh-day Adventists concerning the fall of Adam and Christ's sacrificial atonement on the cross in which he met in full the penalty of the broken law is also similar to the teachings of many other Christians.

When Seventh-day Adventists explain their position concerning authority they declare: "Our Divine authority for teaching the gospel and baptizing in the name of our Lord was received directly from Jesus Christ while He was on earth and has not been lost, but has remained with God's true followers ever since."

CHARLES TAZE RUSSELL

The Watch Tower Bible and Tract Society

Nearly every American at one time or another has encountered "ministers" of the Watch Tower Bible and Tract Society, known as Jehovah's Witnesses. Although this is one of the relatively small denominations in America, such a contact is not surprising considering that every member of this faith is literally a missionary. Every Bible student devotes approximately ten hours or more each month to proselyting activities, including selling *The Watchtower* on busy streets, circulating tracts and magazines from house to house, and teaching a distinct Christian message to all who will listen. Even though most adults living in urban America have been approached by these missionaries and many have heard that these people endorse a strange belief (originating from the book of Revelation) concerning 144,000, most Americans have never seriously examined the history and beliefs of this religious community. As individuals reflect on their encounter with the Jehovah's Witnesses, many might recall hearing their warning and prediction that the millennial reign of Christ is imminent.

Like many other religious communities, the Watch Tower Bible and Tract Society was founded by an industrious leader, Charles Taze Russell (1852-1916), who through conscientious work and personal sacrifice attracted many to the movement which he launched. While Joseph Smith, Ellen G. White, and Mary Baker Eddy published guides for their followers to the mysteries of the Bible, Russell followed in the steps of Alexander Campbell in rejecting all such latter-day works. Echoing a popular belief of the Disciples, Russell denounced all claims to modern-day visions and revelations, claiming that such miracles ceased with the death of the apostles. Many of Russell's interpretations of the Bible, however, were in sharp contrast to teachings of the restorationist theologians of the nineteenth century and of other Christians of his age.

The controversial founder of this society was born in Allegheny (now part of the city of Pittsburgh), Pennsylvania, during the decade preceding the disruption of American democracy. Three years after the Civil War, Charles Taze Russell launched a personal quest for religious truth. Although he had been raised a Presbyterian and as a teenager had joined the Congregational Church, in 1868, at the age of sixteen, Charles Russell withdrew his membership from the Allegheny Congregational Church. About the same time that Mary Baker Eddy was challenging the traditional view of predestination, Russell also rejected it and became an avowed skeptic. Although he temporarily discarded the Bible and the historic creeds of Christendom, the seventeen-year-old boy, who had become a partner with his father in a growing chain of men's clothing stores, had not lost all interest in the religious societies of America.[1]

Charles Russell's search for religious truth directed him to various Christian churches. One of his earliest contacts was with a group of Pittsburgh Adventists, a remnant of the Millerite movement. After the "Great Disappointment" of 1844, these Adventists had reexamined the scriptures and predicted that Christ would return in 1873 or 1874. Although Russell soon learned that these Second Adventists had again erred in their calculations, during his association with them he developed a keen interest in biblical chronology, the Second Coming, and the millennium.

After reviewing biblical prophecies, Russell decided that Christ had returned in 1874, but not physically as the Second Adventists had anticipated. This coming, he announced, was as an invisible, spiritual being. Moreover, Russell predicted that the separation of the wheat from the tares had begun and this gathering of God's children would continue until 1914. In October of that year, he declared, the Battle of Armageddon would inaugurate the millennial reign.

During the 1870s, the decade when Russell presented his view "that Christ's second presence began invisibly in the fall of 1874," he participated in a systematic study of the Bible with a small group of students.[2] In 1876, after this group had increased to about thirty members, Russell was elected as their chairman or pastor. In the fall of that year, Russell embarked upon a successful lecture tour through the New England states where he popularized his eschatological views and enlisted a few converts. As the decade drew to a close, Russell began publishing his most influential magazine, *Zion's Watch Tower,* and commenced organizing his followers into a distinct religious community. Within one year, thirty congregations had been constituted in seven states. Loosely united, these groups accepted the leadership of Russell and the directions which he issued from his congregation in Pittsburgh.[3]

The year 1879 was significant in Russell's life not only because he initiated a new religious movement but also because at the age of twenty-seven he met and married one of his Bible students, Maria F. Ackley. Immediately, Maria

Russell became deeply involved in this new religion, assisting her husband in editing and publishing his journal, and acting as first secretary-treasurer of the Watch Tower Society after its incorporation. She remained an enthusiastic supporter of this faith until her separation from Pastor Russell in 1897.

The task of organizing a religious community continued throughout the 1880s. After many were converted to Russell's biblical messages, they were authorized and encouraged to go forth as missionaries, teaching and warning others. In order to finance various proselyting activities, Russell liberally spent money earned from his successful mercantile business. In 1884, three years after organizing an unincorporated Bible society, the young man became president of a legal corporation, designated as Zion's Watch Tower Bible and Tract Society. Twelve years later the name "Zion" was dropped from the organization's official title. Although a Board of Directors assisted him in guiding the movement, Pastor Russell was throughout his life the dominant leader of this society. Russell did not pretend to establish a new church; Jehovah's Witnesses currently insist that they are not affiliated with a church but are members of a Bible society.

Even though membership in the Bible society continued to increase under Russell's direction, throughout the thirty-seven years in which he guided the movement Pastor Russell encountered much opposition and many trials. After being accused of fraudulent business dealings and profiteering, Russell was subjected to a series of legal trials; in the midst of many reported scandals, his character was defamed. His personal burdens were further magnified by his separation from his wife and dissension within the leadership of the society. Nevertheless, in the midst of external pressures and internal conflict, Russell continued to promulgate his beliefs by preaching frequently and writing profusely.

In 1909 Russell transferred the headquarters of the Bible society from Allegheny, Pennsylvania, to the Henry Ward Beecher mansion in Brooklyn, New York. From this new center, the movement spread throughout the United States and into many foreign lands. Converts to this new native American religion became missionaries not only in the neighborhoods where they earned their livings, but some accepted the challenge to labor overseas without financial remuneration. [4]

As October 1914, the calculated beginning of the millennial reign of Christ, approached, Russell sensed that he might have erred in his analysis of Bible chronology and announced that a mistake on the precise date of the Battle of Armageddon would not invalidate his interpretations of other major themes of the scriptures. After World War I erupted, Russell confidently proclaimed that death, anarchy, and revolution would continue until Christ returned to rule on earth. [5]

When 1914 brought no end to the world in its present state and some of Russell's predictions proved premature, he insisted that within a couple of years the millennium would begin. The biblical prediction, he explained, describing the forces of Satan combatting the soldiers of God was imminent. But Russell did not live to witness the creation of a new world. On 31 October 1916, two years before the cessation of hostilities in Europe, Russell died. The Watch Tower Society had lost its founder and president, a man who had traveled more than a million miles, delivered more than 30,000 sermons, published books totaling over 50,000 pages, and left an established society of approximately 50,000 adherents. Eulogizing Russell's accomplishments, his followers declared, "Not since the Apostle Paul has there lived in the world a greater and better man than Pastor Russell." [6]

After considering the qualifications for members of the Board of Directors, leaders of the Watch Tower Corporation nominated Joseph F. Rutherford (1869-1942) as second president of the society; he was unanimously approved by the members who voted. This attorney had served for many years as member of the board and had been a legal counsellor for Pastor Russell. Since he had served briefly as a special judge in the fourteenth judicial district in Missouri, he was often referred to as Judge Rutherford.

While president of the Bible society, Rutherford introduced a number of doctrinal themes that were not taught by the founder of the movement. In the 1930s, he proclaimed that a central message of the Bible was the vindication of Jehovah's name, meaning that eventually God would defeat Satan and restore the earth to a state of its original perfection.

For centuries, Rutherford explained, Christians had taught that the principal mission of Jehovah (meaning Almighty God) was to save mankind by bringing individuals into heaven. "The Lord now makes it plain," he proclaimed, that "[He] will take drastic action against His enemies, not for the mere purpose of saving [those who are] consecrated to Him, but because of His own holy name." Equipped with another essential message, Bible students intensified their missionary labors. If mankind neglected to heed their message, the unbelievers would be held accountable while the ardent ambassadors of Jehovah would have accomplished the will of God. [7]

Rutherford also introduced a distinct explanation of events that had transpired between 1874 and 1918. Revising Russell's predictions, the second president asserted that the Battle of Armageddon was not to commence in 1914 or shortly thereafter. In the year World War I erupted, he suggested, the war in heaven described in Revelation began; in 1918 Satan was cast out of heaven and confined to this earth. Jehovah's Witnesses further believe that in 1918 Jehovah placed Christ upon his throne, authorizing him to be king. Prior to this appointment, Christ was sitting on the right hand of God, but now he is ruling from heaven. According to this belief, for a few years the King will permit Satan to continue his reign of terror, and then with the beginning of the millennium Satan's power and influence will be temporarily crushed. [8]

During the presidency of Judge Rutherford, turbulence among the leadership of the Bible society intensified. Replacing four members of the Board of Directors with his appointees, Rutherford worked to gain complete control of the organization. However, some of the original followers of Russell were not only dissatisfied with what they regarded as Rutherford's domineering actions, but they disagreed with the new doctrinal emphasis initiated by the second president in his controversial book, *The Finished Mystery* (1917). Following the publication of *The Finished Mystery,* Rutherford hoped to stem the rising tide of opposition by requesting members to conduct a straw vote. In the November, 1917, referendum, Rutherford received an overwhelming majority. While most Bible students indicated a strong support of their new leader, some members of the movement were not content, and various schisms occurred among the followers of Charles Russell known as "Russellites." One group who claimed to preserve the basic theology of Pastor Russell formed the Dawn Bible Students Association. Other offshoots of this movement are known as the Standfast Movement, Paul Johnson Movement (later renamed the Layman's Home Missionary Movement), Elijah Voice Movement, Eagle Society, and Pastoral Bible Institute of Brooklyn. In 1931, to differentiate the followers of Rutherford from other "Russellites," those who remained loyal to the second president adopted the name "Jehovah's Witnesses." [9]

After winning the internal struggle and securing control of the Bible society, Rutherford and other members of the movement were threatened not only by mobs but also by the United States government. Many thought that the Great War was the beginning of Armageddon and was a necessary prelude to the dissolving of the present evil world and preparation for the millennial reign of Christ. In the midst of wartime hysteria, Bible students were accused of being German agents, of circulating insidious propaganda, and of violating the Federal Espionage Law. (While members of the society were pacifists and refused to serve in the armed forces, they did not support the Germans.) In June 1918, Judge Rutherford and seven members of his staff were arrested and charged with conspiring to cause insubordination and refusal of duty in the United States military and naval forces. After a jury declared that the Witnesses were guilty, the eight men were sentenced to twenty years' imprisonment. For nine months these leaders were incarcerated in a federal penitentiary in Atlanta. After the war ended, they were released; in 1919 their convictions were reversed. Meanwhile, other members of the society were charged with disloyalty; in the midst of oppression, many left the movement. By 1920, Rutherford's following had declined from nearly 50,000 to less than 9,000 members. [10]

The responsibility of members serving as missionaries was emphasized in 1920 when everyone in the local congregations who participated in witness work was requested to submit a weekly report. Prior to 1918, only "pioneers," those who volunteered to serve as full-time nonsalaried missionaries, submitted such records. When the first of these new reports were introduced, more than 8,400 responded, with 350 designated as pioneers. [11]

During Rutherford's administration there was a marked attempt to coordinate the efforts of the Witnesses and to establish increased unity in the society. This objective was partly accomplished by the creation of what Jehovah's Witnesses call a centralized theocracy. This theocracy, which is considered in harmony with New Testament Christianity, became an official structure in the summer of 1938 when leaders of the Watch Tower Bible and Tract Society gained control over the appointment of all local officials. According to the polity of the society, local bodies called congregations are arranged into circuits with traveling ministers assigned to visit regularly the local societies. The circuits are then grouped into districts and all phases of this organization are under the direction of a governing hierarchy.

When individuals unite with this theocracy, they are to disassociate themselves from all activities of the political state and give full allegiance to "Jehovah's organization." Such allegiance includes refusal to salute any national flag, to serve in the armed forces, to vote, or to run for public office. Witnesses generally view nearly every organization outside this theocratic body (including churches, ministers, and international organizations) as a giant conspiracy which is cleverly directed by Satan. [12]

Harassment and persecution of Jehovah's Witnesses continued throughout the 1930s and 1940s. During these two decades more members of this society were imprisoned in this country while practicing their religious convictions than were members of any other religious community. In the 1930s, for example, many Bible students were charged with selling without a license, distributing advertising matter without permission, disturbing the peace, and violating Sabbath laws and other local ordinances. After being convicted, many were jailed for from ten to thirty days and were fined up to $200. Between 1928 and 1934 nearly 700 Witnesses were imprisoned in New Jersey. Hundreds of others were jailed in other states, and in 1936 the society reported 1,149 faithful members arrested. For many Americans, these unorthodox "ministers" were a threat to the existing social order. Some Americans reacted violently because these Bible students vehemently denounced the major religious societies in America, attacked the clergy, and engaged in what they considered repugnant missionary tactics. A brief calm in this tidal wave of oppression, however, was created when the Supreme Court ruled in 1938 that these Christians had the right to distribute their literature in America. [13]

Another type of persecution erupted in the late 1930s when young school children, at the request of their parents, refused to salute the flag. Thousands of children were engulfed in this national controversy and hundreds were expelled from school. After the Supreme Court ruled in 1940 that saluting the flag was a legitimate obligation for every American, the problems of these Christians intensified. Three years later, however, relief from this new form of external pressure was secured when the Supreme Court reversed its decision.[14]

In the midst of the controversy concerning the national flag, Judge Rutherford died. On 13 January 1942, five days after the death of the second president, the Board of Directors elected another conscientious leader to guide the young Bible society, Nathan H. Knorr (1905-   ). Knorr's task was difficult. Mob violence against members of the society was evident in many sections of this nation and in many countries throughout the world. Moreover, during World War II, 3,500 Witnesses were imprisoned for refusal to serve in the armed forces.[15] Recognizing some of the problems which precipitated persecution, Knorr labored to stem the tide of oppression and to make the Bible society more palatable to the American public. While Witnesses continued to denounce organized religions and launched an attack on the United Nations, they gradually altered some of their missionary techniques. Retaining their enthusiasm, Witnesses under Knorr's leadership became less aggressive and subsequently more acceptable to many Americans.

One of the new doctrines introduced during Knorr's presidency was the concept of a "New World Society." This belief refers to the earthly kingdom which will be created following the Battle of Armageddon. According to Jehovah's Witnesses, this New World Society has been functioning since 1919 and presently includes all members of their theocracy. Eventually, they teach, this New Society will encompass all nations of the earth.[16]

Since 1942 leaders of the Watch Tower Society have witnessed a tremendous expansion throughout many parts of the world and acknowledge that their religious community has been one of the fastest growing religious bodies in America. In the year that Nathan Knorr became president, witnessing was conducted in fifty-four countries; in 1944 the society reported a membership of 129,000. Thirty years later, in 1971, more than one and one-half million "ministers" were laboring in 207 countries with a membership in the United States of 416,789. In 1942 approximately 84,000 Witnesses attended the annual Memorial Supper, a service in which those who declare that they are included among the 144,000 mentioned in Revelation partake of the Lord's Supper. In 1971, almost three and one-half million attended this worldwide memorial service. And while Witnesses distributed twenty-eight million books, pamphlets, and magazines in 1948, in 1971 Bible students circulated over eighteen million bound books and Bibles, more than ten and one-half million booklets, and almost 219 million copies of *The Watchtower* and *Awake*.[17]

Under the leadership of Nathan Knorr, the image of the Witnesses has changed and in the opinion of many observers the society is attracting more mature, cultured, and better-educated individuals.[18] Witnesses have gained a reputation in contemporary America of being neat, clean, courteous, honest, and industrious.

While changes have occurred in missionary techniques and the composition of the society, Jehovah's Witnesses have not lost their missionary zeal of warning others of the imminence of the Second Coming. These Bible students are currently emphasizing that "millions now living will never die," that the Battle of Armageddon will begin within a brief span of time, and that many will witness the inauguration of a new millennial era.

Distinguishing Beliefs [19]

Although variations have occurred in the beliefs of members of this movement launched by Russell, there is a harmony of belief concerning many doctrines that are currently advocated by Jehovah's Witnesses; and many of these doctrines are different from the historical Protestant faith. Included among the unusual beliefs that are popular today among Jehovah's Witnesses are the following doctrines and practices.

Members of this Bible society teach that even though the Bible is inerrant, meaning that the scriptures were written by individuals who recorded accurately the message dictated by God, modern versions of the Holy Scriptures contain mistranslations. Consequently, a New World Translation of the Scriptures (1961), based upon what are called preferred texts, has been issued by these Christians. This new version, in the opinion of Jehovah's Witnesses, corrects mistakes appearing in other editions.

While describing their belief concerning the Godhead, Jehovah's Witnesses explain that the Father and Son are separate and distinct spirits and the Holy Ghost is not a member of the Godhead, but is a divine influence or active force. According to members of this Bible society, almighty God, referred to by the ancient prophets as "Jehovah," is the creator of all things. God was once alone in the universe, they say, but after initiating the creation, Jehovah brought forth a son who was called "Michael" or the "Logos" (the "Word") in his pre-mortal existence and Jesus during his journey on earth.

Members of this society further teach that while Jesus was born of a virgin and lived a perfect life void of sin, Jesus was not a God while residing on earth. They reason that since the mission of the Messiah was to provide a ransom, the ransom needed to be equal to the loss. Since Adam was a perfect being while living in Eden and not a God, they hold that God's justice would not permit Jesus to be more than a perfect man.

They also believe that although Jesus rose from the grave and appeared as a man, his true resurrected form was like Jehovah's, a spirit that was neither earthly, human, nor confined to a particular form.

While describing the fall and atonement, members of this faith declare that as a consequence of the fall of Adam, sin and death were transmitted to Adam's posterity, necessitating an atonement. Christ, they add, laid down his life not only to cancel the sins of believing men but to free mankind from death's condemnation by a guarantee that everyone will receive full opportunity during the millennium to embrace the gospel.

There are a few parallels in the views of Seventh-day Adventists and Jehovah's Witnesses regarding life beyond the grave. Members of both of these faiths teach that since man's spirit and body are never separated, the soul sleeps after death. Jehovah's Witnesses further believe that not all mankind will be judged at the same time. They explain that many who have lived an unrighteous life on this earth and have sinned against the Holy Spirit have already been judged. Those beyond reform and correction will not stand before Christ on the day of judgment but will remain asleep forever. The "lake which burneth with fire and brimstone," is considered a scriptural expression which means that there is no recovery or resurrection for the most wicked creatures. Jehovah's Witnesses also teach that at the end of Christ's thousand-year reign on earth, all of God's children, except those beyond reform, will gather for one last test. Satan will then be released from his prison and will cunningly strive to turn men from God. Individuals who succumb to the temptation will be exterminated with Satan and his demons, and all who remain loyal to God during this last trial will be blessed with eternal life. These obedient souls will be free from sickness, sorrow, confusion, and pain, and will be endowed by the pure love of God.

Another distinguishing belief of this religious community is that the 144,000 mentioned in Revelation 7:4 are the only Christians who will inherit heaven. When asked, "How are these men selected," they answer, the spirit of God bears witness to these individuals that they are of this select group. This elite, they continue, will be raised with spiritual bodies (without flesh, bones, or blood) and will assist Christ in ruling the universe. Others who benefit from Christ's ransom will be resurrected with healthy, perfected physical bodies (bodies of flesh, bones, and blood) and will inhabit this earth after the world has been restored to a paradisiacal state.

According to Jehovah's Witnesses, many significant developments will take place during and following the millennium. The period of time extending from 607 B.C., the date Nebuchadnezzar conquered Jerusalem, to 1914 is referred to as the "Times of the Gentiles." During these centuries, the Devil ruled the world without God's interference. In 1914, war erupted in heaven between Michael (Christ) and Satan. After his defeat, the "Dragon" was cast out of heaven and down to earth, and Christ commenced ruling in heaven as King. During the period in which mankind is now living, called the "Time of the End of this World," the gospel will be carried to all nations, kindreds, tongues, and people, and the wicked will be separated from God's people. One of the popular expressions of this group is that millions now living will never die but will live beyond the end of Satan's rule and will reside in a state of peace and happiness in Jehovah's righteous new world. Consequently, they reason that one of the major responsibilities of God's children today is to inform others of the drama described in the Bible, including the birth of God's kingdom, the imminent and final defeat of the Devil, and the creation of a new earth.

Jehovah's Witnesses also teach that everyone who accepts Jehovah as the Almighty God and agrees to serve him should indicate this dedication by being baptized by immersion. Since baptismal fonts are not built in "kingdom halls" (meetinghouses), this rite is generally performed in lakes, rivers, oceans, or municipal baths; and only Witnesses authorized to perform such ordinances may baptize.

Another distinct practice of this faith relates to the Lord's Supper. Individuals who are classified among the 144,000 are the only ones who should partake of the bread and wine as a symbol of the death of Christ and of the dedication to God. All Witnesses and others may attend this important meeting, but only those numbered among the 144,000 partake. It is also their belief that this Memorial of Christ's death should take place on the day corresponding to Nisan 14 of the Jewish calendar (occurring sometime in March or April). In 1972, 10,350 received the Lord's Supper.

Members of this Bible society also refrain from gambling, abstain from the use of tobacco, and hold that drunkenness is a serious sin. They do not celebrate popular holidays, such as Christmas and Easter, and are opposed to blood transfusions. Moreover, their position concerning saluting the flag and serving in the armed forces has not been changed; and they do not vote in civil elections nor hold public office.

17

The Church of Christ, Scientist

One of the most remarkable women to appear on the American horizon during the nineteenth century was the discoverer, founder, and leader of Christian Science, Mary Baker Eddy. While Ellen G. White was a cofounder of one of the major denominations in America, Mary Baker Eddy was the only woman in Christian history to be the sole founder of a religious society that has continued to grow in this country and has expanded into many other parts of the world.

This gifted individual, who founded one of the most unusual religious systems in Christendom, was born on 16 July 1821 in Bow, New Hampshire, a small farm community located a few miles south of Concord. Mary was the youngest child in a family of three girls and three boys. Her parents were highly respected in the communities where they lived and were devoted to the Congregational Church. At the age of seventeen Mary united with that faith even though she did not endorse the Calvinistic doctrine of predestination and unconditional election. On one occasion, as she considered the belief that the nonelect would be perpetually banished from God, she became highly perturbed. Her deep emotions led to such apparant sickness that the family doctor was summoned. Diagnosing her condition, he observed that she was "stricken with fever." After praying to the Lord, however, Mary Baker testified that "a soft glow of ineffable joy" encompassed her and the fever departed. [1]

During her youth, while living in Tilton, New Hampshire, about seventy-five miles from Portland, Maine (the home of Ellen G. White), she showed a genuine interest in intellectual and spiritual themes and, like Ellen G. White, experienced childhood marred by continual illness. Although Mary Baker's education was occasionally interrupted because of her ill health, she studied at home, learned quickly, and possessed an unusual memory. Unlike Ellen G. White, however, Mary Baker had several years of formal education in academies and received periodic instruction from private tutors. Her favorite subjects were natural philosophy, logic, and moral science, and she obtained a few lessons in Hebrew, Greek, and Latin. [2]

Mary Baker Eddy recalled that when she was about eight for about one year she periodically heard a voice, repeating, "Mary." At times she thought her mother was calling, but upon learning that she had not been summoned, she became discouraged, and her mother was perplexed. After reading the narrative of Samuel in the Old Testament, Mary said she understood that the voice was of God. After this the call was not repeated "again to the material senses." [3]

Early in life she gained a desire to write, and during her adolescent years contributed many poems and articles to local papers. It was also at an early age that she remarked that one day she would write a book. Undoubtedly, however, the young woman did not perceive at that time the tremendous influence her work would have on the lives of countless followers.

One of the most significant aspects of her early life that undoubtedly played a major role in her becoming a spiritual leader was her constant suffering from various forms of illness. Her parents turned to many medical doctors, attempting to secure relief for their daughter. Eventually, she was exposed to a variety of healing programs, including exercises of faith and mesmeric practices of that age.

In addition to her protracted illness, her marital hardships undoubtedly caused her to seek relief from suffering. In 1843 she married George W. Glover and was widowed the following year and left with inadequate financial support. After returning to her parents' home and giving birth to her only child, she felt compelled to locate another woman to nurse and raise her son. Later, hoping to regain her boy, she married Daniel Patterson, a dentist and homeopathist. But this union failed to result in a lasting bond of love between husband and wife or an intimate relationship between mother and son. After frequent quarrelling, the marriage ended in divorce in 1873. After inaugurating the Christian Science movement, she was again married, to one of her students, Asa G. Eddy, who died in 1882, five years after their wedding. Mrs. Eddy, however, did win the respect of her son George Glover, toward the end of her life.

During her unpleasant marriage to the itinerant dentist, Mary Baker Patterson sought help from a faith healer, Phineas Parkhurst Quimby, who resided in Maine. While under his care, she secured some relief from her ailments and became genuinely interested in the mental origin of disease.

In February, 1866, shortly after the death of this "magnetic doctor," Mrs. Eddy slipped on an icy street in the manufacturing community of Lynn,

MARY BAKER EDDY

Massachusetts, and sustained a painful injury. An attending physician pronounced the injury fatal but three days after the accident she opened her Bible to a description of one of the Savior's miraculous healings: "And, behold, they brought to him a man sick of the palsy, lying on a bed; and Jesus seeing their faith said unto the sick of the palsy; Son, be of good cheer; thy sins be forgiven thee" (Matthew 9:2). As Mrs. Eddy read, she testified that "the healing Truth dawned upon" her. Subsequently, she continued, "I rose, dressed myself, and ever after was in better health than I had before enjoyed." Although this healing was not permanent and she required therapy following this discovery, a definite change had taken place in her pattern of belief. As Mrs. Eddy recalled, in 1866 "I discovered the Science of divine metaphysical healing which I afterwards named Christian Science. . . . I named it Christian, because it is compassionate, helpful, and spiritual."[4] For twenty years prior to this accident, she had been trying to trace physical effects to a mental cause, but following her recovery she decided that all causation was Mind, and every effect a mental phenomenon. [5]

For three years following her healing, she withdrew from society to ponder her mission in life, to study the Bible, and to develop a new religious system. Employing the Bible as a basic text, Mrs. Eddy unfolded an unusual interpretation of the scriptures, revealing the teachings of Jesus and his accomplishments in light of what she called "the Principle and rule of spiritual Science and metaphysical healing." [6]

One of the central doctrines presented by Mrs. Eddy that helps inquirers better understand the pattern of belief of this religious community was her unique concept of God. While describing the unlimited nature of God's presence, the founder of Christian Science emphasized that "God is All-in-all." According to her convictions, "From this it follows that nothing possesses reality nor existence except the divine Mind and His ideas." She also believed that God is Spirit, pure Love, and pure good, and she reasoned that since God "fills all space" and all is spirit and spiritual then the opposite of these characteristics do not really exist. Therefore, Mrs. Eddy concluded that sin, sickness, matter, and death are unreal. [7]

As her novel religious system emerged, Mrs. Eddy adopted unusual definitions of terms which sometimes create semantic problems when individuals not of this faith communicate with Christian Scientists. In defining various terms, she wrote:

> God I called *immortal Mind*. That which sins, suffers, and dies, I named *mortal mind*. The physical senses, or sensuous nature, I called *error* and *shadow*. Soul I denominated *substance,* because Soul alone is truly substantial. God I characterized as individual entity, but his corporeality I denied. The real I claimed as eternal; and its antipodes, or the temporal, I described as unreal. Spirit I called the *reality;* and matter, the *unreality*.[8]

Although many critics of the Christian Science faith point out parallels in the teachings of Quimby and Mrs. Eddy, Christian Scientists emphasize the differences between their beliefs. Whereas Quimby and many others interested in "mind-cure" concentrated on mind-over-matter with the healing power generated by the individual, Mrs. Eddy taught that the power that heals comes from God and his influence on consciousness. As explained by Christian Scientists, Quimby stressed personal will and Mrs. Eddy concentrated on the influence of what she considered God's "Truth" on the thinking of mankind.

Another significant difference in the teachings of Mrs. Eddy and Quimby is that she viewed creation as "wholly spiritual." As one expositor of Christian Science stated, the need is to "recognize the immutable perfection of Mind's spiritual creation, which could not possibly permit the presence of anything contrary to its own nature." The result, he added, of this "yielding to the divine Mind" is inevitably healing, "a radical changing of the evidence before the senses." [9] As explained by Mrs. Eddy,

> What is the cardinal point of the difference in my metaphysical system? This: that *by knowing the unreality of disease, sin, and death,* you demonstrate the allness of God. This difference wholly separates my system from all others. The reality of these so-called existences I deny, because they are not to be found in God, and this system is built on Him as the sole cause. It would be difficult to name any previous teachers, save Jesus and his apostles, who have thus taught. [10]

In the view of Christian Scientists, disease and pain are mental, not material. They are said to arise from a false concept of existence, and it is held that when an individual learns that sickness and suffering are not God-created and therefore are mortal and illusory, they disappear from his experience. According to this teaching, what appears to be physical healing is really the wiping out of a false belief that disease is real.

"Man's belief produces disease and all its symptons," Mrs. Eddy asserted. "We weep because others weep, we yawn because they yawn, and we have small-pox because others have it; but mortal mind, not matter contains and carries the infection." [11]

After studying, writing, and discussing her religious views with boarders in homes where she resided, Mrs. Eddy organized her first school in 1870, in Lynn, Massachusetts, thereby commencing a career of healing and teaching. To provide for her support, she charged students who could afford to pay a tuition; graduates who subsequently engaged in spiritual healing agreed to pay their tutor ten percent of their income. Shortly after instituting a formal program of instruction, Mary Baker Eddy purchased a home in Lynn, where she continued conducting classes.

The basic beliefs of Mrs. Eddy were widely circulated in what became known as the Christian Science textbook, *Science and Health with Key to the Scriptures.* This work was originally published in 1875 and has passed through many revisions and editions, but the basic theology unfolded in this influential treatise has not been changed. Although Mrs. Eddy taught that the Bible is the only authority for religious truth and a sufficient guide to eternal life, she claimed that men have altered the original text and have developed erroneous interpretations of the scripture. Her textbook, *Science and Health,* does not in the view of Christian Scientists supersede the Bible but is a guide unlocking biblical truths. Moreover, this book is regarded as a complete statement of Christian Science, and, like the Bible in its original form, contains "nothing of human opinion" and is "devoid of man made theories." [12]

In the same year that the first edition of the Christian Science textbook was printed, Sunday services were held in private homes, consisting primarily of a sermon by Mrs. Eddy, prayers, and hymns. For many months, the gatherings remained small, usually numbering fewer than twenty. Although few converts had been gathered, in 1879 about twenty-six people assembled in Boston and endorsed Mrs. Eddy's proposal to establish a church which was named the "Church of Christ, Scientist." Shortly thereafter these members extended a call to Mrs. Eddy to be their pastor and in 1881 she was ordained. [13]

In the decade following the organization of this religious community, Mrs. Eddy founded the Massachusetts Metaphysical College, published and edited *The Christian Science Journal,* and changed the Sunday services from the afternoon to the morning, so that the society would no longer be considered subordinate to any other denomination. In the 1890s, Mrs. Eddy reorganized the church, prepared a church *manual* describing the procedure of church government, and delivered her last public sermon. Although Mrs. Eddy's last appearance behind a pulpit took place on 5 January 1896, this influential woman continued to direct the affairs of the church through written messages after her retirement.

One of the last accomplishments of Mrs. Eddy was the founding in 1908 of the internationally known *Christian Science Monitor.* Two years after initiating this newspaper, on 3 December 1910, the eighty-nine-year-old founder of one of America's most unusual religious societies died, leaving a church with a membership of nearly 100,000 and an estate worth two and one-half million dollars. [14]

Sunday services of this religious community are different from those held in many other Christian churches. There are no pastors and no sermons delivered from the pulpits on their Sabbath day. A First and a Second Reader, however, read selections from the Bible and *Science and Health with Key to the Scriptures.* These "lesson-sermons," covering twenty-six subjects, are published in advance of the meetings, are studied by members the week before they are read at the Sunday service, and are uniformly presented in the various branches located throughout the world. Services also include congregational singing (no choirs), a song by a professional vocalist, silent prayer, and the recitation of the Lord's Prayer with Mrs. Eddy's spiritual interpretation of it.

On Wednesday, at noon or in the evening, another meeting is held, in which members testify of their healing experiences and describe how they have benefited from the application of the principles unfolded by the author of *Science and Health*.[15]

Throughout the history of this denomination, world headquarters have been located in Boston, Massachusetts. Envisioning that the central or "mother" church would draw members from various countries, Mrs. Eddy reorganized her church under a title that has continued to the present day, "The Mother Church, The First Church of Christ, Scientist, in Boston, Massachusetts." The central government of the Mother Church consists of a Board of Directors who were originally appointed by Mrs. Eddy and then became a self-perpetuating body. These men and women have the responsibility of administering church affairs according to the constitution and laws published in Mrs. Eddy's *Manual of the Mother Church*. Another national group of administrators, known as the Board of Trustees, has the responsibility of supervising the publishing activities of the denomination.

While Christian Scientists living throughout the world may become members of the Mother Church, they also maintain membership in one of the 3,300 branches located in more than fifty countries. Each branch is an independent, self-governing body. In this essentially democratic polity, members elect a rotating board of directors who manage local ecclesiastical affairs according to the guidelines found in The Mother Church manual. The two Readers are also elected by the membership from among their own number.[16]

Currently this church publishes a weekly periodical, *The Christian Science Sentinel;* a monthly periodical, *The Christian Science Journal;* a foreign periodical, *The Christian Science Herald;* and continues to publish its daily newspaper, *The Christian Science Monitor*. The society also authorizes thousands of Christian Science practitioners to assist individuals in applying the beliefs of their faith to illness and other problems afflicting mankind. Repudiating the principles governing the actions of medical doctors (including treatment in hospitals), Christian Scientists turn to practitioners for assistance. After demonstrating evidence of successful work of healing, practitioners are registered by the officers of the Mother Church at Boston; these men and women continue to heal what they classify as "human errors and ills."

While members of this faith may seek the special skills of doctors for childbirth, secure the services of dentists, and ask for medical help following a bone fracture, they insist that correct application of Christian Science would eliminate the need for these specialists. Many members testify, for example, that broken bones following accidents have mended perfectly without the aid of medical doctors. These Christians are also opposed to compulsory vaccination for their members on the ground that such laws infringe upon their religious convictions. Believing in obeying the laws of the land, however, they comply with the statutes which are enacted and enforced.

It is incorrect to say that Christian Science is a religion which concentrates only on helping those with physical illness, for members of this denomination teach that their religion gives relevant answers concerning life and salvation, including man's preexistence and the road to an eternal life with God. The proper implementation of this Science, they add, will not only heal people of sickness and sin but of all forms of discord. One of the central themes which Christian Scientists are proclaiming to the world is that all problems of society can be resolved through proper utilization of spiritual power.

Distinguishing Beliefs

While many Americans associate the Christian Science faith with a system of healing, the teachings of this church encompass a wide spectrum of religious thought. Partly because members of this faith have adopted unique definitions for many terms, the teachings of the Christian Scientists are difficult for the average American to comprehend. After inquirers learn a few basic concepts held by these Christians, however, their doctrines and practices seem less confusing.

One of the best approaches to an understanding of Christian Science belief is to begin with their unusual concept of God. Members of this religious community teach that "Life, Truth, and Love constitute the triune Person called God." This one God is a Spirit, they explain, and is supreme good, is love, and is "multiform in office: God the Father-Mother; Christ the spiritual idea of sonship; divine Science or the Holy Comforter." They say that the supreme Deity is properly called "Father-Mother" because this name identifies God's "tender relationship to His spiritual creation." They further hold that Jesus was born of the virgin Mary, was the reflection of God, was appointed to speak God's word to humanity in a form which man could understand, and expressed the Christ, the true idea voicing good to man. They do not believe, however, that Jesus and Christ are synonyms, for they say Jesus is the name of the human man and Christ refers to the divine idea.[17]

Christian Scientists also teach that the "Scriptures imply that God is All-in-all" and "declare that God is spirit." Therefore, they explain that "in Spirit all is harmony, and there can be no discord; all is Life, and there is no death. . . . He fills all space, and it is impossible to conceive of such omnipresence and individuality except as infinite Spirit or Mind. Hence all is Spirit and spiritual."[18] Therefore, Christian Scientists insist that sin, sickness, matter, pain, and death are illusions of the mind or misconceptions of man.

Although Christian Scientists teach that the Bible is a sufficient guide to eternal life, they maintain that their publication *Science and Health* serves as a guide for a proper interpretation of the Bible.

According to members of this religious community, the Genesis account of the creation and fall of Adam is an allegory, a myth, or a dream narrative. Adam was not created a mortal being by God, they add, for "the mortality of man is a myth"; and, since man is immortal, man was never born. The belief that spirit was submerged in matter to be emancipated at a future date is considered erroneous. Adam is regarded as the scriptural term for error and stands for a belief of material mind. Since God, they reason, is eternal and made all that was created, they state that "man and the spiritual universe co-exist with God." [19]

Another distinguishing belief of these Christians is that salvation is understanding God and demonstrating one's convictions by surmounting sin, sickness, and death. [20]

While describing life beyond the grave, Christian Scientists teach that there is no death, meaning that life is indestructible; man, they say, in his real definition, is never separate from his maker. In their opinion, since God is eternal, so is man. Death is sometimes compared to another incident in the dream of mortality or another experience of mortal mind. "The sinner makes his own hell by doing evil," Mrs. Eddy declared, "and the saint his own heaven by doing right." While our thoughts are evil, she continued, we are in hell, which is a self-imposed agony, a self-inflicted belief in sin, sickness, death, and suffering. As we come close to God in thought, we experience more of that spiritual harmony which is heaven. And, she concluded, there is no final judgment, for "the judgment-day of wisdom comes hourly and continually, even the judgment by which mortal man is divested of all material error." [21]

There are no physical sacraments in this church. Baptism is considered as a continuous act, a perpetual purification from all error; and twice a year, active members participate in a communion service. Instead of partaking of bread and wine, which is part of the regular sabbath service activity, during this semiannual meeting Christian Scientists commune silently with God.

Miscellaneous Beliefs

Like many other Christians, Christian Scientists also believe in daily prayer, frequent communication with diety, and living a life governed by the principle of love.

The Holiness-Pentecostal Movement

18

While Americans concentrated on the challenges created by the post-Civil War social, industrial, and intellectual revolutions, leaders of a Holiness-Pentecostal movement sought to preserve what they regarded as the central truths of classical Christianity. The rise of this new movement paralleled the reforms of labor leaders, prohibitionists, socialists, populists, and progressives. In the midst of demands for political and social changes, Holiness and Pentecostal leaders sounded their protests concerning the evils of their generation. Reacting against the growing popularity of contemporary theology, especially trends in biblical criticism and the rise of the social gospel, these orthodox Protestants claimed that the moral degeneracy of their time was the result of man's departure from traditional Christian principles. These preachers further declared that the mounting problems of urban America could be resolved by rekindling historic Christian truths. [1]

One of the specific doctrines that one group of Holiness preachers sought to revitalize was the Methodist belief in sanctification. John Wesley had emphasized two distinct stages in a Christian's religious experience. The first was an individual's initial conversion, called his justification, and the second was a sanctification, a perfecting of a Christian or a person's becoming holy. According to this belief, when an individual was converted he was forgiven of his sins of commission but retained within himself a "residue of sin." The sin which persisted was the inbred sin resulting from Adam's fall and had to be removed by receiving a second rebirth. This second blessing purified the believer from his inward sin and enabled him to secure perfect love of God and of his fellowmen. Although Wesley recognized that believers continued to sin, the perfection which he advanced was one of motives and desires. Even though he taught that this holiness could be attained instantly "as a second work of grace," he held that it usually was preceded and followed by a "gradual growth in grace." [2]

Methodist preachers not only transplanted to America the doctrine of entire sanctification, but also popularized in this land a pentecostal type of religious enthusiasm. Ministers of this denomination undoubtedly conducted more camp meetings in the early republic and initiated more revivals than did preachers of any other Protestant society. During some of these Methodist-directed spiritual quickenings, participants expressed their emotional aspirations with a variety of outward manifestations. While one group of participants was weeping, wailing, and praying vocally, others were fainting, jerking, or speaking in an unknown tongue.

The last general awakening which preceded the Civil War occurred in the North in 1858. Hundreds of prayer meetings were held in the rapidly growing northern cities with clergy and lay members participating in the services. During this revival thousands united with the major Protestant churches of America. Endowed with a motivating spiritual zeal, the new converts stimulated the crusades against slavery, intemperance, and Sabbath negligence. During this urban enlivenment several preachers also published works on Christian holiness, encouraging Christians of all faiths to live in closer harmony with the example set by the Savior of mankind. [3]

Although the Holiness movement was temporarily disrupted by the holocaust of the Civil War, following Appomattox another wave of revivals swept across the nation; amidst the flames of these quickenings, an emphasis on Wesley's doctrine of sanctification was renewed. Most clergy who spoke on this holiness theme were of the Methodist persuasion, but a few Presbyterian and Baptist preachers incorporated the doctrine into their sermons. From 1867 to 1894, "holiness associations" were formed to promote the doctrine of the second rebirth. After leaders of these interdenominational groups decided that the Methodist Church had failed to reestablish the doctrine of sanctification as emphasized by Wesley, they withdrew from this and other Protestant denominations and organized independent religious societies. [4]

The major divisions within Methodism occurred after 1894, at a time when the Methodist society was the largest Protestant denomination in America, and during an era when the percentage of church membership was growing rapidly. Since influential leaders of the Holiness movement could not agree on the precise nature of the new religious communities, they failed to establish one major denomination.

Further divisions in this movement occurred during the first decade of the twentieth century. Between 1901 and 1906, a theological rupture within the Holiness communions gave birth to the Pentecostal movement. One of the doctrines precipitating this schism was the "evidence required to prove that one had been baptized by the Holy Spirit." While Holiness preachers emphasized the doctrine of sanctification, one faction within the communion specified that Christians secured full holiness only when the second baptism, the baptism of the Spirit, was accompanied by an outward, emotional reaction. Although Pentecostals generally agree that speaking in tongues is a major evidence that a convert has been baptized by the Holy Spirit, members of this religious community have not been unified on the propriety of other forms of manifestations.[5]

One of the foremost leaders in the rise of the modern Pentecostal movement was Charles F. Parham (1873-1929). Born in Muscatine, Iowa, Parham testified that when he was nine years of age, he was called to the ministry. "Though unconverted," he recalled, "I realized as certainly as did Samuel that God had laid His hand on me." For many years, he added, he felt like Paul when that apostle of Christendom declared, "Woe is me, if I preach not the gospel."[6]

After his conversion, Parham united with the Congregational Church, and two years later, when he was fifteen, became a lay preacher. His interest in the ministry was temporarily interrupted after entering Southwestern, a college in Kansas; but after being stricken with rheumatic fever and failing to respond to medical treatment, he decided that his illness was caused by a rebellion against his Heavenly Father. After dedicating his life to God and deciding to serve him in the capacity of a minister, Parham felt that he had been miraculously healed. He further declared that this experience was one of the most significant spiritual events in his life and was an immediate predecessor to his becoming a well-known faith healer.

After graduating from college, Parham became a minister in the Methodist Church, but his nonsectarian views and desire to retain characteristics of John Wesley's Methodism led him away from that denomination and into Holiness circles.

A number of the basic teachings of Parham were eventually incorporated into most Pentecostal societies. While many preachers in America were teaching that conversion was a gradual process, Parham returned to Wesley's emphasis on salvation as a crisis experience. He further held that sanctification was an important second work of grace and completely destroyed the inbred sin. This second rebirth, he added, should be sought by all Christians so that their sinful desires would be eradicated. Two additional doctrines popularized by the Pentecostal leaders were healing through faith and premillennialism. Although some Christians were teaching a postmillennialism, that Christ would return following a man-made millennium, Parham taught that Christ would suddenly return, that the world would be transformed by divine intervention and that a thousand years of peace would continue, followed by the final judgment.[7]

One of Parham's most controversial beliefs that eventually led to various schisms within the Pentecostal movement was his insistence that speaking in tongues was necessary as the only biblical evidence of the baptism by the Holy Spirit. This belief, though controversial, gave to the Pentecostal community a powerful thrust. While members of the communion were trying to decide the visible forms that the second rebirth should take, some claiming that it should be by shouting, leaping, jumping, or falling into trances, Parham argued that speaking in tongues was an unmistakable motor expression which guaranteed that a Christian had received his second rebirth.[8]

Like the Holiness societies, the Pentecostal movement has experienced a number of permanent divisions. Influential leaders have gathered their own followers, and theological diversities have kept groups apart. Currently there are more than twenty religious societies in the United States that are classified as Holiness-Pentecostal or Baptistic-Pentecostal bodies. The largest of these denominations is the Assemblies of God, whose leaders enumerated a membership of more than one million in 1972. Other major wings of this movement which reported a membership of from one-fourth to a half-million members are the Church of God in Christ, International; the Church of God in Christ; the Church of God (Cleveland, Tennessee); and the Church of the Nazarene, the latter group endorsing the Wesleyan view of holiness but opposing the practice of speaking in tongues.

Since the 1920s many Pentecostal bodies have witnessed a phenomenal growth not only in the United States but in other parts of the world. From 1926 to 1970, for example, the Assemblies of God increased in this nation from 47,950 converts to 626,660 members; the Church of God in Christ from 30,263 to 425,500; the Church of God (Cleveland, Tennessee) from 23,247 to 243,532; and the Pentecostal Holiness society from 8,096 to 66,750. In percentage, a number of these groups are among the fastest growing denominations in the United States.[9]

One of the best-known Pentecostal leaders of mid-twentieth-century America is Oral Roberts. After gaining notice as a revivalist and faith healer, Roberts established a school that was originally referred to as the first distinctly Pentecostal university, the Oral Roberts University, in Tulsa, Oklahoma. Shortly after this school was founded, Roberts shocked many people by joining the Methodist Church. After uniting with this popular faith in 1968, the evangelist vowed that he would never depart from the basic teachings of Pentecostalism.[10]

Since there is such a wide latitude of belief among members of the Holiness and Pentecostal societies, it is difficult to summarize their distinguishing beliefs. Basically most members of these churches endorse the classical Protestant faith. In fact, many accept the fundamentalist view of the Bible (and many other beliefs which fundamentalists popularized) but they do not generally support the fundamentalist crusade, a movement that was primarily directed by leaders of the major Protestant faiths.

Although doctrinal diversities have kept the Holiness and Pentecostal communions from uniting into several denominations, a large majority of these Christians agree on a number of doctrines. In addition to endorsing the view of John Wesley concerning sanctification, nearly all these Christians assert that there is one God and that the Father, Son, and Holy Ghost are three persons of one essence. Although most endorse a belief that harmonizes with the traditional Catholic and Protestant view of the Godhead, they generally reject the use of the term "Trinity," claiming that it is unscriptural. Most teach that the Bible in all its parts is divinely inspired and is the sole norm of faith, containing all truth necessary to faith and proper Christian conduct. In harmony with the classical Arminian spectrum of Protestantism, most members of these religious circles declare that because of the fall, man is born with a fallen nature and an inclination to evil, that Christ took upon himself the sins of all believers who persevere to the end, that heaven is a place where all believers, who benefit from Christ's action on Calvary, will reside, and that hell is a place of everlasting punishment for all unregenerates. Most believe in the priesthood of all believers and that the Lord's Supper is a memorial commemorating the death and sacrifice of the Savior.

One doctrine which currently serves as a wedge preventing the unification of some of these religious bodies is baptism. While Nazarenes believe that sprinkling, pouring, and immersion are proper modes of baptism and that young children may be baptized upon recommendations of their parents or guardians, most members of the Pentecostal movement teach that only believers should be baptized and that immersion is the only proper mode for this ordinance.

The orthodox flavor of Pentecostalism is further reflected by the recommendations of these Christians concerning observance of the Lord's Day and their emphasis on simplicity and modesty in dress. Most members refrain from dancing, attending movies, and participating in games of chance. Moreover, most members are opposed to the sale, distribution, and consumption of intoxicating liquors, and many do not use tobacco in any of its popular forms. Some of the adherents of these two evangelistic faiths earnestly believe that they are conscientiously preparing for the imminent return of the Savior of mankind.[11]

The tremendous growth of the Holiness and Pentecostal movement and many other religious societies of modern America, including the Latter-day Saints, the Jehovah's Witnesses, and the Seventh-day Adventists, is striking evidence that man's quest for religious truth has continued and that many people in the modern world are earnestly striving to recapture the essence of New Testament Christianity.

Notes and
Appendixes

Notes

Introduction

1. Constant H. Jacquet, Jr., ed., *Yearbook of American Churches, Edition for 1972* (New York: Abingdon Press, 1972), pp. 229-31.
2. George Gallup, Jr. and John O. Davies, III, eds., *Religion in America. The Gallup Opinion Index,* April, 1971 (Princeton: Gallup International, Inc., 1971), p. 69.
3. Edwin Scott Gaustad, *A Religious History of America* (New York: Harper and Row, 1974), p. 350.
4. Eusebius, "The Life of Constantine," *A Select Library of Nicene and Post-Nicene* Rand McNally and Co., 1965), pp. 72-84.
5. Constant H. Jacquet, Jr., ed., *Yearbook of American and Canadian Churches, Edition for 1974* (New York: Abingdon Press, 1974), p. 262; Constant H. Jacquet, Jr., ed., *Yearbook of American Churches, Edition for 1970* (New York: Council Press, 1970), p. 227.

Chapter 1

1. John 20:21. See also Matthew 28:18-20. This and the reference in Footnote 2 are from the Revised Standard version of the Bible. All other scriptures cited herein are from the King James version.
2. Matthew 16:17-19.
3. Leo J. Trese, *The Faith Explained* (Notre Dame, Indiana: Fides Publishers, Inc., 1962), pp. 146-47, 159-65.
4. Eusebius, "The Life of Constantine," *A Select Library of Nicene and Post-Nicene Fathers of the Christian Church,* Philip Schaff and Henry Wace trans. (2nd ser., New York, 1890), vol. 1, pp. 521-24; Philip Hughes, *The Church in Crisis: A History of the General Councils 325-1870* (Garden City, New York: Image Books, 1964), pp. 33-38.
5. N. Q. King, *The Emperor Theodosius and the Establishment of Christianity* (London: SCM Press, 1961), pp. 77-79, 84-86, 93-96; Philip Hughes, *A Popular History of the Catholic Church* (New York: MacMillan, 1962), p. 37.
6. John P. Kleinz, "Vatican II on Religious Freedom," *The Catholic Lawyer,* vol. 13 (Summer, 1967), pp. 180-81.
7. John Tracy Ellis, ed., *Documents of American Catholic History* (Milwaukee: Bruce Publishing Co., 1956), pp. 115-17.
8. James Bisset, *Abridgment and Collection of the Acts of the Assembly of the Province of Maryland at Present in Force* (Philadelphia, 1759), pp. 12-17, 39.
9. Frederick Lewis Weis, *The Colonial Churches and the Colonial Clergy of the Middle and Southern Colonies, 1697-1776* (Lancaster, 1938), p. 18.
10. Ellis, *Documents of American Catholic History,* pp. 151-54.
11. Ibid., pp. 140-45.
12. Theodore Maynard, *The Story of American Catholicism* (Garden City, New York: Image Books, 1960), p. 255-56.
13. J.D.S. DeBow, *Statistical View of the United States* (Washington, 1854), p. 138;

Department of the Interior, Census Office, *Report on Statistics of Churches in the United States at the Eleventh Census: 1890* (Washington: Government Printing Office, 1894), p. xviii; U.S. Department of Commerce, *Religious Bodies: 1936* (Washington: Government Printing Office, 1941), vol. 2, part 2, p. 1,530; Lauris B. Whitman, ed., *Yearbook of American Churches: Edition for 1968* (New York: National Council of Churches, 1968), p. 200.

14. *The Official Catholic Directory: 1973* (New York: P. J. Kennedy and Sons, 1973), General Summary, pp. 1-2.

15. Trese, p. 147.

16. E. M. Burke, "Omniscience," *New Catholic Encyclopedia* (New York: McGraw-Hill Book Co., 1967), vol. 10, p. 690, hereafter cited as *NCE*.

17. M. F. Morry, "Omnipresence," *NCE*, vol. 10, p. 689.

18. S. Tsuji, "Iconography," *NCE*, vol. 1, p. 515; J. Michl, "Theology of Angels," *NCE*, vol. 1, pp. 509-10, 514.

19. Trese, pp. 17, 560; Karl Rahner, *Inspiration in the Bible* (New York: Herder and Herder, 1964), pp. 10-14.

20. J. F. Whealon, "Bible," *NCE*, vol. 2, pp. 513-14.

21. *Instructions for Non-Catholics* (Orland Park, Ill.: United Book Service, 1954), pp. 30-32.

22. T. R. Heath, "Adam," *NCE*, vol. 1, pp. 114-15; I. Hunt, "Fall of Man," *NCE*, vol. 5, pp. 814-16.

23. Ludwig Ott, *Fundamentals of Catholic Dogma* (St. Louis: B. Herder Book Co., 1964), p. 189.

24. Robert S. Franks, *The Work of Christ: A Historical Study of Christian Doctrine* (New York: Thomas Nelson and Sons, 1962), pp. 40, 83.

25. Ibid., pp. 128-35.

26. Ibid., pp. 220-21.

27. Vincent Taylor, *Jesus and His Sacrifices* (London: MacMillan, 1951), pp. 299-300.

28. H. M. McElwain, "Theology of Resurrection of the Dead," *NCE*, vol. 12, p. 425; C. J. Corcoran, "Glorified Body," *NCE*, vol. 6, p. 512; Yves Congar, *The Wide World My Parish*, Donald Attwater, trans. (Baltimore: Helicon Press, 1962), pp. 176-77.

29. Ott, p. 485; Congar, pp. 67-68.

30. Philip Hughes, *The Catholic Faith in Practice* (Wilkes-Barre, Pa.: Dimension Books, Inc., 1965), p. 116.

31. George J. Dyer, *Limbo: Unsettled Question* (New York: Sheed and Ward, 1964), pp. 109-10, 147, 169, 178-82.

32. *Instructions for Non-Catholics*, pp. 44-45; Congar, p. 72.

33. Karl Rahner, *The Church and the Sacraments* (New York: Herder and Herder, 1964), p. 9; Hughes, *The Catholic Faith in Practice*, pp. 79-83.

Chapter 2

This chapter was published in *The Ensign*, vol. 1 (May 1971), pp. 48-53 and appears in this work with approval of the publishers.

1. Steven Runciman, *The Eastern Schism* (Oxford, Claredon Press, 1955), pp. 159-60.

2. Bureau of the Census, *Special Reports, Religious Bodies: 1906* (Washington, 1910, p. 25. The reported membership of the Eastern Church in 1890 was only 600. Benson Y. Landis, ed., *Yearbook of American Churches: Edition for 1957* (New York: National Council of the Churches of Christ in the U.S.A., 1956), p. 271.

3. Constant H. Jacquet, Jr., ed., *Yearbook of American Churches: Edition for 1967* (New York: National Council of the Churches of Christ in the USA, 1967), p. 211.

4. Timothy Ware, *The Orthodox Church* (Baltimore: Penguin Books, Inc., 1967), pp.

180-90; R. M. French, *The Eastern Orthodox Church* (London: Hutchinson University Library, 1964), pp. 162-63; Ernst Benz, *The Eastern Orthodox Church: Its Thought and Life* (Garden City, New York: Doubleday and Co., 1963), pp. 83-84.

5. Ware, p. 139.

6. Idem.; *The World Almanac* (New York: *New York World-Telegram* and *The Sun,* 1966), p. 491.

7. John Meyendorff, "St. Peter in Byzantine Theology," *The Primacy of Peter* (London: The Faith Press, 1963), pp. 11, 14, 18, 23.

8. Ignatius to the Smyrnaeans, quoted in C. C. Richardson, ed. and trans., *Early Christian Fathers,* "Library of Christian Classics" (Philadelphia Westminster Press, 1953), vol. 1, p. 115.

9. Ibid., pp. 20, 26; Demetrios J. Constantelos, *An Old Faith For Modern Man* (n.p., 1964), pp. 18-20.

10. Meyendorff, pp. 10, 14.

11. Ware, pp. 204-14; Gerasimos Papadopoulos, "The Revelatory Character of the New Testament and Holy Tradition in the Orthodox Church," *The Orthodox Ethos,* A. J. Philippon, ed. (Oxford, England: Holywell Press, 1964), vol. 1, pp. 98-99.

12. French, pp. 88-89; Sergius Bulgakov, *The Orthodox Church* (New York, 1953), pp. 47, 119.

13. John of Damascus, "Exposition of the Orthodox Faith," Philip Schaff and Henry Wace, ed., *A Select Library of Nicene and Post-Nicene Fathers of the Christian Church* (2nd series, New York, 1899), vol. 9. pp. 1-4; Ware, p. 217.

14. Nicolas Zernov, *Eastern Christendom* (New York: G. P. Putman's Sons, 1961), p. 230.

15. Frank Gavin, *Some Aspects of Contemporary Greek Orthodox Thought* (Milwaukee, 1923), pp. 219-20, 276; Ware, pp. 281-82.

16. Zernov, p. 249; Ware, p. 281.

17. Zernov, pp. 250-51; Ware, pp. 285-86.

18. Ware, pp. 292-94.

19. Zernov, pp. 251-53, 268.

20. Ibid., pp. 253-55, 271.

21. Benz., pp. 1-2.

22. Timothy Ware, "The Communion of Saints," *The Orthodox Ethos,* vol. 1, pp. 143-48.

23. Jerome Kotsonis, "Fundamental Principles of Orthodox Morality," *The Orthodox Ethos,* vol. 1, pp. 230-31; Gavin, pp. 166-69.

24. Gavin, pp. 236, 395-97; Bulgakov, pp. 210-12.

Chapter 3

1. Jeffrey K. Hadden, *The Gathering Storm in the Churches* (New York: Doubleday, 1969), ch. 2.

2. Charles Y. Glock and Rodney Stark, *Religion and Society in Tension* (Chicago: Rand McNally and Co., 1971), p. 41. *See* 5.

3. John L. Thomas, *Religion and the American People* (Westminster, Maryland: Newman Press, 1963); George W. Hanson, "Patterns of Belief of 104 Protestant Ministers from Utah" (Master's thesis, Brigham Young University, 1970); Merton P. Strommen, *Profiles of Church Youth* (Saint Louis: Concordia Publishing House, 1963), pp. 50-52.

4. Glock and Stark, pp. 102, 104, 112.

5. A similar analysis appears in Richard C. Wolf, "1900-1950 Survey: Religious Trends in the United States," *Christianity Today* (April 27, 1959), p. 5, and in Glock and Stark's *Religion and Society in Tension,* p. 120.

204

6. Constant H. Jacquet, Jr., ed., *Yearbook of American Churches: 1972* (New York: Abingdon Press, 1972), pp. 220-31.

7. Wolf. p. 5. Information on church membership in Tables 1 - 4 are taken from the annual yearbooks published by the National Council of Churches.

8. John Dillenberger, ed., *Martin Luther: Selections from His Writings* (Garden City, New York: Doubleday and Co., 1961), pp. 408-9.

9. Ibid., xxxiii; Cyril Eastwood, *The Priesthood of Believers* (Minneapolis: Augsburg Publishing House, 1962), pp. x, 1-3.

10. Dillenberger, pp. 408-9.

11. Ibid., p. 408.

12. Ibid., pp. 346, 349; Eastwood, pp. 40-41.

13. Eastwood, pp. ix, 70, 75, 90.

14. Dillenberger, pp. xvii, 69.

15. Hadden, p. 47; Glock and Stark, p. 99; Hanson, pp. 27-29.

16. *The Baptist Faith and Message* (Nashville, Tennessee: Sunday School Board of the Southern Baptist Convention, 1963), p. 10.

17. Dillenberger, p. 211.

18. Benson Y. Landis, *Religion in the United States* (New York: Barnes and Noble, 1966), pp. 98, 100; Van A. Harvey, *A Handbook of Theological Terms* (New York: Macmillan Co., 1964), pp. 135-37, 210-12, 214-25.

19. Samuel G. Craig, *Christianity Rightly So Called* (Philadelphia: Presbyterian and Reformed Publishing Co., 1957), pp. 74, 83-84, 158; Warfield, *The Person and Work of Christ,* pp. 308-9.

20. Harvey, pp. 136, 214-25.

21. Ibid., pp. 108-10.

22. Ibid., p. 109.

23. Dillenberger, p. xxvi.

24. *The Baptist Faith and Message,* p. 23.

25. Dillenberger, p. 69.

26. Robert Campbell, ed., *Spectrum of Protestant Beliefs* (Milwaukee: Bruce Publishing Co., 1968), pp. 57-60; Craig, pp. 152-54.

27. Dillenberger, p. xxxi; John H. Leith, ed., *Creeds of the Churches* (Garden City, New York: Doubleday and Co., 1963), pp. 70, 124.

28. Dillenberger, pp. 256-91.

29. Ibid., pp. xxi, xxii, 160-62, 412, 415-17.

30. Ernest R. Sandeen, *The Origins of Fundamentalism* (Philadelphia: Fortress Press, 1968), pp. v, 26. In some respects, Sandeen disagrees with interpretations concerning the origin of fundamentalism as discussed in two other well-known works on this subject: Stewart G. Cole, *History of Fundamentalism* (New York: R. R. Smith, Inc., 1931) and Norman F. Furniss, *The Fundamentalist Controversy 1918-1931* (New Haven: Yale University Press, 1954).

31. Charles L. Feinberg, ed., *The Fundamentals for Today* (3rd ed., Grand Rapids, Michigan: Kregel Publications, 1964).

32. Sandeen, pp. 13-14.

33. W. B. Riley, "Is the Bible a Human or a Divine Book?" *The Christian Fundamentalist,* vol. 5 (December 1931), pp. 214-15.

34. "The Scriptures Verbally Inspired," *The Christian Fundamentalist,* vol. 5 (December 1931), pp. 232-33.

35. J. Gresham Machen, "The Bible," *The Christian Fundamentalist,* vol. 3 (November 1929), p. 427.

36. "The Scriptures Verbally Inspired," *The Christian Fundamentalist,* vol. 5 (December 1931), p. 232.

37. W. B. Riley, "What is the Meaning of Modernism?" *The Christian Fundamentalist,* vol. 4 (July 1930), pp. 30-31.

38. "The Scriptures Verbally Inspired," *The Christian Fundamentalist,* vol. 5 (December 1931), p. 233.

39. Edward John Cornell, *The Case for Orthodox Theology* (Philadelphia: Westminster Press, 1959), pp. 33, 36-39, 42, 65.

40. Hadden, p. 41.

41. "Christian Fundamentals Associations. Doctrinal Statement," *Christian Fundamentals in School and Church,* vol. 5 (January-March 1923), pp. 18-19.

42. Cornell, p. 94.

43. F. Ernest Johnson, ed., *Patterns of Faith in America Today* (New York: Collier Books, 1962), pp. 47-48.

Chapter 4

1. Bernard Towers, *Teilhard de Chardin* (Richmond, Virginia: John Knox Press, 1966), pp. 5, 29.

2. William Newton Clarke, *Sixty Years with the Bible* (New York, 1909), pp. 157-58.

3. Ibid., pp. 160, 210, 241.

4. Ibid., p. 184.

5. Ibid., pp. 56, 210.

6. William Adams Brown, *Christian Theology in Outline* (New York, 1924), pp. 54-55.

7. Ibid., p. 56.

8. Albert Schweitzer, *The Quest of the Historical Jesus* (New York: Macmillan, 1961), p. 10. The first German edition of this book appeared in 1906.

9. William A. Scott, *Historical Protestantism: An Historical Introduction to Protestant Theology* (Englewood Cliffs, New Jersey: Prentice-Hall, Inc., 1971), p. 120.

10. David Friedrich Strauss, *Life of Jesus,* J. L. M'Ilraith, trans. (London, n.d.), pp. 106, 116.

11. Ibid., p. 165.

12. Schweitzer, pp. 399-402.

13. Ibid., p. 399.

14. Fritz Buri, "Albert Schweitzer," *A Handbook of Christian Theologians,* Dean G. Peerman and Martin E. Marty, eds. (New York: World Publishing Co., 1965), pp. 115-16.

15. Martin J. Heinecken, "Soren Kierkegaard," *Handbook of Christian Theologians,* p. 141.

16. Friedrich Schleiermacher, *On Religion,* John Oman, trans. (New York: Harper and Row, 1958), pp. 105-106; Friedrich Schleiermacher, *The Christian Faith,* H. R. Mackintosh and J. S. Stewart, eds., (Edinburgh: T & T. Clark, 1956), pp. 6-8; Stephen Sykes, *Friedrich Schleiermacher* (Richmond, Virginia: John Knox Press, 1971), pp. 25-26: Richard R. Niebuhr, "Friedrich Schleiermacher," *A Handbook of Christian Theologians,* p. 28-29.

17. Sykes, *Friedrich Schleiermacher,* pp. 25-27; Schleiermacher, *On Religion,* pp. 36, 42-46, 72; Richard Niebuhr, "Friedrich Schleiermacher," *Handbook of Christian Theologians,* p. 29-33.

18. Schleiermacher, *The Christian Faith,* p. 425; Lloyd J. Averill, *American Theology in the Liberal Tradition* (Philadelphia: Westminster Press, 1967), pp. 38-39.

19. Scott, *Historical Protestantism,* p. 123-28: Averill, *American Theology,* p. 39.

20. Albert Ritschl, *The Christian Doctrine of Justification and Reconciliation,* H. R. Mackintosh and A. B. Macaulay, eds. (Clifton, New Jersey: Reference Book Publishers, 1966), vol. 3, pp. 336-39, 348-49 (originally published 1870-1874); Averill, *American Theology,* pp. 40, 43.

21. Ritschl, *Christian Doctrine of Justification and Reconciliation,* vol. 3, p. 10, 85, 406; Averill, *American Theology,* pp. 39-40.

22. Ritschl, *Christian Doctrine of Justification and Reconciliation,* vol. 3, pp. 8-13.

23. Henry P. Van Dusen, *The Vindication of Liberal Theology* (New York: Charles Scribner's Sons, 1963), pp. 178-80, 183-85.

Chapter 5

1. Rudolf Bultmann, *Jesus and the Word* (New York: Charles Scribner's Sons, 1958), pp. 172-73; Rudolf Bultmann, "New Testament and Mythology," *Kerygma and Myth,* Hans Werner Bartsch, ed. (New York: Harper and Row, 1961), pp. 35-36.

2. Bultmann, "New Testament and Mythology," pp. 38-39.

3. Ibid., pp. 10, 16.

4. George W. Davis, *Existentialism and Theology* (New York: Philosophical Library, 1957), pp. 9-10; Van A. Harvey, *A Handbook of Theological Terms* (New York: Macmillan, 1964), pp. 138-39.

5. Bultmann, "New Testament and Mythology," p. 1.

6. Ibid., p. 3.

7. Bultmann, *Jesus and the Word,* pp. 8-9, 12; Bultmann, "New Testament and Mythology," pp. 34-35; John Macquarrie, "Rudolf Bultmann," *A Handbook of Christian Theologians,* pp. 445-46.

8. Bultmann, "New Testament and Mythology," pp. 10, 16; Macquarrie, "Rudolf Bultmann," pp. 448-49.

9. Bultmann, "New Testament and Mythology," p. 29.

10. Ibid., p. 33.

11. Macquarrie, "Rudolf Bultmann," p. 454.

12. Ibid., p. 453.

13. Ibid., pp. 458-59, 462-63.

14. Daniel Jenkins, "Karl Barth," *Handbook of Christian Theologians,* pp. 396-98; Scott, *Historical Protestantism,* pp. 130-32.

15. Karl Barth, *Dogmatics in Outline,* G. T. Thomson, trans. (New York: Harper and Row, 1959), pp. 96-98.

16. Karl Barth, *The Word of God and the Word of Man,* Douglas Horton, trans. (New York: Harper and Row, 1957), p. 45.

17. Barth, *Dogmatics in Outline,* p. 118; Herbert Hartwell, *The Theology of Karl Barth* (Philadelphia: Westminster Press, 1964), p. 51, 57.

18. Barth, *Dogmatics in Outline,* pp. 119-22.

19. Arnold B. Come, *An Introduction to Barth's Dogmatics for Preachers* (Philadelphia: Westminster Press, 1963), pp. 201-3.

20. Hans Hofmann, "Reinhold Niebuhr," *Handbook of Christian Theologians,* pp. 355-56. For a more complete biographical sketch of Reinhold Niebuhr see June Bingham's excellent work, *Courage to Change: An Introduction to the Life and Thought of Reinhold Niebuhr* (New York: Charles Scribner's Sons, 1961).

21. Bingham, *Courage to Change,* p. 339.

22. Ibid., 172-73; Reinhold Niebuhr, *Moral Man and Immoral Society* (New York: Charles Scribner's Sons, 1932), pp. xi-xii, 9, 25, 36, 38.

23. Hofmann, "Reinhold Niebuhr," pp. 359-60.

24. L. Harold De Wolf, *A Theology of the Living Church* (New York: Harper and Brothers, 1953), p. 128.

25. Ibid., pp. 104, 108-9, 118-23.

26. Henry P. Van Dusen, *The Vindication of Liberal Theology* (New York: Charles Scribner's Sons, 1963), pp. 17, 41-44, 47, 130.

27. For an excellent survey of the popular patterns of belief currently held by many

contemporaries see Daniel Day Williams, *What Present-Day Theologians are Thinking* (New York: Harper and Row, 1967).

Chapter 6

1. *Martin Luther: Selections from his Writings,* John Dillenberger, ed. (Anchor Books, Garden City, New York: Doubleday, 1961), pp. 490-500.
2. Roland H. Bainton, *Here I Stand: A Life of Martin Luther* (Mentor, New York: New American Library of World Literature, 1961), pp. 72-73.
3. Ibid., p. 144.
4. John H. Tietjen, *Which Way to Lutheran Unity?* (Saint Louis, Missouri: Concordia Publishing House, 1966), pp. 6-7, 28.
5. Ibid., pp. 7-8

Chapter 7

1. John Calvin, *Institutes of the Christian Religion,* Henry Beveridge, trans. (Grand Rapids, Mich: Wm. B. Erdmans Publishing Co., 1957), vol. 2, pp. 558-71 (4:17:3, 4, 9, 10, 18, 19).
2. James Arminius, *The Writings of James Arminius,* W. R. Bagnall, trans. (3 vols., Grand Rapids, Michigan: Baker Book House, 1956), vol. 1, p. 526; vol. 2, pp. 472-73.
3. In 1750 almost one-third of all religious societies (excluding Quaker congregations) were Congregational and only 11 of their 465 local churches were situated outside New England. Edwin Scott Gaustad, *Historical Atlas of Religion in America* (New York: Harper and Row, 1962), p. 167.
4. Gaius Jackson Slosser, ed., *They Seek a Country* (New York: Macmillan Co., 1955), p. 169.
5. The Christian Reformed Church teaches many basic beliefs taught by John Calvin. For example, the ground for man's election is not anything merited by man but solely the good pleasure of God. God will not suffer those who are joined to Christ to totally fall away from faith and grace; the body which in death is separated from the soul will be raised on the Last day and be reunited with the soul, and that the righteous will enjoy perfect bliss and the ungodly will be sent into eternal condemnation. They also teach that the bread and wine in the Lord's Supper represent the body and blood of Christ, but instead of specifying, as did Calvin, that communicants receive Christ spiritually, they declare that believers will grow in grace and knowledge of the Savior. *The Christian Reformed Church: What It Teaches* (Grand Rapids, Michigan: Back to God Tract Committee, n.d.).

Chapter 8

1. Norman Sykes, *The Crisis of the Reformation* (London: Geoffrey Bles, 1950), pp. 80-85; G. R. Elton, *England under the Tudors* (London: Methuen and Co., 1963), pp. 102-11; Philip Hughes, *The Reformation in England* (3 vols., London: Hollis and Carter, 1954), vol. 1, chaps. 3 and 4; vol. 2, chap. 2.
2. Edwin Scott Gaustad, *Historical Atlas of Religion in America* (New York: Harper and Row, 1962), p. 167.
3. Walter M. Stowe, "The Clergy of the Episcopal Church in 1785" *The Protestant Episcopal Church Historical Magazine* 20(September 1951):253; James Thayer Addison, *The Episcopal Church in the United States* (New York: Charles Scribner's Sons, 1951), pp. 51-52.
4. Addison, pp. 60-61, 65-74.

5. Two excellent summaries of the popular contemporary views concerning the faith and worship of the Episcopal Church are Massey M. Shepherd, Jr., *The Worship of the Church* (New York: Seabury Press, 1965) and James A. Pike and W. Norman Pittenger, *The Faith of the Church* (New York: Seabury Press, 1965).

Chapter 9

1. Albert C. Outler, ed., *John Wesley* (New York: Oxford University Press, 1964), p. vii.

2. Ibid., p. 13; Rupert E. Davies, *Methodism* (Baltimore, Md.: Penguin Books, 1963), p. 57; Ole E. Borgen, *John Wesley: An Autobiographical Sketch of the Man and His Thought, Chiefly from His Letters* (Leiden, Netherlands: E. J. Brill, 1960), pp. 32-34.

3. John Wesley, *Interesting Extracts, from the Journals of the Rev. John Wesley* (Boston, 1819), p. 29; Davies, p. 58.

4. Davies, p. 78.

5. Outler, pp. 177-78.

6. Davies, p. 126.

7. Davies, pp. 128-29.

8. Among the best works on the early history of Methodism in America are William Warren Sweet, *Methodism in American History* (New York: Abingdon Press, 1953); Wade Crawford Barclay, *Early American Methodism, 1768-1844* (2 vols., New York: Board of Missions and Church Extension of the Methodist Church, 1949); and Emory Stevens Bucke, ed., *The History of American Methodism* (3 vols., New York: Abingdon Press, 1964).

9. Edwin Scott Gaustad, *Historical Atlas of Religion in America* (New York: Harper and Row, 1962), p. 162.

10. Peter Cartwright, *Autobiography of Peter Cartwright,* W. P. Strickland, ed. (New York, 1857) pp. 484-86.

11. Ibid., pp. 45-46, 49-51.

12. Abel Stevens, *A Compendious History of American Methodism* (New York, n.d.), p. 607; William Warren Sweet, *Methodism in American History* (New York: Abingdon Press, 1953) pp. 176-77; John O. Gross, *The Beginnings of American Methodism* (New York: Abingdon Press, 1961), pp. 66-69; *Historical Statistics of the United States* (Washington, D.C.: U.S. Bureau of Census, 1960), p. 229.

13. The Methodist emphasis on humanitarian programs is in part reflected by the wide variety of institutions currently supported by the United Methodist Church which includes educational institutions, hospitals, children's homes, and homes for the senior citizens.

Chapter 10

1. *The 1973 World Almanac and Book of Facts* (New York: Newspaper Enterprise Association, Inc., 1973), p. 342. Some Baptists do not classify themselves as Protestants.

2. Edward H. Overbey, *A Brief History of the Baptists* (Niles, Ill.: Independent Baptist Publications, 1962), pp. 45-61.

3. Robert G. Torbet, *A History of the Baptists* (Valley Forge: Judson Press, 1973), pp. 18-19; W. Morgan Patterson, "The Development of the Baptist Successionist Formula," *Foundations,* vol. 5 (October 1962), pp. 331, 335.

4. Torbet, *History of the Baptists,* pp. 25-32.

5. Ibid., pp. 25-32.

6. Reuben Aldridge Guild, "A Biographical Introduction to the Writings of Roger Williams," *The Complete Writings of Roger Williams* (New York: Russell and Russell, 1963), vol. 1, pp. 35-37.

7. Roger Williams to John Winthrop, December 10, 1649, quoted in *Writings of Roger Williams,* vol. 6, pp. 187-89.

8. Ibid., vol. 5, p. 103.

9. John Callender, *An Historical Discourse, on the Civil and Religious Affairs of the Colony of Rhode Island and Providence Plantations* (Boston, 1739), reprinted in *Collections of the Rhode Island Historical Society* (Providence, 1838), vol. 4, pp. 109-11; John Winthrop, *History of New England,* James Kendall Hosmer, ed. (2 vols., New York: Barnes and Noble, 1946), vol. 1, p. 309.

10. Torbet, *History of the Baptists,* p. 203.

11. Edwin Scott Gaustad, *Historical Atlas of Religion in America* (New York: Harper and Row, 1962), pp. 10-12, 52-53; Milton V. Backman, Jr., *American Religions and the Rise of Mormonism* (Salt Lake City: Deseret Book Co., 1970), p. 277; John Asplund, *The Universal Annual Register of the Baptist Denomination . . . for . . . 1794 and 1795* (Hanover, 1796), p. 82.

12. W. W. Barnes, *The Southern Baptist Convention 1845-1953* (Nashville: Broadman Press, 1954), pp. 18-33.

13. Frank S. Mead, *Handbook of Denominations in the United States* (Nashville: Abingdon Press, 1970), p. 38; Edwin Scott Gaustad, *Historical Atlas of Religion in America* (New York: Harper and Row, 1962), p. 159.

Chapter 11

1. Rufus M. Jones, *The Quaker's Faith* (n.p., n.d.), p. 1.

2. George Fox, *An Autobiography,* Rufus M. Jones, ed. (Philadelphia, 1919), pp. 66-67.

3. Ibid., p. 68.

4. Ibid., pp. 68-69.

5. Ibid., pp. 76, 82, 100.

6. Ibid., pp. 125-26.

7. William C. Braithwaite, *The Beginnings of Quakerism* (London, 1912), pp. 22, 57, 73, 132, 307.

8. Vernon Noble, *The Man in Leather Breeches* (New York: Philosophical Library, 1953), pp. 136, 161, 167.

9. Braithwaite, p. 512; Noble, p. 275; Frederick B. Tolles, *Quakers and the Atlantic Culture* (New York: Macmillan Co., 1960), p. 24.

10. Edwin B. Bronner, ed., *American Quakers Today* (Lebanon, Pa.: Sowers Printing Co., 1966), p. 17.

11. Edwin B. Bronner, *Quakerism and Christianity* (Lebanon, Pa.: Sowers Printing Co., 1967), pp. 5-6; The leaders of these three Quaker movements were Elias Hicks (1748-1830), John Gurney (1788-1846), and John Wilbur (1774-1856). For additional information on the history of this faith see Elbert Russell, *The History of Quakerism* (New York, 1942).

12. William Hubben, *Who Are the Friends?* (Alburtis, Pa.: Hemlock Press, n.d.), pp. 11-12.

13. Lawrence McK. Miller, Jr., *The Practice of Quaker Worship* (n.p., n.d.), p. 2.

14. Hubben, p. 18. Not all Friends would agree with Hubben's deemphasis on doctrine. Much diversity of belief currently exists among Quakers regarding the tenets outlined by this Quaker writer.

Chapter 12

1. Earl Morse Wilbur, *The Two Treatises of Servetus on the Trinity* (vol. 16 of the Harvard Theological Studies. (Cambridge: Harvard University Press 1932): Earl Morse

Wilbur, *A History of Unitarianism* (Cambridge: Harvard University Press, 1947), vol. 1, pp. 62-63.

2. Roland H. Bainton, *Hunted Heretic: The Life and Death of Michael Servetus 1511-1553* (Boston: Beacon Press, 1953), p. 168; Stefan Zweig, *The Right to Heresy,* Eden and Cedar Paul, trans. (New York: Viking Press, 1936), pp. 115-18, 123-24; Carl Theophilus Odhner, *Michael Servetus: His Life and Teachings* (Philadelphia, 1910), pp. 25-26.

3. Bainton, pp. 207-12; Zweig, pp. 131-36.

4. Wilbur, *History of Unitarianism,* vol. 2, pp. 167-77.

5. Ibid., pp. 29-32, 38-41. Blandrata is also spelled Biandrata.

6. Ibid., vol. 1, pp. 413-16.

7. Ibid., vol. 2, pp. 184, 194-95, 207.

8. John Milton, "Christian Doctrine," *Works of John Milton,* ed. J. A. St. John London, 1890), vol. 4, pp. 79, 85-87, 90-95.

9. Ibid., p. 240; Conrad Wright, *The Beginnings of Unitarianism in America* (Boston: Beacon Press, 1955), p. 201.

10. Wilbur, *History of Unitarianism,* vol. 2, p. 285.

11. Wright, p. 211, 253-55; William W. Fenn, "The Unitarians," *The Religious History of New England* (Cambridge: Harvard University Press, 1917), pp. 99, 102.

12. Wright, p. 210; Elizabeth M. Geffen, *Philadelphia Unitarianism* (Philadelphia: University of Pennsylvania Press, 1961), pp. 34, 46, 239.

13. Fenn, pp. 122-23, William E. Channing, *The Works of William E. Channing* (Boston, 1894), pp. 369, 486-89, 1010-12; Robert Leet Patterson, *The Philosophy of William Ellery Channing* (New York: Bookman Associates, 1952), p. 175.

14. Fenn, pp. 120-21; Channing, pp. 380, 621, 993.

15. John Nicholls Booth, *Introducing Unitarian Universalism* (Boston: Unitarian Universalist Association, 1965), pp. 7-8; A. Powell Davies, *Unitarianism: What Is It?* (Boston American Unitarian Association, n.d.), pp. 6-7; Karl M. Chworowsky, "What Is a Unitarian?" *Religions in America,* ed. Leo Rosten (New York: Simon and Schuster, 1963), p. 194; Jack Medelsohn, *Meet the Unitarians* (Boston: American Unitarian Association, 1960), pp. 22-23.

16. Milton V. Backman, Jr., *American Religions and the Rise of Mormonism* (Salt Lake City: Deseret Book Co., 1970), pp. 216-23.

17. Ibid., p. 219.

18. *Newsweek,* May 25, 1964, p. 73; Lauris B. Whitman, ed., *Yearbook of American Churches: Edition for 1968* (New York: National Council of Churches, 1968), p. 207.

19. Davies, p. 4; Booth, pp. 3, 13-17; *Newsweek,* May 25, 1964, p. 73.

20. Davies, pp. 8-11.

21. *The Hamburg Sun,* June 10, 1965.

22. Booth, pp. 3, 13; Duncan Howlett, *A Loose-Leaf Bible* (Boston: Unitarian Universalist Association, 1963), pp. 9-10.

23. George N. Marshall, *Unitarians and Universalists Believe* (Boston: Unitarian Universalist Association, n.d.), pp. 1-2; Booth, pp. 13, 16.

24. Chworowsky, pp. 190-91.

25. Booth, pp. 15-16.

Chapter 13

1. Charles Franklin Kilgore, *The James O'Kelly Schism in the Methodist Episcopal Church* (Mexico: Casa Unida De Publicaciones, 1963), pp. 5, 31, 34, 38.

2. Alfred Thomas DeGroot, "The Grounds of Divisions among the Disciples of Christ" (Ph.D. dissertation, University of Chicago, 1939), pp. 58-59.

3. Kilgore, pp. 35-37; "Sketch of the Denomination who Claim to be Styled 'Christians,' " *Christian Palladium,* vol. 3 (August 1, 1834), pp. 107-9.

4. Barton W. Stone, *Works of Elder B. W. Stone,* James Mathes, ed. (Cincinnati, 1859), pp. 19, 68, 83-84. See also the excellent biography of Stone, W. G. West, *Barton Warren Stone* (Nashville: Disciples of Christ Historical Society, 1954).

5. Alexander Campbell, *The Christian Baptist* (7 vols., Cincinnati, 1835), vol. 1, pp. 192-93; *Minutes of the Redstone Baptist Association, 1815* (Pittsburg, 1815), pp. 4-5.

6. Campbell, *The Christian Baptist,* pp. 127-28.

7. Amos Sutton Hayden, *Early History of the Disciples in the Western Reserve, Ohio* (Cincinnati, 1876), p. 143.

8. Mary A. Smith, "History of the Mahoning Baptist Association" (Master's thesis, West Virginia University, 1943), p. 93.

9. Alexander Campbell, *The Millennial Harbinger,* vol. 1 (July 5, 1830), p. 307.

10. Ibid., vol. 1 (August 2, 1830), pp. 372-73; Campbell, *The Christian Baptist,* vol. 1, p. 561.

11. W. E. Garrison and A. T. DeGroot, *The Disciples of Christ* (St. Louis, Mo.: Bethany Press, 1958), pp. 207-11.

12. DeGroot, "Grounds of Divisions Among the Disciples," pp. 66-67; *Department of Commerce and Labor Bureau of the Census: Religious Bodies: 1906* (Washington: Government Printing Office, 1910), p. 25.

13. In 1906 the body referred to as the Disciples or Christians was the fifth largest Protestant family of churches in the United States. Ibid., pp. 25-26.

Chapter 14

1. Joseph Smith, *History of the Church of Jesus Christ of Latter-day Saints,* B. H. Roberts, ed. (7 vols., Salt Lake City: Deseret Book Co., 1959), vol. 1, p. 3; Milton V. Backman, Jr., *Joseph Smith's First Vision: The First Vision in its Historical Context* (Salt Lake City: Bookcraft, 1971), pp. 182-83; Richard Anderson, *Joseph Smith's New England Heritage* (Salt Lake City: Deseret Book Co., 1971), pp. 105-6.

2. Smith, vol. 1, pp. 2-5; vol. 4, p. 536.

3. Ibid., vol. 4, p. 536; Backman, *Joseph Smith's First Vision,* pp. 154-69.

4. Smith, vol. 1, pp. 18-71.

5. The Book of Mormon (Palmyra, 1830). The testimony of the witnesses of the Book of Mormon was placed at the back of the original edition of this work and is currently at the beginning of the book.

6. Backman, *Joseph Smith's First Vision,* pp. 140-46.

7. Smith, vol. 1, pp. 39-43.

8. Gustive O. Larson, *The "Americanization" of Utah for Statehood* (San Marino, Calif.: Huntington Library, 1971), pp. 211, 263-64; Leonard Arrington, *Great Basin Kingdom: An Economic History of the Latter-day Saints 1830-1900* (Lincoln: University of Nebraska Press, 1968), pp. 376-80.

9. For additional information on the beliefs of the Latter-day Saints see James E. Talmage, *Articles of Faith* (Salt Lake City: Deseret News Press, 1966); Bruce R. McConkie, *Mormon Doctrine* (Salt Lake City: Bookcraft, 1966); Lowell L. Bennion, *An Introduction to the Gospel* (Salt Lake City: Deseret Sunday School Union Board, 1955).

Chapter 15

1. William Miller, *Evidence from Scripture and History of the Second Coming of Christ About the Year 1843* (Boston, 1840), p. 54; Ellen G. White, *The Great Controversy Between Christ and Satan* (Mountain View, Calif.: Pacific Press Publishing Association, 1950), pp. 325-27.

2. James White, *Sketches of the Christian Life and Public Labors of William Miller* (Battle Creek, Michigan, 1875), pp. 182-83.

3. Ibid., p. 184; Francis D. Nichol, *The Midnight Cry* (Takoma Park, Washington, D.C.: Review and Herald Publishing Association, 1945), p. 171.

4. James White, p. 296.

5. Nichol, pp. 239, 251-52; James White, p. 299.

6. Don F. Neufeld and Julia Neuffer, eds., *Seventh-day Adventist Encyclopedia* (Washington, D.C.: Review and Herald Publishing Association, 1966), vol. 10, pp. 364-65.

7. Ibid., vol. 10, pp. 107-8.

8. Ibid., vol. 10, p. 1406.

9. Ellen G. White, *Testimonies for the Church* (Mountain View, Calif., n.d.), pp. 58-61.

10. Ibid., p. 62. See also pages 9-12, 55, 67, 80, 86, 87, 92, and 93 for references to Mrs. White's physical and emotional problems. After adopting a program of diet reform her health improved and during the later years of her life she enjoyed average good health.

11. Ellen G. White, *The Great Controversy,* p. 480.

12. Richard H. Utt, *A Century of Miracles* (Mountain View, Calif.: Pacific Press Publishing Association, 1963), p. 15.

13. Ibid., pp. 16-17.

14. *Seventh-day Adventist Fact Book* (Nashville, Tenn.: Southern Publishing Association, 1967), pp. 19-23.

15. Utt, pp. 17-18.

16. One of the best descriptions of Seventh-day Adventist theology is in *Seventh-day Adventists Answer Questions on Doctrine* (Washington, D.C.: Review and Herald, 1957).

17. *Seventh-day Adventist Fact Book,* pp. 71-72.

Chapter 16

1. *Qualified to be Ministers* (Brooklyn, New York: Watchtower Bible and Tract Society, Inc., 1955), pp. 298-99.

2. Ibid., p. 300.

3. Ibid., p. 302.

4. Ibid., p. 309.

5. William H. Cumberland, "A History of the Jehovah's Witnesses" (Ph.D. dissertation, University of Iowa, 1958), pp. 83-84.

6. *Qualified to be Ministers,* p. 310-11; Alan Rogerson, *Millions Now Living Will Never Die* (London: Constable, 1969), p. 15, quoted from *Zion's Watch Tower,* May 1, 1917.

7. Cumberland, pp. 158-59; Marley Cole, *Jehovah's Witnesses* (New York: Vantage Press, 1957), pp. 148-49.

8. Cumberland, p. 167.

9. Rogerson, p. 39.

10. *Qualified to be Ministers,* pp. 314-16, 319.

11. Ibid., p. 319.

12. Cumberland, pp. 204, 208.

13. Ibid., pp. 226, 229-31; *Qualified to be Ministers,* p. 322.

14. *Qualified to be Ministers,* pp. 323-24.

15. Ibid., p. 331. "From 1933, when figures of arrests began to be kept by the Watch Tower Society," to 1951, there is a record of 18,886 individual arrests of Witnesses and at least 1,500 mobbings occurred in the United States involving members of this faith. Ibid., p. 330.

16. Cumberland, pp. 295-96.

17. Ibid., p. 263; Rogerson, pp. 75, 163; *1972 Yearbook of Jehovah's Witnesses* (Brooklyn, New York: Watchtower Bible and Tract Society, 1972), pp. 33-41.

18. Cumberland, pp. 295-96.

19. One of the best works available summarizing the patterns of belief of members of this faith is *Things In Which It is Impossible For God To Lie* (Brooklyn, New York: Watchtower Bible and Tract Society, 1965). There are also a number of references to the beliefs of members of this Bible society in *Jehovah's Witnesses in the Divine Purpose* (Brooklyn: Watchtower Bible and Tract Society, 1959), a work that describes the history of this religious community from the Witnesses' point of view.

Chapter 17

1. Mary Baker Eddy, *Retrospection and Introspection* (Boston, 1915), p. 13. Many controversial biographies have been written about Mary Baker Eddy. One of the most factual and complete accounts of her life is the multi-volume work written by Robert Peel, *Mary Baker Eddy: The Years of Discovery* (New York: Holt, Rinehart and Winston, 1971) and *Mary Baker Eddy: The Years of Trial* (New York: Holt, Rinehart and Winston, 1971), the latter volume covering the pivotal years 1876-1891. Two other sympathetic accounts of this religious leader are Sibyl Wilbur's *The Life of Mary Baker Eddy* (New York, 1907) and Norman Beasley's *The Cross and the Crown* (Boston: Little, Brown and Co., 1953). The most popular critical biographies are E. F. Dakin, *Mrs. Eddy: The Biography of a Virginal Mind* (New York, 1929) and Fleta Campbell Springer, *According to the Flesh* (New York, 1930). An excellent brief sketch of her life is Allen Johnson, "Mary Morse Baker Eddy," *Dictionary of American Biography,* Allen Johnson and Dumas Malone, eds. (20 vols., New York: Charles Scribner's Sons, 1958), vol. 3, part 2, pp. 7-15.

2. Eddy, *Retrospection and Introspection,* p. 10.

3. Ibid., pp. 8-9.

4. Ibid., pp. 24-25; Mary Baker Eddy, *Miscellaneous Writings* (Boston, 1905), p. 24.

5. Eddy, *Retrospection and Introspection,* p. 24.

6. Ibid., p. 25.

7. Mary Baker Eddy, *Science and Health with Key to the Scriptures* (Boston: Trustees under the Will of Mary Baker G. Eddy, 1934), pp. 331-32.

8. Eddy, *Retrospection and Introspection,* p. 25.

9. Robert Peel, *Christian Science: Its Encounter with American Culture* (New York: Henry Holt and Co., 1958), pp. 91, 94.

10. Mary Baker Eddy, *Unity of Good* (Boston, 1915), pp. 9-10.

11. Eddy, *Science and Health,* pp. 153, 159.

12. Ibid., pp. 126, 497; *Christian Science Quarterly,* vol. 75 (1964), p. ii.

13. Eddy, *Retrospection and Introspection,* p. 16.

14. Allen Johnson, "Mary Morse Baker Eddy," *Dictionary of American Biography,* vol. 3, part 2, p. 14.

15. Thomas Linton Leishman, *Why I Am A Christian Scientist* (Boston: Beacon Press, 1966), Ch. 4.

16. Ibid., pp. 194-96, 223.

17. Eddy, *Science and Health,* pp. 331-33.

18. Ibid., p. 331.

19. Ibid., pp. 73, 267, 529-31, 545-46.

20. Ibid., p. 593.

21. Ibid., pp. 266, 291, 588.

Chapter 18

1. Vinson Synan, *The Holiness-Pentecostal Movement in the United States* (Grand Rapids, Michigan: William B. Eerdmans Publishing Co., 1971), pp. 217-19; Klaude Kendrick, *The Promise Fulfilled: A History of the Modern Pentecostal Movement* (Springfield, Mo.: Gospel Publishing House, 1961), pp. 25-34.

2. Synan, pp. 17-18; Thomas Jackson, ed., *The Works of John Wesley* (Grand Rapids, Michigan: Zondervan, 1958), vol. 9, pp. 366-488.

3. Timothy L. Smith, *Called Unto Holiness* (Kansas City, Mo.: Nazarene Publishing House, 1963), pp. 11-12.

4. Synan, pp. 37-47.

5. Ibid., pp. 219-220.

6. Kendrick, p. 37.

7. Ibid., pp. 37-43. A third view of the millennium is called a millennialism, a belief that the church is the Kingdom of God and that the millennium is experienced by men at the present age.

8. Synan, pp. 121-22.

9. Ibid., p. 203.

10. Ibid., pp. 210-11.

11. An excellent description of the patterns of belief of members of the Pentecostal Assemblies is found in Nils Bloch-Hoell, *The Pentecostal Movement* (New York: Humanities Press, 1964).

Appendix A:
Selected Bibliography
on American Religions

SOURCE BOOKS AND BIBLIOGRAPHICAL GUIDES

Burr, Nelson R. *A Critical Bibliography of Religion in America.* Vol. 4 of Religion in American Life. Edited by James W. Smith and A. Leland Jamison. Princeton University, 1961.
_____. *Religion in American Life.* Appleton-Century-Crofts, 1971.
Mode, P.G. *Sourcebook and Bibliographical Guide for American History.* George Banta Publishing Co., 1921.
Schaff, Philip. *The Creeds of Christendom.* 3 vols. Harper, 1919.
Smith, H. S., Handy, R. T., and Loetscher, L. A. *American Christianity: An Historical Interpretation with Representative Documents.* 2 vols. Scribner, 1960-63.

GENERAL HISTORIES OF RELIGION IN THE UNITED STATES

Ahlstrom, Sydney E. *A Religious History of the American People.* Yale, 1973. (Includes excellent bibliography.)
Gaustad, Edwin S. *Historical Atlas of Religion in America.* Harper, 1962.
_____. *A Religious History of America.* Harper, 1966.
Hudson, Winthrop S. *Religion in America.* Scribner's, 1965.
Mead, Sidney E. *The Lively Experiment: The Shaping of Christianity in America.* Harper, 1963.
Olmstead, Clifton E. *History of Religion in the United States.* Prentice-Hall, 1960.
Sweet, William W. *The Story of Religion in America.* Harper, 1950.

GENERAL DESCRIPTIONS OF BELIEFS

Backman, Milton V., Jr. *American Religions and the Rise of Mormonism.* Deseret Book, 1970.
Harvey, Van A. *A Handbook of Theological Terms.* Macmillan, 1964.
Mead, Frank S. *Handbook of Denominations in the United States.* Abingdon, 1961.
Rosten, Leo C. *Religions in America.* Simon and Schuster, 1963.
Spence, Hartzell. *The Story of America's Religions.* Holt, Rinehart, and Winston, 1960.
Williams, J. Paul. *What Americans Believe and How They Worship.* Harper, 1962.

DENOMINATIONAL HISTORIES AND DESCRIPTIONS OF BELIEF

Baptist

Armstrong, O. K. and Marjorie M. *The Indomitable Baptists: A Narrative of Their Role in Shaping American History.* Doubleday, 1967.
Barnes, William Wright. *The Southern Baptist Convention,* 1845-1953. Broadman, 1954.
Baxter, N. A. *History of the Freewill Baptists.* American Baptist Historical Society, 1957.
Hill, Samuel S., and Torbet, Robert G. *Baptists North and South.* Judson, 1964.
Maring, Norman H., and Hudson, Winthrop S. *A Baptist Manual of Polity and Practice.* Judson, 1963.

Newton, Louie Devotie. *Why I Am a Baptist.* Nelson, 1957.
Torbet, Robert G. *A History of the Baptists.* Judson, 1955.

CATHOLIC (ROMAN)

Burghardt, S. J., and Lynch, S. J. *The Idea of Catholicism. An Introduction to the Thought and Worship of the Church.* Meridian Books, 1960.
Conway, Bertrand L. *The Question Box.* All Saints, 1962.
Daniel-Rops, Henri (ed.). *Twentieth Century Encyclopedia of Catholicism.* Hawthorn, 1958.
Ellis, John Tracy. *American Catholicism.* University of Chicago, 1956.
Maynard, Theodore. *The Story of American Catholicism.* Macmillan, 1951.
McAuliffe, Clarence. *Sacramental Theology.* B. Herder Book Co., 1958.
McDonald, William J., et al. (ed). *New Catholic Encyclopedia.* 15 vols. McGraw-Hill, 1967.
Ott, Ludwig. *Fundamentals of Catholic Dogma.* B. Herder, 1964.
Roemer, Theodore. *The Catholic Church in the United States.* B. Herder Book Co., 1950.
Trese, Leo J. *The Faith Explained.* Fides, 1962.

CHRISTIAN SCIENTIST

Beasley, Norman. *The Cross and the Crown: The History of Christian Science.* Little, Brown and Co., 1953.
Braden, Charles S. *Christian Science Today,* Southern Methodist University, 1958.
DeWitt, John, and Conham, Erwin D. *The Christian Science Way of Life.* Prentice-Hall, 1962.
Eddy, Mary Baker. *Science and Health with Key to the Scriptures.* Trustees under the Will of Mary B. Eddy, 1934.
Leishman, Thomas Linton. *Why I Am a Christian Scientist.* Nelson, 1958.
Peel, Robert. *Christian Science: Its Encounter with American Culture.* New York: Henry Holt, 1958.

CONGREGATIONAL

Atkins, Gaius G., and Fagley, Frederick L. *History of American Congregationalism.* Pilgrim Press, 1942.
Horton, Douglas. *The United Church of Christ.* T. Nelson, 1962.
Jenkins, Daniel. *Congregationalism: A Restatement.* Harper, 1954.
Rouner, Arthur A. *The Congregational Way of Life.* Prentice-Hall, 1960.

DISCIPLES OF CHRIST

Abbott, Byrdine Akers. *The Disciples: An Interpretation.* Bethany Press, 1964.
Adams, Hampton. *Why I Am a Disciple of Christ.* Nelson, 1957.
Garrison, Winfred E., and DeGroat, Alfred. *The Disciples of Christ.* Bethany Press, 1958.
Harrell, David Edwin. *A Social History of the Disciples of Christ.* 2 vols. Disciples of Christ Historical Society, 1966.
Humbert, Royal. *A Compend of Alexander Campbell's Theology.* Bethany Press, 1961.
Lair, Loren. *The Christian Churches and Their Work.* Bethany Press, 1963
Murch, James DeForest. *Christian Only: A History of the Restoration Movement.* Standard Publications, 1962.
Whitley, Oliver Read. *Trumpet Call of Reformation.* Bethany Press, 1959.

EASTERN ORTHODOX

Benz, Ernst. *The Eastern Orthodox Church: Its Thought and Life.* Doubleday, 1963.
Bulgakov, Sergius, *The Orthodox Church.* American Orthodox Press, 1964.
Ware, Timothy. *The Orthodox Church.* Penguin, 1967.
Zankov, Stefan. *The Eastern Orthodox Church.* Translated by Donald A. Lowrie. Student Christian Movement, 1929.
Zernov, Nicolas. *Eastern Christendom.* Weidenfeld and Nicholson, 1963.

EPISCOPALIAN

Addison, James Thayer. *The Episcopal Church in the United States.* Scribner, 1951.
Albright, Raymond Wolf. *A History of the Protestant Episcopal Church.* MacMillan, 1964.
Krumm, John McGill. *Why I Am an Episcopalian.* Nelson, 1957.
Moss, Claude Beaufort. *Answer Me This.* Longmans, Green and Co., 1959.
Pike, James A., and Pettenger, W. Norman. *The Faith of the Church.* Seabury, 1965.
Sheperd, Massey H. *The Worship of the Church.* Seabury, 1965.

EVANGELICAL AND REFORMED

Arndt, Elmer J. F. *The Faith We Proclaim: The Doctrinal Viewpoint Generally Prevailing in the Evangelical and Reformed Church.* Christian Education, 1960.
Dunn, David, et al. *A History of the Evangelical and Reformed Church.* Christian Education, 1961.

HOLINESS-PENTECOSTAL MOVEMENT

Bloch-Hoell, Nils. *The Pentecostal Movement.* Humanities, 1964.
Kendrick, Klaude. *The Promise Fulfilled: A History of the Modern Pentecostal Movement.* Gospel Publishing House, 1961.
Nichol, John Thomas. *Pentecostalism.* Harper, 1966.
Smith, Timothy L. *Called unto Holiness.* Nazarene, 1963
Synan, Vinson. *The Holiness-Pentecostal Movement in the United States.* Eerdmans, 1971.
Kendrick, Klaude. *The Promise Fulfilled: A History of the Modern Pentecostal Movement.* Gospel Publishing House, 1961.

JEHOVAH'S WITNESSES

Cole, Marley. *Jehovah's Witnesses.* Vantage, 1957.
From Paradise Lost to Paradise Regained. Watch Tower Bible and Tract Society, 1959.
Jehovah's Witnesses in the Divine Purpose. Watch Tower Bible and Tract Society, 195-.
Qualified to be Ministers. Watch Tower Bible and Tract Society, 1955.
Rogerson, Alan. *Millions Now Living Will Never Die.* Constable, 1969.
Things In Which It Is Impossible For God To Lie. Watch Tower Bible and Tract Society, 1959.
Stroup, Herbert Hewitt. *The Jehovah's Witnesses.* Russell and Russell, 1967.
White, Timothy. *A People for His Name: A History of the Jehovah's Witnesses and an Evaluation.* Vantage Press, 1968.

LATTER-DAY SAINTS

Arrington, Leonard J. *Great Basin Kingdom: An Economic History of the Latter-day Saints.* University of Nebraska, 1968.

Barrett, Ivan J. *Joseph Smith and the Restoration.* Brigham Young University, 1973.
Bennion, Lowell. *An Introduction to the Gospel.* Deseret Sunday School, 1955.
McConkie, Bruce R. *Mormon Doctrine.* Bookcraft, 1966.
Rich, Russell R. *Ensign to the Nations.* Brigham Young University Publications, 1972.
Talmage, James E. *Articles of Faith.* Deseret News Press, 1966.

LUTHERAN

Arden, Gothard Everett. *Meet the Lutherans: Introducing the Lutheran Church in North America.* Augustana Press, Saint Louis: 1962.
Beck, Victor Emanuel. *Why I Am a Lutheran.* Nelson, 1956.
Ferm, Bergilius. *The Crisis in American Lutheran Theology.* Century Co., 1927.
Lazareth, William H. and Garhart. Marjorie F. *Helping Children to Know Doctrine.* Lutheran Church Press, 1962.
Schmid, Heinrich. *The Doctrinal Theology of the Evangelical Lutheran Church.* Translated by C. A. Hay and Henry E. Jacobs. Augsburg Publishing House, 1961.
Tappert, Theodore (trans.). *The Book of Concord.* Mulenberg, 1959.
Tietjen, John H. *Which Way to Lutheran Unity?* Concordia, 1966.
Wentz, Abdel Ross. *A Basic History of Lutheranism in America.* Mulenberg, 1955.

METHODIST

Barclay, Wade Crawford. *Early American Methodism, 1768-1844.* 2 vols., Board of Missions and Church Extension of the Methodist Church, 1949.
Bucke, Emory S. (ed.). *The History of American Methodism.* 3 vols. Abingdon, 1964.
Gross, John C. *The Beginnings of American Methodism.* Abingdon, 1961.
Hawley, Bostwick. *Manual of Methodism.* Hunt and Eaton, 1868.
Smith, Roy L. *Why I Am a Methodist.* Hermitage House, 1955.
Williams, Colin W. *John Wesley's Theology Today.* Abingdon, 1960.

PRESBYTERIAN

Clark, Gordon H. *What Presbyterians Believe.* Presbyterian and Reformed Publishing Co., 1956.
Hendry, George S. *The Westminster Confession for Today: A Contemporary Interpretation.* John Knox, 1960.
Loetscher, Lefforts A. *A Brief History of the Presbyterians.* Westminster, 1958.
_____. *The Broadening Church: A Study of Theological Issues in the Presbyterian Church since 1869.* University of Pennsylvania, 1957.
Mackay, John A. *The Presbyterian Way of Life.* Prentice-Hall, 1960.
Miller, Park Hays. *Why I Am a Presbyterian.* Nelson, 1958.
Slosser, Gaius J. *They Seek a Country: The American Presbyterians.* Macmillan, 1955.

QUAKER

Bronner, Edwin B. *American Quakers Today.* Friends World Committee, 1966.
_____. *Quakerism and Christianity.* Walling Ford, Pa.: Pendle Hill Publications, 1967.
Jones, Rufus M. *The Faith and Practice of the Quakers.* Philadelphia. Yearly Meeting of the Religious Society of Friends, 1958.
Lucas, Sidney. *The Quaker Story.* Harper, 1949.
Russell, Elbert. *The History of Quakerism.* Macmillan, 1942.
Tolles, Frederick B. *Quakers and the Atlantic Culture.* Macmillan, 1960.

West, Jessamyn. *The Quaker Reader.* Viking, 1962.
Williams, Walter Rollin. *The Rich Heritage of Quakerism.* Eerdmans, 1962.

SEVENTH-DAY ADVENTISTS

Herndon, Booton. *The Seventh Day: The Story of the Seventh-day Adventists.* McGraw-Hill, 1960.
Seventh-day Adventists Answer Questions on Doctrine: An Explanation of Certain Major Aspects of Seventh-day Adventist Belief. Review and Herald, 1957.
Spalding, Arthur Whitefield. *Origin and History of Seventh-day Adventists.* Review and Herald Pub., 1961.
Utt, Richard H. *A Century of Miracles.* Pacific Press, 1963.

UNITARIAN

Mendelsohn, Jack. *Why I Am a Unitarian.* Nelson, 1960.
Parke, David B. *The Epic of Unitarianism.* Starr King, 1957.
Wilbur, Morse. *A History of Unitarianism.* 2 vols. Harvard University, 1947.
Wright, Conrad. *The Beginning of Unitarianism in America.* Beacon, 1955.

LEADERS OF RELIGIOUS MOVEMENTS

Bainton, Roland H. *Here I Stand: A Life of Martin Luther.* New American Library, 1950.
Bingham, June. *Courage to Change: An Introduction to the Life and Thought of Reinhold Niebuhr.* Scribner, 1961.
Brown, Arthur W. *Always Young for Liberty: A Biography of William Ellery Channing.* Syracuse University, 1956.
Cannon, George Q. *Life of Joseph Smith.* Deseret News, 1907.
Lee, Umphery. *The Lord's Horseman: John Wesley the Man.* Abingdon, 1954.
Lindley, Denton R. *Apostle of Freedom.* (A biography of Alexander Campbell.) Bethany Press, 1957.
Mackinnon, James. *Calvin and the Reformation.* Russell and Russell, 1962.
Marty, Martin E., and Peerman, Dean G. *A Handbook of Christian Theologians.* Meridian Books, 1965.
McConnell, Francis J. *John Wesley.* Abingdon, 1939.
Noble, Wilfred V. *The Man in Leather Breeches: The Life and Times of George Fox.* Philosophical Library, 1953.
Peel, Robert. *Mary Baker Eddy: The Years of Discovery.* Holt, Rinehart and Winston, 1971.
———. *Mary Baker Eddy: The Years of Trial.* Holt, Rinehart and Winston, 1971.
Powell, Lyman P. *Mary Baker Eddy: A Life-Size Portrait.* Christian Science Publishers, 1950.
Springer, Fleta C. *According to the Flesh: A Biography of Mary Baker Eddy.* Coward-McCann, Inc., 1930.
West, William G. *Barton Warren Stone: Early American Advocate of Christian Unity.* Disciples of Christ Historical Society, 1954.
Whitley, Elizabeth. *Plain Mr. Knox.* John Knox, 1960.

Appendix B: Patterns of Faith in America Today

BELIEFS OF 7,441 CLERGY POLLED IN 1965

	M	E	P	AmB	AmL	LMs
			Per Cent Agreeing			
I believe in a literal or nearly literal interpretation of the Bible.	18	11	19	43	43	76
Adam and Eve were individual historical persons.	18	3	16	45	49	90
Scriptures are the inspired and inerrant Word of God not only in matters of faith but also in historical, geographical, and other secular matters.	13	5	12	33	23	76
I believe that the virgin birth of Jesus was a biological miracle.	40	56	51	66	81	95
I accept Jesus' physical resurrection as an objective historical fact in the same sense that Lincoln's physical death was a historical fact.	49	70	65	67	87	93
I believe in a divine judgment after death where some shall be rewarded and others punished.	52	55	57	71	91	94
Hell does not refer to a special location after death, but to the experience of self-estrangement, guilt, and meaninglessness in this life.	58	60	54	35	22	6
Man by himself is incapable of anything but sin.	36	45	47	40	73	85
I believe in the demonic as a personal power in the world.	38	63	53	67	86	91

Younger Clergy Are Less Likely to Believe in A Literal Interpretation of Scriptures

I believe in a literal or nearly literal interpretation of the Bible.

	M	E	P	AmB	AmL	LMs
Under age 35	11	5	14	27	24	72
35-44	16	11	16	41	43	73
45-54	23	14	23	55	60	79
Over 55	23	14	31	47	74	84

Younger Clergy Are Less Likely to Accept the Doctrine of Miraculous Conception of Jesus

I believe that the virgin birth of Jesus was a biological miracle

Under age 35	31	49	38	58	70	94
35-44	43	53	52	64	84	95
45-54	42	57	57	75	92	96
Over 55	48	65	61	68	92	98

Comparison of Beliefs of Laity and Clergy

Beliefs of Clergy based on poll of 7,440 Clergy and Laity based on random sample of about 3,000 church members residing in four metropolitan counties of the San Francisco Bay Area.

Laity: Jesus was born of a virgin.	34	39	57	69	66	92
Ministers: I believe that the virgin birth of Jesus was a biological miracle.	28	40	36	58	68	90
Laity: The devil actually exists.	13	17	31	49	49	77
Ministers: I believe in the demonic as a personal power in the world.	21	38	30	49	66	78
Laity: Man cannot help doing evil.	22	30	35	36	52	63
Ministers: Man by himself is incapable of anything but sin.	19	25	25	22	53	72

M: Methodist, **E:** Episcopalian   **P:** Presbyterian, USA   **AmB:** American Baptist
AmL: American Lutheran   **LMs:** Lutheran, Missouri Synod

Jeffrey K. Hadden, *The Gathering Storm in the Churches* (New York: Doubleday, 1969), pp. 39-53, 63; Charles Y. Glock and Rodney Stark, *Religion and Society in Tension* (Chicago: Rand McNally & Co., 1965), Chapter 5.

222

Index